Praise for *At All Costs*

"With verve and empathy . . . Moses gives WWII's Operation Pedestal . . . its
first book-length treatment since Peter Smith's 1970 volume *Pedestal*. . . .
An exciting, imperative read for anyone interested in WWII."
                                        —*Publishers Weekly* (starred review)

"A first-class retelling of the story of Operation Pedestal . . . a solid addition
to WWII naval literature by anyone's lights."   —*Booklist*

"*At All Costs* is an extraordinary work of research and an exciting read.
Sam Moses has brought the ghastliness of war and the beauty of heroism
together, in jarring union."   —FRANK DEFORD

ALSO BY SAM MOSES

Fast Guys, Rich Guys and Idiots

AT ALL COSTS · · ·

How a Crippled Ship
and Two American Merchant Mariners
Turned the Tide of World War II

RANDOM HOUSE TRADE PAPERBACKS
NEW YORK

AT ALL COSTS

SAM MOSES

2007 Random House Trade Paperback Edition

Published in the United States by Random House Trade Paperbacks,
an imprint of The Random House Publishing Group,
a division of Random House, Inc., New York.

RANDOM HOUSE TRADE PAPERBACKS and colophon are registered
trademarks of Random House, Inc.

Originally published in hardcover in the United States by Random
House, an imprint of The Random House Publishing Group,
a division of Random House, Inc., in 2006.

ISBN 978-0-345-47674-6

*Grateful acknowledgment is made to the following for permission to reprint
previously published material:*

CONSTABLE & ROBINSON LTD.: Excerpts from *Churchill: The Struggle for
Survival* by Lord Moran (Constable & Robinson, 2006). Reprinted by
permission of Constable & Robinson Ltd.

HOLLY GILL: Excerpts from "A Reporter at Large" by Brendan Gill
(*The New Yorker,* July 3, 1943). Reprinted by permission of Holly Gill.

HOUGHTON MIFFLIN COMPANY AND CURTIS BROWN LIMITED: Excerpts
from *Memoirs of the Second World War* by Winston Churchill,
copyright © 1959 by Houghton Mifflin Company and copyright
renewed 1987 by Lady Mary Soames. Rights outside of the United
States are controlled by Curtis Brown Limited, London. Reprinted by
permission of Houghton Mifflin Company and Curtis Brown Limited.

PERISCOPE PUBLISHING LTD.: Excerpts from *Destroyer Captain* by Roger
Hill. Reprinted by permission of Periscope Publishing Ltd.,
Penzance, Cornwall, UK.

MARY JEANNE SUPPIGER: Excerpts from *The Malta Convoy* by Gerhart S.
Suppiger, Jr., Commander U.S.N.R. Reprinted by permission of
Mary Jeanne Suppiger.

LIBRARY OF CONGRESS CATALOGING-IN-PUBLICATION DATA
Moses, Sam
    At all costs: how a crippled ship and two American
merchant mariners turned the tide of World War II /
by Sam Moses.
        p.   cm.
Includes index.
ISBN 978-0-345-47674-6
    1. World War, 1939–1945—Campaigns—Mediterranean Sea.
2. World War, 1939–1945—Transportation—Mediterranean Sea.
3. World War, 1939–1945—Naval operations, American. 4. World
War, 1939–1945—Naval operations, British. 5. Merchant
marine—United States—History. 6. Naval convoys—
Mediterranean Sea—History. 7. Larsen, Frederick August, 1915–
8. Dales, Francis. 9. World War, 1939–1945—Norway. I. Title.
D772.M23M67 2006   940.54'21585—dc22   2006040425

Printed in the United States of America

www.atrandom.com

9 8 7 6 5

Book design by Simon M. Sullivan

For Grandma Moses, who lived to see it

Operation Pedestal

- ••••••▸ Convoy route
- Axis aircraft
- Axis submarines
- Axis torpedo boats
- ✠ Axis airfields

FRANCE

Barcelona

Minorca

Majorca

Ibiza

SPAIN

Alicante

Gibraltar
August 10,
1942

Algiers

MOROCCO

ALGERIA

1 Carrier *Eagle* sunk.
2 Freighter *Deucalion* sunk.
3 Italian submarine rammed/sunk.
4 Carrier *Indomitable* damaged, destroyer *Foresight* sunk.
5 Cruiser *Nigeria* damaged, cruiser *Cairo* sunk, freighter *Clan Ferguson* sunk,
   freighter *Empire Hope* bombed, freighter *Brisbane Star* torpedoed, cruiser
   Kenya torpedoed, tanker *Ohio* torpedoed.
6 Freighters *Almeria Lykes*, *Wairangi*, *Glenorchy,* sunk.
7 Freighter *Santa Elisa* sunk, cruiser *Manchester* torpedoed (later sunk),
   freighter *Rochester Castle* damaged.
8 Freighter *Waimarama* torpedoed.
9 *Ohio* bombed, abandoned.
10 Destroyer *Penn* begins tow of *Ohio*, Larsen and Dales board *Ohio*, freighter *Dorset*
   damaged (later sunk), *Rochester Castle* damaged.
11 *Ohio* survives final attack.

Map by Cosmographics, Watford, UK

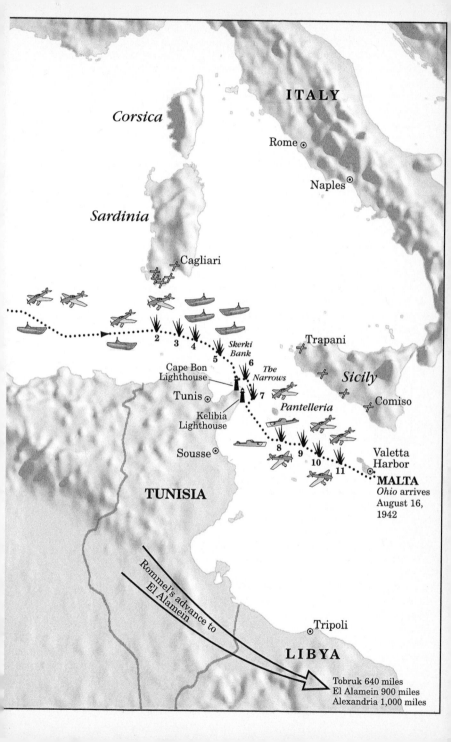

CORSICA

ITALY

Rome

Naples

Sardinia

Cagliari

2 3 4

Skerki
Bank

5   6

The
Narrows

Cape Bon
Lighthouse

Tunis

Kelibia
Lighthouse

7

Pantelleria

Sousse

8   9

10   11

TUNISIA

Trapani

Sicily

Comiso

Valetta
Harbor

MALTA
Ohio arrives
August 16,
1942

Rommel's advance to
El Alamein

Tripoli

LIBYA

Tobruk 640 miles
El Alamein 900 miles
Alexandria 1,000 miles

CONTENTS • • •

PART IV **OPERATION PEDESTAL**

PART V **INTO THE MEDITERRANEAN**

PART VI **HELL IN THE NARROWS**

PART VII **SURVIVORS**

PART VIII **TWO MEN, ONE WARRIOR**

PART I

FATE IN THE CONVERGENCE

CHAPTER 1 • • •

MALTA, SUMMER OF 1942

In the summer of 1942, scores of thousands of men, women, and children were starving and living in caves and tunnels on Malta, a block of limestone the size of Cape Cod rising out of the Mediterranean like a little white pebble kicked by the toe of the boot of Italy.

The island had been under siege for two years. Malta was the most heavily bombed place on Earth, with more bombs falling in April and May than during the entire summer and fall of the Battle of Britain. German and Italian planes flew from airfields on Sicily, just sixty miles north of Malta. If Italy was the boot kicking Malta, Sicily hung over the island like the massive other shoe, ready to drop.

"Malta is not only as bright a gem as shines in the King's Crown, but its effective action against the enemy communications with Libya and Egypt is essential to the whole strategic position in the Middle East," Prime Minister Winston Churchill told the House of Commons. It was an understatement for him. Sometimes stubborn but never alone on the issue, Churchill believed that Malta must survive for the war to be won. He might have echoed Admiral Lord Horatio Nelson, who wrote, "Malta, my dear sir, is in my thoughts sleeping and waking," to the Russian prime minister in 1799.

"It was evident that Malta, laying as it does in the very center of the Mediterranean, and flanking the Italian lifeline between Italy and North Africa, was not only of the greatest importance, but was, in fact, the vital key point which must be held at all costs," said Governor-General William Dobbie. "Its loss would obviously open the door to disasters of the first magnitude, the outcome of which was not good to contemplate."

"I cannot believe that Malta was more desirable a prize [for the Axis] than Moscow, but there was really no comparison," said Air Marshal Hugh Lloyd, the Royal Air Force commander on Malta in 1942. "Malta stood athwart the path to Cairo and our oil in Iraq, and had to be eliminated first of all."

It was all about oil, again. Churchill called Malta the "windlass of the tourniquet" on the supply lines of General Erwin Rommel's Afrika Korps, and Rommel was after the Mideast oil, which fueled the British war effort. Axis convoys from Italy to North Africa kept Rommel in supplies, but submarines and bombers from Malta destroyed much of that shipping; bombers also made runs over North Africa, striking truck convoys. If Malta were to fall, and the Luftwaffe and Italian Navy were to move in where the Royal Air Force and Royal Navy were desperately hanging on, Churchill believed it would be impossible for the British Army to keep Rommel from marching across North Africa and taking Egypt. After that, the Mideast oil fields would be lost. Syria, Turkey, Iraq, and Persia (Iran) would be Hitler's.

This was Hitler's "Great Plan," in which his army would conquer Russia, come down through the Caucasus, and meet the Afrika Korps to complete a Nazi wall encircling Europe, looping clockwise from Scandinavia to Spain, confining and enslaving Europe.

"With Malta in our hands, the British would have had little chance of exercising any further control over convoy traffic in the Central Mediterranean," said Rommel, who pushed Hitler for an invasion of the island, to get it out of his way.

"Malta was really the linchpin of the campaign in the Mediterranean," said Admiral Andrew Cunningham, Commander in Chief of the British naval forces in the Mediterranean and Britain's greatest admiral since Nelson. "The island served as the principal operational base for the surface ships, submarines and aircraft working against the Axis supply line to North Africa. The Navy had always regarded the island as the keystone of victory in the Mediterranean, and considered it should be held at all costs."

Cunningham's German counterpart, Admiral Eberhard Weichold, wrote in a report to Hitler, "It cannot be emphasized sufficiently often, that a Malta capable of fighting is essential to the possibility of effective action against the African supply route for the Panzer army, and, moreover, a cornerstone in the whole defense of Egypt and the English position in the

Mediterranean and the Middle East. I see only one possibility, and that is through a strategical offensive: The British Air Force in the Central Mediterranean, that is Malta, must be obliterated."

"There was no lasting solution for the enemy short of the conquest of Malta," said Churchill.

The stomachs of the Maltese might have been empty, but their hearts were pure and their faith indomitable, and they didn't die easily. They had been digging into the limestone and living in caves forever, and their tolerance was nearly as strong as their belief in the power of the Virgin Mary. There are limestone temples on Malta five thousand years old, the most ancient man-made structures in Europe, older than the Egyptian Pyramids. They were built like bomb shelters ahead of their time, with altars believed to be for worship.

Seventy-eight churches, thirteen hospitals, and twenty-one schools had been bombed in the two years since the beginning of the siege. Luftwaffe and Regia Aeronautica bombers had made thousands of runs over Malta, destroying an uncountable number of other buildings and killing more than five hundred people in April alone. The magnificent Opera House in Valletta had been reduced to rubble, and it remains a monument in ruin to this day. A 500-pound bomb fell through the Mosta Dome in the ancient walled city of Mdina, skidded across the floor of the church as three hundred people were praying, and came to a stop without exploding. It was clearly a miracle, they all said.

The bombers turned the towns to mountains of limestone rubble, and then turned the big blocks of rubble into smaller blocks: rubble to rubble, dust to dust. Sometimes a house that had been bombed to rubble became a family's new home, its limestone blocks rearranged into a limestone cave. Or sometimes a family moved out of a perfectly good home and into the security of a cave, which they often dug themselves. Some of the caves were no more than big dents in a cliff, which the Maltese called "caterpillar caves." They also called them "ready-made graves."

The soft limestone hardened when exposed to the salt air. Irish coal miners were brought in to help dig the caves, because they had the skills, and because the Maltese men worked all day in the dockyards or manned the antiaircraft guns around the harbor and at the edges of the island. The possibilities for tunnels were endless. Passageways led to one- and two-room homes and communal areas. People in the cities around the harbor lived their hungry lives underground, sharing all the sights, sounds, and smells, all the fighting and loving and living and dying and sometimes birthing, and always the praying, with the Virgin Mary hovering in every cave.

Sand flies flew out of the cracks in the limestone, carrying their fever. Cockroaches, bedbugs, and lice ruled. The "Malta Dog," a virulent form of dysentery, barked in the corners. The hunger never went away.

Lacking a river, forests, and rich soil, Malta could provide little of its own food and none of its fuel, so its survival depended upon cargo ships. Supplies coming from Gibraltar, 999 miles to the west, and Alexandria, 866 miles east, had been cut off by Axis air forces and navies. Some foodstuffs trickled in over the "Magic Carpet," a slim trail of fast minesweepers and minelaying submarines from Alexandria, but not nearly enough to sustain the island's 270,000 people.

The Maltese lived mostly on rationed bread, olive oil, and tomato paste, drank homemade wine they called "screech," and smoked bamboo for want of tobacco. The macaroni factory operated only when there was flour. Citrus, fig, date, and almond trees grew wild on the island, but they were perpetually picked clean. Adult males received a weekly ration of six ounces of rice, six ounces of preserved meat, six ounces of preserved fish, and five ounces of cheese. Women and children received less. Victory kitchens served one thin meal a day, maybe a skinny sausage and some peas; the goats had all been eaten, and the spring potato crop had failed. Chickens, eggs, milk, and fruit were sold on the black market, but the price was beyond reach to all but a few. Beasts of burden killed by bombs were bled and butchered if it could be done before they began to rot.

By the summer of 1942, any freighter sent to Malta was virtually on a suicide run. The sea was prowled by vicious "wolfpacks" of Axis submarines. The sky was blotched by aircraft from Sicily, Sardinia, and Libya, the Italian colony stretching much of the length of the North African coast. Fast and deadly torpedo boats, which the Italians called E-boats, owned the night.

The 10th Submarine Flotilla on Malta had done its best to protect the cargo ships coming in, but a handful of subs running on empty wasn't enough for the job. The flotilla's home was on the fifty-acre Manoel Island in Marsamxett Harbor, where its personnel hunkered down against the bombing in the sheltered limestone buildings of a former *lazzaretto*, which had quarantined victims of the plague in the sixteenth century, and more recently been a leper hospital. But the Luftwaffe blitz in April had chased the "Fighting Tenth" to Alexandria, with its five remaining subs. There wasn't enough diesel fuel left on Malta for them, anyhow.

That left the defense of the island up to the Royal Malta Artillery and the struggling Royal Air Force, which flew from three primitive bases on the island. But diesel fuel was needed by the generators making electricity for the RMA antiaircraft batteries, which were connected by wires strung across the island and could be controlled by one man in a bunker, like a wizard showering the sky with shrapnel and big bangs. Generators also powered the searchlights and radar stations that spotted enemy aircraft.

Meanwhile, the RAF bombers and fighters were running on fumes. The RAF was so low on aviation fuel that planes were towed by a tractor to the runway, to save the pints used by taxiing. When the last tractor was blown up by bombs, the ground crews began pushing the planes.

In addition to the diesel needed by the submarine fleet, fuel oil was needed by the Royal Navy warships, minesweepers, and tugboats, a few of which were based on Malta, with others coming and going. The movement of the fleet into the central Mediterranean from Gibraltar or Alexandria required the refueling in Malta of destroyers and sometimes a battleship. But by the summer of 1942, the fuel was no longer there for them.

Kerosene was also needed on the island, for heat, light, and cooking. It was rationed and sold from carts guarded by policemen, to prevent black market sales.

The diesel, fuel oil, and kerosene were often blended, leaving little distinction. The submarines, warships, freighters, and antiaircraft guns used any and all of it for fuel. Malta's survival was down to one thing: a tanker carrying oil must get in.

It had been nine months since a convoy with freighters had made it to Valletta, Malta's harbor city. Eight solo cargo ships had trickled through in that time, but that scarcely postponed the reckoning. Malta's days were numbered, literally; a secret countdown was on, to September 7. Governor Dobbie had recently taken an inventory of the food and fuel, and had informed Prime Minister Churchill that if a convoy didn't get through by then, Malta would be forced to capitulate to the Axis.

CHAPTER 2

FRED AND MINDA

Frederick August Larsen, Jr., was born in Newark, New Jersey, in 1915, to a Norwegian father and Irish mother. His spine began turning to steel when he was three years and nine months old, when in one deadly week in December 1918, his father, mother, a sister, and Irish grandmother died at home, victims of the great influenza pandemic that made orphans out of 21,000 children in New York alone. A month later his Irish grandfather, who carved model ships out of wood for a living, also died from the flu.

Children were rarely struck by this flu, but they were severely affected by what they saw; and in his parents' small house, young Freddie couldn't be sheltered from pain.

The symptoms of the virus were unimaginable. Delirium was common and pain was intense. Blood ran from eye sockets, eardrums burst, and ribs cracked during violent coughing fits. Air bubbles in lung tissue popped with a sound like Rice Krispies. By the time victims died, they often wanted to.

When the boy looked out the window to escape the suffering in the rooms behind him, he saw horse-drawn wagons with black-clad drivers clopping down empty streets, calling for families in shuttered houses to bring out their dead, to be buried in mass graves dug by steam shovels.

For about a year after his parents, sister, and grandmother died, Freddie lived with his Norwegian grandmother in Brooklyn, along with his sister, Christina, fourteen years of age, and brother, Clarence, only two. Money from the sale of his family's furniture was used to buy him a steamship ticket to Norway, where he was raised by an uncle and aunt.

They lived in a little white house clustered with others like it, exposed to the icy wind on the rocky seaside cliffs of remote Sandessjoen, on the western coast.

His uncle John Tonnessen was a big man with a big heart. As one of Norway's chief customs inspectors, he knew almost every ship's master in the Norwegian fleet. His work sometimes took him to sea, and he took Fred along whenever he could. He and the boy became inseparable. But Tonnessen's big heart failed him when Fred was fourteen. Two dads down, in ten years.

At seventeen, Fred left home for a life of his own at sea. He signed on as a deck boy on the MV *Attila,* a Norwegian tanker sailing for California and China. Six years later he came back to Norway, to attend the Mates and Masters Maritime College in Farsund, on the southern tip of Norway. By now he was a handsome, strapping young man, five feet eleven and 180 pounds, with clear blue eyes and sandy hair, with curls that appeared to be piled on top of his head because he cut the sides so short. He could flash a smile that looked almost feminine, but he didn't give it up easily. He also had a don't-mess-with-me glare that made men around him think he could break them like sticks, if he needed to.

He met the love of his life during his first semester at the Mates and Masters College, in 1937. He was looking out to sea when Cupid smacked him between the eyes with a snowball lobbed by a beautiful girl, which is how Minda Heskestad got his attention. She was twenty-one, the ninth of ten children born on a farm over a period of twenty-eight years, and until the day Fred died, he called her "my Norwegian princess."

He married Minda, graduated, and went back to sea, all in the busy spring and summer of 1939. As they kissed good-bye on the dock in Farsund, Minda was already pregnant. He boarded a steamship bound for Germany, where he traveled across the country by train, getting a scary look at life under Nazi control, and then caught a freighter from Amsterdam to New York.

He had left Minda in Norway only because they agreed it was best for her to have the baby in Farsund, with family and friends around her. They hadn't been thinking of war, which broke out in September when Germany invaded Poland. And they had never imagined that Norway would be occupied by Nazis.

"The only thing Fred wanted to do was go to sea," said Minda. "He had to earn some money. He thought he could send for me to come to the U.S. as soon as our child was born."

Germany invaded Norway by sea on April 9, 1940. That was their first wedding anniversary, and streets full of Nazis weren't much of a gift for Minda. Larsen was quartermaster on the *City of Norfolk*, a 1918 freighter converted to carry passengers, steaming between New York and Liverpool. He immediately petitioned the ship's owners, United States Lines, to carry his wife and baby son back from Liverpool, if he could get them there. There was family in New York waiting for them, including his sister and brother, whom he had scarcely seen in the years since influenza had ripped them apart.

Larsen applied to the U.S. Immigration and Naturalization Service for immigration visas for Minda and Jan. He received a letter granting Minda's visa, but it was stamped "Approval was not given your son, Jan F."

Jan was caught in a Catch-22. The letter stated, "Through your birth in the United States, your child Jan Frederick is apparently a citizen of this country, and, if so, he is entitled to an American passport. Therefore, you should forward to him documentary evidence of birth here, which he may present to the nearest American consul abroad."

That wasn't so easy, with Larsen at sea so much and the German Gestapo controlling the mail to and from Norway. It took months, and each day that his family was in the hands of the Germans, Larsen grew less patient.

As quartermaster on the *City of Norfolk*, his duties at sea included shifts at the helm as the ship crossed the North Atlantic. When he wasn't on watch, there was too much time to think about Minda and Jan, and their safety. He came up with a plan.

He thought he could take a fishing boat from Liverpool and motor north through the Irish Sea, then around Scotland and the Orkney Islands to the Scandinavian-speaking Shetland Islands, about two hundred miles off the western coast of Norway, where the North Sea meets the Norwegian Sea. He remembered those rough waters; his uncle John Tonnessen had taken him to Zetland when he was a boy. And he knew the rocky coves around Farsund. He believed he could anchor there under cover of darkness, slip into Farsund in a dinghy, steal away his wife and child, and race back to Zetland in the fishing boat.

He applied for a furlough from U.S. Lines and stayed in Liverpool to plan the escape. But everyone he spoke to told him the scheme was insane; between the vicious sea and the German planes and boats, the chances of survival were nought, they said. He couldn't do it alone, so he reluctantly steamed back to the United States on the next ship, and returned to the bureaucratic paper trail.

He began writing letters to Washington and traveling there on the train from New York whenever he could, knocking on doors at the Department of State, aggressively using diplomatic channels, trying to get his family out of Norway. He spent much of his small salary on cables, phone calls, and travel expenses. By the time he finally got the passport for Jan, Minda's immigration visa had expired. He couldn't reach them by mail and had no idea what was happening to them under the Nazi boot in Farsund. He was left with little but his fears.

When an opportunity arose to work for the Grace Line, whose fleet of modern freighters in New York City made it the best steamship company in the country, he quit the *City of Norfolk*. Larsen had been driven by the desire to command his own ship ever since his first day at sea as a seventeen-year-old, and Grace Line was the place where he could achieve that dream. Hard work and intelligence were rewarded at Grace Line.

Larsen held an officer's license with the Norwegian Merchant Navy, but that didn't carry weight in the U.S. Merchant Marine; he still needed to take the exam to get a U.S. license. With eight years of experience at sea—from the engine room of the *Attila* to the helm of the *City of Norfolk*—and two recent years of mariners' college in Norway, he didn't need to go to school to prepare for the difficult three-day test, but he enrolled in a private crash course in Connecticut anyhow, because he was always hungry to learn. Grace Line was pleased when he passed the exam easily and it was able to make him an officer.

In early 1941, Larsen sailed as cargo mate on the freighter SS *Nightingale*, which was chartered by Grace Line. It was a busy job with heavy responsibility, including some functions of the chief mate, supervising the loading and off-loading of cargo. The *Nightingale* sailed to Valparaíso, Chile, stopping at every little port on the way back to load strategic metals from South American mines, coffee from Colombian plantations, and fruit, which was good moneymaking cargo, carried home in the *Nightingale*'s refrigerated holds in the 'tween decks.

After three months on that run, he got sweet duty as junior third mate on a spring cruise to the Caribbean with the SS *Santa Rosa*, a 225-passenger ocean liner advertised as being "sexier than Rita Hayworth." He served two more months as junior third mate on the SS *Siletz*, another chartered cargo ship sailing out of New York.

He was making nearly $100 per week, and saving it all because he had no living expenses; and unlike other sailors, he didn't go out to bars when his ship was in port. He knew he would need cash to get Minda and Jan to the United States, although he still didn't know how he could. He wasn't counting on the State Department.

In Norway, German officers had taken over the Heskestad farmhouse, located six miles from Farsund. Minda's aged father and mother were moved into an upstairs bedroom, while Nazis ate the harvest from Heskestad farm. Minda and Jan, who was about eighteen months old at this time, lived in a small apartment in town.

Their bedroom window was against the sidewalk, which was traveled by goose-stepping soldiers whose barracks were just down the street in a school building. The daytime marching was intimidating, but the nights were downright scary, as the soldiers often staggered home loud and drunk. Minda said it was like having Nazis in her bedroom. She held her son, stroked his cornsilk curls, and told him his father would protect him.

She supported herself by cutting hair in the front room of their apartment. "One time a Nazi officer came right in and took off his cap and his gun belt, and told me to give him a haircut," she said. "I got so angry. I said, 'I don't do men's hair.' He insisted, but I refused, and I held the door open for him. He took his cap and his gun and left."

The other girls there were terrified, but Minda was too firm to be afraid. She was more worried that the Nazis would find the radio her brother kept in the barn, where he listened to the BBC. The penalty for having a radio was death.

Fred wrote dozens of letters to Minda during this time, but she received few of them. The mail to Norway was opened by the Gestapo and read by "little quislings," said Minda. She clung to her favorite funny memory of their courtship, the time Fred had ridden his bicycle a hundred miles from his aunt's house along the coast to visit Minda in Farsund one weekend, sleeping overnight in the woods. When he got there, she was out on a ship with her sister until Monday, so he had turned around and ridden back.

But she did get one package from her husband. "There were some clothes for Jan and a pink satin robe for me," she said. "It was beautiful, and I treasured it for a long, long, long time. It was quilted, and it fit me perfectly. Oh, I was happy. I thought I was a queen."

Larsen had heard that the Norwegian Resistance was recruiting, and he wanted to join. Other Norwegian mariners had told him about the Lingekompani, a group of commandos led by Kaptein Martin Linge, called "ice cold" and "heroic" by his men. Since his scheme to take a fishing boat from Liverpool to the western coast of Norway wasn't possible, he now wanted to go to Farsund on a commando mission, and rescue Jan and Minda by sneaking them through the forest across the border to Sweden. The *Siletz* sailed to England, where it was easy for any Norwegian mariner to find the Resistance; but when he volunteered, the Resistance wouldn't take him because he wasn't a native Norwegian. The betrayal by Vidkun Quisling, the Norwegian politician who had sold out his country to the Nazis, burned in the hearts of Norwegians and kept their suspicion high.

In May 1941, Larsen was assigned to the ship that would take him to war: the shiny new SS *Santa Elisa*. She was launched that month from the shipyards in Kearny, New Jersey, and in July joined other Grace Line ships running military stores to South America, with ports of call in Panama, Colombia, Ecuador, Peru, Bolivia, Chile, and Argentina. Mostly, she brought back copper and other metals from Chile and coffee from Colombia.

In September he joined the U.S. Naval Reserve and was commissioned an ensign; it was a requirement by Grace Line that all its officers belong to the USNR, although it didn't change their status in the merchant marine.

He also finally succeeded in getting the travel documents for Minda and Jan. For $525, he bought them tickets on a Pan American Clipper, scheduled to fly from Lisbon to New York on Minda's twenty-fifth birthday. But getting from Farsund to Lisbon with a toddler—Jan was nearly three years old now—was the hard part. There were half a dozen legs in which anything could go wrong, with trains and ferries to Berlin, a flight from Berlin to Madrid, and another train to Lisbon. The Gestapo stood at every corner and doorway along the way. And even if Minda and Jan made it to Lisbon, the flight over the ocean in a monstrous "flying boat" was a scary step for a farm girl who had never been away from home and family.

"My friends talked me out of it," she said. "It was tempting, but I didn't want to take a chance like that."

Three months later, Japan attacked Pearl Harbor, bringing the United

States into the war. Larsen heard the news over the radio on the bridge of the *Santa Elisa,* anchored in the harbor of Valparaíso. After that, his attempts to get his family out of Norway grew in desperation. But the replies from the government weren't very promising.

Department of State
Washington

My dear Mr. Larsen:

The Department of Justice has referred to this Department your letter of January 5, 1942 regarding the visa case of your wife, Minda Heskestad Larsen, and your son, Jan Frederick Larsen, who are residing at Farsund, Norway.

Because of the withdrawal of the Department's representatives from enemy-controlled territory, there is no action which can be taken at this time with a review to providing Mrs. Larsen with an appropriate visa for admission into the United States or passport facilities for your son, who, it is understood, is an American citizen.

While the possibility of American citizens proceeding from enemy-controlled territory is being investigated, no assurance can be given that it will be found possible to arrange for American citizens to come to the United States from Norway. You will be properly informed should the Department be able to make such arrangements.

CHAPTER 3 • • •

FIRE DOWN BELOW

At twenty-eight, Lieutenant Reinhard Hardegen, a German U-boat captain, was a loose cannon. He carried unchecked ambition and relentless intensity along with his war wounds—a short leg and bleeding stomach—from the aviation crash that had ended his previous career as a naval pilot. He had concealed the injuries in order to qualify for command of U-123, and then began an impatient rampage of sinkings with the neutral Portuguese freighter *Ganda.* The 4,300-ton ship didn't go down after two torpedo hits, so Hardegen surfaced U-123 and sank her with its four-inch gun. When the attack became an international incident, Admiral Karl Dönitz, commander of Germany's U-boat fleet, claimed it was a British sub that had sunk *Ganda.*

Dönitz chose U-123 to be among the first five U-boats with orders to attack the eastern seaboard of the United States. He had begun planning the attack four days after Pearl Harbor, on instructions from Hitler to destroy merchant ships from New York to Cape Hatteras. Five 1,050-ton Type 9B U-boats, with a range of 12,000 nautical miles cruising at 10 knots on the surface, left their pens at the port of Lorient in France on separate dates around Christmas 1941. Dönitz called the operation "Drumbeat," for the effect he expected it to have.

The Submarine Tracking Room at the Operational Intelligence Centre of the British Admiralty in London, Royal Navy headquarters, had located the U-boats crossing the surface of the ocean, and their positions were passed on to the U.S. Navy and charted on the wall in the headquarters of the Eastern Sea Frontier in New York City. But a vicious winter hurricane hit the Atlantic with winds of 100 mph, tossing the subs like surfboards off the lips of big waves, and enabling them to lose the Americans tracking them.

The Eastern Sea Frontier, commanded by Admiral Adolphus "Dolly" Andrews, didn't have much of a fleet: Coast Guard cutters with wooden hulls, turn-of-the-century gunboats, and converted yachts with a machine gun and maybe a few depth charges on deck. The boats were often broken down in port. The day before the first U-boat left France, Admiral Andrews complained in a memo to Admiral Ernest King, commander in chief of the U.S. Navy: "It is submitted that should enemy submarines operate off this coast, this command has no forces available to take adequate action against them, either offensive or defensive."

Early on the morning of January 12, 1942, off the coast of Nova Scotia, U-123 sank the 9,100-ton British freighter *Cyclops*. Ninety-eight men died, almost all of them freezing in lifeboats. Operation Drumbeat was supposed to be a sneak attack off New York, coordinated with the other U-boats, and by attacking the *Cyclops*, Hardegen had disobeyed Dönitz's orders and blew the element of surprise; not that it mattered, because the Eastern Sea Frontier was so unprepared.

The New York Times ran a two-paragraph story, picked up from a boast by Radio Berlin, but the story didn't attract much attention. The U.S. Navy issued a lying press release claiming to have "liquidated" U-boats off the coast, adding that national security prevented the disclosure of more information. "This is a phase of the game of war secrecy into which every American should enter enthusiastically," said the navy's statement, printed by the *Times*. The release added that the media and civilians could make the same "great, patriotic contribution" by not mentioning what they might see with their own eyes.

The next day, U-123 traveled south from Nova Scotia, steaming at 18 knots in broad daylight. It submerged a couple of times when aircraft flew over, but the ESF's Fleet Air Arm was no more of a threat to U-boats than its bathtub navy. U-123 had traveled more than 3,300 nautical miles from France, only 55 of them submerged, without being challenged. The big U-boat passed south of Nantucket late in the afternoon, and that night was beckoned down the coast by Montauk Point Lighthouse.

Kapitan Hardegen was excited by the glow from the lights on shore, exposing his targets. "Don't they know there's a war on?" he asked his chief mate. The U.S. Navy had suggested cities and towns along the coast to black themselves out, but merchants declined because business would suffer.

After midnight, Hardegen spotted the *Norness*, a 9,600-ton Norwegian tanker, and split her apart with three torpedoes. He continued to New York and submerged at sunrise in the harbor. U-123 spent the day on the bottom, ninety feet down in the mud.

The New York Times was still on the street with a headline now shouting TANKER TORPEDOED 60 MILES OFF LONG ISLAND when Hardegen surfaced after dark, awed by the dome of white light rising almost religiously into the black sky above Manhattan. He knew the moment was profound. "We were the first to be here, and for the first time in this war a German soldier looked out upon the coast of the U.S.A.," he said.

Later that night, during an icy nor'easter, he torpedoed the 6,800-ton British tanker *Coimbra*, whose 80,000 barrels of oil exploded in a giant fireball, killing thirty-six. Witnesses saw flames from the beach at Southampton. Admiral Andrews told the press that the navy knew nothing about it, which was almost the truth. His feeble fleet was grasping at the wisps and ghosts of ocean spray in its lame attempt to find U-123.

Fred Larsen's Irish grandfather, the woodcarver Christopher Melia, and William Russell Grace, who founded Grace Line after emigrating from Ireland, were about the same age and had the same eye for beauty. Had they lived long enough to see the *Santa Elisa*, Melia might have carved her, and Grace would have been proud of her.

A flurry of shipbuilding was triggered by the Merchant Marine Act of 1936, passed in order to increase the size of the U.S. merchant fleet. As President Franklin D. Roosevelt prepared for the growing possibility of war, the pace increased. The *Santa Elisa* was one of 173 freighters built between 1940 and 1945 to Maritime Commission designs for the class called C2. She was 459 feet from bow to stern, 63 feet at beam, and 40 feet between main deck and keel bottom, with a loaded draft of 26 feet and freeboard of 14. Her five holds gave her a gross weight of 8,380 tons, with the ability to stow 8,620 tons of cargo.

Because she was specially built for Grace Line, she had some custom touches shared by only her sister ship, the *Santa Rita*. Her bridge was enclosed, keeping the helmsman out of the weather and providing protection against shrapnel from bombs. Powered by a double reduction General

Electric turbine making 6,000 horsepower and driving a single screw, she could run all day and night at 17 knots.

Larsen was junior third officer on the *Santa Elisa*, in charge of the lifeboats and lifesaving equipment, but the chief officer also assigned him to supervise the fire equipment. He did much more than the manual described for a third mate, simply because he could. At twenty-seven, he had done it all. He'd been a teenage prodigy in the engine room of his first ship, the *Attila*, working with diesel, steam, and hydraulic systems. He could navigate and operate radios. He'd been a quartermaster, purser, bosun, and cargo mate; he was certified in firefighting and lifeboats, and liked guns. He'd even been a stevedore on the San Pedro wharf in California. He could speak English, Norwegian, Danish, Swedish, and Spanish, and was beginning to study German, although he despised it.

He acted with a natural sense of authority based on experience, and carried himself with conspicuous self-discipline. When he stepped into territory that was not a third mate's, other officers could usually see that his involvement was driven by efficiency, not ego, but his rigidity could be difficult. "He was a square-head all the way," said Peter Forcanser, the junior engineer who maintained the deck machinery. "A real sonofabitch. He was only the third mate, but he acted like he owned the ship."

After the attack on Pearl Harbor, the *Santa Elisa* had returned to Brooklyn, where she was armed by the War Shipping Administration, primarily with two .30-caliber Browning machine guns on the afterdeck. Armor plating thirty-six inches high was added to the bridge, on each wing just outside the wheelhouse door. A steel visor projecting downward at 45 degrees was welded to the top of the wheelhouse, and a crow's nest with a telephone to the bridge was built between the two fifty-foot-tall king posts at the forward end of the number one hatch. Steel gun tubs were welded to the bow and four corners of the bridge, intended for 20-millimeter Oerlikon rapid-fire cannons, but the tubs were empty, because the guns weren't available so early in the war.

On the afternoon of Saturday, January 17, 1942, Kapitan Hardegen and his U-boat were lurking off the New Jersey coast as the *Santa Elisa* steamed south from Gravesend Bay in Brooklyn after loading ammunition for her machine guns. She was headed for Cristobal, at the mouth of the Panama

Canal, where an attack by the enemy was feared, and then to Arica, Antofagasta, Valparaíso, and San Antonio, Chile. There were 552 cases of safety matches in wooden crates stowed on the starboard side of the upper 'tween deck level of her number one hold, the most forward of five. In the lower 'tween deck of that same hold there were 1,900 drums of highly explosive carbide crystals. Such drums had been used during the Spanish Civil War like rolling depth charges; republican forces sent them barreling down steep hillsides onto rebel encampments.

Word of the U-boat sinkings had moved over the merchant fleet's radios. Small craft hugged the coast, but the freighters still ran offshore. At about 7:15 that evening, the *Santa Elisa* was steaming at 16 knots in choppy seas and big swells, running without lights, approximately ten miles off Atlantic City. The chief mate, Tommy Thomson, was decoding a message with the master in his cabin next to the bridge as Kapitan Hardegen peered into the periscope of U-123, searching the icy blackness and hoping to light it up with flames.

"I heard a loud crash and the vessel listed to starboard," reported Thomson. "I immediately ran out of the captain's room by way of the after door, and up the fore and aft alleyway into the wheelhouse, followed by the captain. I ran to the telegraph in the wheelhouse and put the engine full astern.

"Just as I put the engine telegraph full astern, there was a heavy explosion forward, followed by flame. Then almost immediately followed by a second explosion and more flame. About this time the master arrived on the bridge and remarked that it was a torpedo."

"There was a rocketing explosion on the *Santa Elisa* that blew half-ton hatch covers twenty feet into the air," reported *The Grace Log*, a Grace Line magazine. "The rush of all hands to meet the emergency was immediate. Along tilted passageways, ladders now inclined at an illogical angle, as the crew fought its way to the outer decks. A gutting fire tore through her forward cargo holds. Her steel hull was ragged and rent, and searing flames threatened to buckle her bulkheads."

As the *Santa Elisa* listed to starboard, Thomson saw green and red lights drifting eerily past the port bridge wing. He saw the lights again, about four hundred yards away, as Larsen followed the captain's orders and lowered a lifeboat to stand by what appeared to be another ship. It was the last time anyone saw the lights.

An old banana boat, the 3,400-ton freighter SS *San Jose*—a pioneer "reefer," with refrigerated holds—had been chugging north from Guatemala in the same waters. *The New York Times* reported that the *San Jose* had rammed the *Santa Elisa* and then sunk. *The Grace Log* said that the *Santa Elisa* had rammed the *San Jose* "with such fury as to send her abruptly to the bottom."

Kapitan Hardegen claimed that U-123 had torpedoed and sunk a ship that could only have been either the *San Jose* or *Santa Elisa*. All thirty-nine crewmen of the *San Jose* made it to lifeboats and were rescued by ships in the area that had received an SOS sent by Thomson on the *Santa Elisa*.

There were many dark mysteries during the war. Unexplained explosions in the dead of night—a mine, a torpedo, a collision—were all the same to the men. Sometimes they never knew. Sometimes a torpedo aimed for one ship hit another. And through a periscope at night, one freighter can look like any other.

Whatever hit the *Santa Elisa* blew a twenty-foot hole in her hull at the waterline, and set off the 1,900 drums of carbide.

Hardegen said he had fired at a heavily loaded freighter with a stern torpedo from six hundred meters. "After 57 seconds there is a mighty detonation and a huge, pitch-black explosion column," he wrote in his diary and shooting report. "The hit was under the bridge. With its high speed, the steamer ran itself under water. When the smoke lifted, only the mast tops were still visible and shortly afterwards they disappeared, too."

As U-123 raced from the scene of its shot, the *Santa Elisa* began listing to port and her mast tops dropped behind the large swells as black smoke belched from the fire. Water rushed into the forward hold, and the ship's bow dipped so steeply that her rudder rose out of the water. Flames spouted thirty feet out of the holes made by the blown-off hatch covers, painting vertical orange stripes over the black horizon. The fire's glow could be seen from the Atlantic City boardwalk as the ship burned.

When lives were at stake, Fred Larsen was the first to arrive and the last to leave. He and his friend Thomson led the firefight in hold number one.

"I gave orders for all hands to come forward and fight the fire," said Thomson. "I shouted up to the captain and suggested that he back the ship up into the wind to keep the fire and smoke forward of No. 1 hatch so we could get at the flame with the hose. Hoses were being brought into position from the amidship superstructure and the after deck. In all, 8 streams of water were playing on the fire within ten minutes. The deck on the starboard side was red hot to a distance of approximately 7 to 8 feet aft of No. 1 after hatch. The port side was also hot, but it was not red hot."

Thomson and Larsen each donned an OBA—oxygen breathing apparatus—which consisted of a rubber mask and an oxygen tank strapped to the wearer's back, and they scrambled toward the hold, the rubber soles of their shoes melting on the burning paint as they struggled with the bucking brass nozzles of 2½-inch hoses. A hatch in the mast house led down to the hold, but they couldn't get near it. "Throughout this time, there were several small explosions in the hatch," said Thomson.

The fire burned through the cold black night until 5:40 A.M., with the SS *Wellhart* and SS *Charles O'Connor* arriving and training more hoses on the *Santa Elisa*'s foredeck. Twice the captain went full ahead on the engines in order to flood the hold with seawater. At daybreak the foredeck was awash, and 37 of the ship's crew of 54 men were placed on the *Wellhart* and *Charles O'Connor* by U.S. Coast Guard boats. Just before noon on Sunday, the tugboats *Relief, Resolute,* and *Wabla* began towing the *Santa Elisa* back to Bay Ridge Flats in Brooklyn, where she was run aground on the sandy bottom, to be unloaded and towed off later. She would smolder for three more days.

Kapitan Hardegen headed south to Hatteras, again steaming in daylight, within sight of the shore. He broke silence to send a gloating message to Dönitz when he passed the naval base at Norfolk. That night he sank three more ships, killing forty-four of forty-seven on the *City of Atlanta,* and shot up a fourth. On the way back to France he got two more ships in the Atlantic, for a total of nine. Hitler draped the Iron Cross around Hardegen's neck.

As the attacks against merchant ships along the coast continued, the U.S. Navy got away with hiding them. Merchant mariners were ordered not to talk about it. Keeping a journal aboard ship was a violation of the Trading with the Enemy Act, punishable by ten years in prison.

When President Roosevelt finally installed the convoy system with destroyer escorts in the summer of 1942, the U-boats were forced to find victims elsewhere. But 609 ships had been sunk in the Eastern, Gulf, and Caribbean Sea Frontiers, and thousands of merchant mariners had lost their lives. Eleven U-boats were sunk.

The *Santa Elisa* was repaired at the Brooklyn Navy Yard that spring. Her

Grace Line colors, black hull and green funnel with a white band, were covered by a drab coat of "gull gray" warpaint. Four new Oerlikon cannons, effective against dive-bombers and fast torpedo boats, were installed on the corners of the bridge in the empty gun tubs. A three-inch antiaircraft gun was mounted in the tub on the bow, and a four-inch low-angle gun was bolted to the afterdeck. The four-inch had been used against tanks in World War I, and could blow a very big hole in a thin-skinned U-boat.

Fred Larsen was promoted to senior third officer. With his previous experience as a cargo officer, he was asked by chief mate Thomson to help supervise the loading of cargo for the *Santa Elisa*'s next voyage. On May 5, at the Brooklyn Army Depot, stevedores began loading her holds with ammunition and war stores, including bombs, mines, and about 5,000 drums of kerosene and diesel fuel, in hold number one. Tanks and heavy trucks were shackled to her foredecks. Fourteen new U.S. Navy Armed Guard joined the ship's crew, and forty soldiers—searchlight specialists, headed for duty in Britain, Egypt, and Malta—came aboard as passengers. It took one week to load all the equipment, fuel, and ammo.

On May 12, 1942, Larsen cast off the lines that held the stern of his ship to the pier. The *Santa Elisa* was going to war.

Although the Department of State had told Fred Larsen that "there is no action that can be taken at this time" regarding his visa application for Minda, he had refused to accept it. Maybe the government couldn't take action, but he could.

He learned that the International Red Cross in Switzerland was arranging exchanges between American noncombatants and German prisoners, with details being handled by the American Red Cross. With the help of his sister, Christina, who lived in Brooklyn, he wrote a letter to the Red Cross explaining the situation, and received a reply with forms that he completed. The Red Cross continued the process, and on May 15 the State Department sent a promising letter, which Christina received as the *Santa Elisa* was steaming across the Atlantic.

> With reference to the inquiry in your letter of March 24, 1942, as to the possibility of your wife and son coming to the United States, I take pleasure in informing you that the S.S. Drottningholm is expected to sail shortly from Goteberg, Sweden for New York in connection with the exchange of official and non-official persons between the United States and the Axis Powers. It is understood that the German authorities may permit Americans to return from Norway and Denmark on the S.S. Drottningholm and that those desiring to proceed from these countries to Goteberg to embark may accordingly be granted exit permits.

On the *Santa Elisa*'s first night at sea after leaving New York, Captain Vladimir Cernesco came down with a case of the shingles. Given the cargo of ammunition and fuel, the fire in January, and the U-boats known to be lying in wait in the North Atlantic, his shingles might have been triggered by nerves. The *Santa Elisa* had to make an unscheduled stop in Boston, where he was hospitalized and declared unfit for further duty.

The *Santa Elisa*'s chief mate, Tommy Thomson, had been an officer with Grace Line since his graduation from the Maritime Academy of New York State University ten years earlier. He held his master's license, although because there weren't many Grace Line ships, promotions to master had been scarce. But now his time had come.

"It was all a fluke," said Thomson. "This is an ocean-going war, and the bosses needed a man who'd seen a ship's bridge. There I was. No one could figure out where to dig up another captain."

Thomson's overnight promotion made him the youngest master in the U.S. Merchant Marine, at thirty-three. He was tall and soft spoken, with platinum hair and sharp blue eyes. He had proved his bravery, having fought the fire in hold number one alongside the third mate, Larsen. His full name was Theodore Roosevelt Thomson, but the link to TR had little to do with political values. When Roosevelt was New York City police commissioner, he had granted a request by Thomson's father, a Brooklyn cop, to be placed on the bicycle squad.

Thomson and Larsen had now worked together for nearly a year. They liked, respected, and trusted each other. They each had young sons, although Larsen had never seen his, and they shared Danish blood. Thomson knew he could count on Larsen, and relied on his experience and skills. When a new chief mate came aboard in Boston, bringing unknown chemistry and introducing an awkward element to the chain of command, little changed between them. But Thomson told Larsen that he would now need him more than ever.

The ship's departure from Boston was delayed until 5 P.M. by the sighting of a possible U-boat outside the harbor. So as soon as it got out to sea, the crew tested the guns. "Tried several times to fire 20mm Oerlikons guns but jammed each time," reported the U.S. Navy ensign whose fourteen-man crew had been assigned to man the guns. Ensign Gerhart Suppiger, Jr., was fresh out of one of the Navy's hastily established armed guard schools, which hadn't included training in the Oerlikons. His shock at the imperfection of war was just beginning.

"He was a hell of a nice boy," said Peter Forcanser, the junior engineer.

"But that's what he was, a boy. He should have taken his mama with him. I knew more about the guns than he did."

The *Santa Elisa* steamed thirty-six hours to Nova Scotia and anchored at dawn in Halifax Harbor, where there were about thirty ships waiting for convoys. An Oerlikon expert with a DEMS—Defensively Equipped Merchant Ship—rating came aboard and said it was no wonder the guns hadn't fired; "They gave you the wrong grease for the shells in Brooklyn," he told Suppiger. He gave the gun crew some cans of the correct grease, along with six smoke floats, to be used if the ship were torpedoed and sunk. "Make that '*when*' the ship is sunk," the DEMS rating said with a smirk.

They swung at anchor in Halifax Harbor for six uneventful days. The only place to go at night was the Green Lantern bar, where a couple of the guys met two local girls, who got them drunk and took them home and grilled them. How many ships were in the convoy? Where was it headed? What was its speed? The boys ran back to the ship, believing they were lucky to have survived such a close call with German spies.

Twenty-six freighters escorted by two Canadian corvettes and two destroyers left Halifax on a foggy Sunday morning, with church bells ringing them good-bye from shore.

The convoy system was new, and few of the masters had any experience at running so close together, let alone zigzagging to make their ships harder for U-boats to hit with torpedoes. It was especially difficult for the speedy *Santa Elisa*, because the convoy moved at the pace of its slowest ship, in this case 9 knots. "You don't know how jumpy it makes you to have a fast ship throttled down by a lot of tubs," said Thomson.

It took the convoy thirteen days to cross the Atlantic, creeping through extended fog, which made navigation difficult but was a blessing because it hid the ships from U-boats. Larsen worked in the wheelhouse a lot, navigating and taking readings with his sextant when he could see the sun or stars. He had bought the sextant secondhand in San Pedro, and it was his most treasured possession, after a pewter-framed photo of Minda and Jan. On the clear days, lookouts often spotted what they believed were torpedo tracks, although to a scared seaman, every bubble on the water looked like the trail of a torpedo zooming past. Wind over the swells made "white horses," which dashed past the lookouts and blurred any periscope feathers. One night they got a radio message that a ship had been torpedoed about twenty miles from their course.

There was a small poker game in the wardroom each night, and sometimes the officers tapped the keg of Jamaican rum that the purser had bought in Halifax and stowed in the head (toilet) in Thomson's cabin. The new chief mate was a hard-drinking Swede, and the mix with the rest of the crew, most of whom had been together since the ship's launch, was already growing edgy. Larsen, especially, had to take a deep breath. He couldn't forget that the Swedes had allowed the Germans to sneak across the border into Norway during that invasion; and he didn't approve of heavy drinking. He avoided the wardroom at night, retreating abovedecks to the wheelhouse, where he worked on his nighttime navigation and took extra watches at the helm on the bridge, steering in the dark.

In the lingering Irish twilight of June 5, 1942, Fred Larsen let go the anchor of the *Santa Elisa* in Belfast Lough. At almost the same moment, Minda's train from Kristiansand screeched to a stop at the station in Oslo, Norway. Belfast and Oslo, seven hundred miles apart, were as close as they'd been to each other in three years.

When Larsen had left Brooklyn twenty-five days earlier, he had known that the *Santa Elisa* was headed to war, but not where. Minda's journey had begun that morning at her home in Farsund. She hoped that it would end in her husband's strong arms in America. She was traveling on faith, with a vague itinerary that made no promises. She only knew that when she and her child got off the train in Oslo, the Gestapo would be there to watch them.

She had received a telegram from an Oslo attorney that morning that said, "Have just received instruction that you and your son have received traveling permission to America." She would have to leave that day, and, for all she knew, it would be for forever. She didn't know if the lawyer, who had been retained by the Red Cross, was even real.

Again, her friends and family all wanted her to stay; in Farsund they could look after her. Her sister Alice begged her not to go; it was a trick by the Gestapo, she said, and the train from Kristiansand would take them straight to Grini, the concentration camp that the Germans had established near Oslo. "But what would the Germans want with a three-year-old?" Minda asked, with reasonable naiveté.

The previous September, when she had feared to take the flight to New York on the Pan Am Clipper, Norway had been an occupied country, but life had still been livable. Since then, the United States had entered the war. Now her son, an American citizen, was the enemy of the Nazis. The first whispers and rumors about the Grini concentration camp had grown into horrible stories. She had second thoughts about what the Germans might want with a three-year-old.

So she quickly packed one suitcase with clothes and one with food, as the cable instructed. Her pink quilted satin robe, which Fred had sent her, filled half the suitcase for clothes. Her girlfriend's father fired up his old London cab, which had been converted to burn wood for fuel, and off they went to Kristiansand. She was racing to catch a train to the unknown, on the belief that it had been sent by her husband to get her.

The Oslo station was full of German soldiers. Plainclothes Gestapo agents watched the passengers get off the train and asked for identification and travel papers from those whose looks seemed suspicious to them. She clutched Jan in her arms as she disembarked, and to her great relief she wasn't challenged. Another passenger carried their suitcases off the train, and for a few fearful minutes she stood by the tracks, alone with her child and all their worldly possessions, worrying that the Gestapo would notice them and question her. "They were all over the place, but you didn't really know who they were," she said.

Then the mysterious lawyer appeared. His name was Mr. Nansen, and he told Minda that she and Jan would be traveling to America, with other Norwegians. But first they had to pass through Nazi Germany.

T he *Santa Elisa* docked at the Belfast pier, off-loaded the tanks, trucks, and military equipment, and began waiting for orders. Fred Larsen and the rest of the crew could only guess where they would be sent next. Maybe back to New York if they were lucky, or Australia or Africa, but a convoy to Murmansk or Malta was more likely. The thought of a run to Murmansk was especially worrisome, because if the ship were torpedoed and sunk in the Barents Sea at the edge of the Arctic Ocean, it meant certain death in the frigid water. Malta sounded better, because you could survive a sinking in the Mediterranean Sea, with its calm water and balmy air; but the possibility of being attacked in the Med was greater, because the fighting around Malta was intense. Like so much of war, it was hell if you did, hell if you didn't.

With so many soldiers and sailors passing through Belfast, news from the corners of the war moved like stray cats along the cobblestone streets, sometimes with the same stealth. Rumors and secrets were whispered in the bars and hangouts, which were haunted by operators and spies. Merchant mariners were plied for information, because they passed through so many ports around the world.

It had been one year since Larsen had tried to join the Norwegian Resistance but been rejected because he wasn't a native of Norway. The commando leader, the heroic and cold-as-ice Kaptein Martin Linge, had been killed in a raid in December, and the Resistance needed fresh blood. There was a new commando unit being formed called "Inter-Allies," with men from the occupied countries of France, the Netherlands, Belgium, Poland, Yugoslavia, and Norway. Larsen's American citizenship was no longer a

barrier. The Resistance found him in Belfast, and this time it tried to re-
cruit him.

But the only way he could now join the Resistance would be to jump
ship, and that was out of the question. He was now an officer, and had
signed ship's articles, a binding contract between the crew and the captain. He was committed to the *Santa Elisa* and his shipmates. His friend
Tommy Thomson needed him.

However, there was another possibility. Larsen's allegedly insane previ-
ous plan, to take a fishing boat from the Shetland Islands onto the shore of
Norway and pick up his family in the night, was now an actual operation.
It was called the "Shetland Bus" and was led by a Norwegian Navy captain
named Leif Larsen, who had trained with the commando Linge and the
Lingekompani. Fred heard about the Shetland Bus in Belfast and was
excited by the idea, but faced two problems: he had only a few days in
Belfast, and in that brief time it would be impossible to organize passage
for Minda and Jan on the Shetland Bus; and if anyone was going to rescue
Minda and Jan in a fishing boat by sea, it would have to be Fred.

But anyhow, Larsen didn't know that his efforts to gain their release
through the Red Cross had succeeded. He wasn't aware that Minda and
Jan were already on their way to America.

There was a lot to do in Belfast. Larsen also wanted to find his Irish
roots. His Irish grandfather, the woodcarver Christopher Melia, had been
born about 250 miles south of Belfast along the Irish Sea, where he had
married Fred's grandmother, Maria Mooney. Larsen wanted to know more
about his grandparents. But it would have taken at least two days to travel
that far, and the crew was required to return to the *Santa Elisa* each night,
so he had to let it go, knowing only what little he had been told about his
Irish background.

Captain Thomson was informed that the British Merchant Navy was
making its Anti-Aircraft Gunnery Course available to any interested
seamen. He went straight to Larsen, knowing that his third mate would
welcome the opportunity to learn more about the *Santa Elisa*'s
weaponry—and that there was no one better to know the ship's guns.
Larsen chose five men and signed up for the course, which qualified them
for the firing and maintenance of the Oerlikons.

The first man he chose was his protégé, an all-American boy named
Francis Alonzo Dales. Larsen and Dales had met just two weeks before the

Santa Elisa left New York. Dales was a cadet-midshipman, fresh out of the new U.S. Merchant Marine Cadet Corps, and he strode up the gangway of the *Santa Elisa* with his seabag over his left shoulder, so he could salute smartly with his right hand. He was sent straight off to report to Larsen, because he was a deck cadet.

"Lonnie" Dales was a handsome boy, almost pretty, with wavy hair, full lips that curved into a smile beyond his years, and a cleft chin that made the girls say he looked like Cary Grant. He had weighed ten and a half pounds at birth and the baby fat had turned into a fine physique, but he still had the baby face, except for penetrating eyes. He looked as if he were studying the future and thinking about what he should do about it.

Lonnie and his older brother, Bert, had been raised by their mother in Augusta, Georgia. It wasn't easy being a single mom with two boys in the rural South during the Depression, not that it ever is, especially when you're deaf. Evelyn had lost her hearing before Lonnie was born, and she slept with her hand on his chest so she could feel when he cried.

She was twenty-one and a schoolteacher when she had her June wedding. According to the announcement in the *Augusta Herald,* Evelyn Denning Dales was "a very charming and most attractive woman, with a dainty winsomeness that is most typically Southern. That she will win the hearts of all who meet her is a foregone conclusion."

Her husband, Bertram Dales, didn't win so many hearts, but the paper found nice things to say about him. "Mr. Dales is the older son of Mrs. Florence Burdell Dales and is a splendid young man in every way. The marriage is the culmination of a romance that has been going on for several years and which reaches its happy climax now that the groom has attained his majority and his fortune."

Straight from the wedding they set out to spend part of that fortune, which came from Irish linen in Belfast. They caught a train from Augusta to Atlanta to Boston, where they boarded the magnificent new Royal Majesty's Steamship *Aquatania,* the only four-funnel ocean liner in the world, and steamed to Belfast. But World War I broke out while they were there. They explored Ireland a bit, and hurried home.

When Lonnie was young, his father fled home, into the swamps of Florida to build roads and bridges, never to return and never to explain, at least not to Lonnie. Evelyn and the boys traveled to see him just once. What remains of their visit is a photo of them all looking uncomfortable—

a smirk clenching the stub of a cigar is almost all that Bertram Dales left of himself. He spent the rest of his life there, dying of a heart attack just after the war, alone on a sidewalk in Dade City.

He sent a couple of postcards to Lonnie after that one visit. "Remember the Gators last summer. Daddy." And later, "Indians in the Everglades. Daddy."

In the first grade, Lonnie was learning to write in cursive, and he practiced his chosen word: *Dad, Daddy, Daddy,* he wrote, again and again.

When Lonnie was eight, the other kids called him "Admiral." His uncle Reggie was a tugboat captain, pushing barges loaded with bales of cotton, bundles of tobacco, and bricks of red Georgia clay down the languid Savannah River; sometimes he took Lonnie with him, and allowed the boy to take the helm. But that wasn't the reason the other kids called him "Admiral." It was because of his attitude.

Larsen and Dales clicked from the beginning. The new cadet-midshipman was a "slow-talking but hard-slugging native of the Cracker state," as the *Augusta Herald* had said in reporting his assignment to the *Santa Elisa,* and that suited the taciturn third mate just fine. Dales respected Larsen's knowledge and authority, and looked up to him as he looked up to his own brother, Bert, who was the same age as Larsen and who was now serving on General George Patton's staff.

Dales was a lot like Larsen. He displayed a seriousness and work ethic beyond his years, and carried himself with an unspoken sense of authority. His focus on self-improvement was intense. He could fix almost anything, using his gift for mechanics, which apparently came from his maternal great-grandfather William Walker Hardman, who had emigrated from England in 1845 to work on the Georgia Railroad, repairing steam locomotives, and who was said to have invented the cowcatcher.

"Lonnie was smart, for sure, I'll tell you that," said a shipmate who worked in the engine room of the *Santa Elisa.* "He had a photographic memory. He read my engineering book in about two nights, and then he coached me. A really likable kind of guy."

As Larsen and Dales got to know each other in Belfast, they discovered they had more than personality traits in common. They had both lost their fathers when they were young, and spent formative time at sea with uncles. And they both had Irish grandfathers.

Lonnie's paternal grandfather, Hugh James Dales, had left Belfast on a cargo steamship when he was twenty-three, sent to Georgia by his wealthy father to learn about growing cotton for their Irish linen company. But the boy learned about love with a southern belle and died at thirty-two, before Lonnie was born. Lonnie's father might have received some of the Irish linen fortune—Evelyn did have a car and black driver, in the beginning—but if so, it never made its way into Lonnie's bank account.

Lonnie had relatives in Belfast, a family with three daughters. So on the days that he and Larsen weren't in gunnery school studying the Oerlikons, they rowed a lifeboat across the water to visit the relatives, bearing chocolate bars and cigarettes. Dales learned how to handle and command a lifeboat. He might have been just eighteen, but he was an officer. Larsen gathered a crew and put Dales in charge, and they trained with the lifeboat by releasing and lowering it against the clock, before rowing away as if they were escaping a burning ship.

Larsen and Dales also shared stories about the uncles who had molded them. Larsen told Dales about his uncle John in Sandessjoen, and Dales replied with Uncle Cliff in Waynesboro. The two places were worlds apart and the uncles spoke different languages, but the values were the same.

As a role model, Cliff Hatcher was as solid as an island of rock. He'd been an army lieutenant during World War I and returned to active duty as a major in 1940, organizing the selective service system in Georgia. But when Lonnie was growing up, his uncle Cliff was a small-town lawyer and the mayor of Waynesboro, a gentle man who lived by the Golden Rule and held strong beliefs. Every morning at sunrise he raised the American flag on the tall flagpole next to his prolific pecan tree, in the yard along Liberty Street. He was committed to physical fitness and University of Georgia football, where he'd been a 165-pound end, in the days before the forward pass—a Bulldog's bulldog. No smoking, no drinking, no cursing, and Methodist church every Sunday morning and Wednesday night, with meetings in between. Much of Uncle Cliff—Major Hatcher to the rest of Waynesboro—had rubbed off on Lonnie.

Hatcher's wife, Mattie, was Evelyn Dales's sister. Cliff and Mattie had lost their only son in infancy, so it was a natural fit. Lonnie spent summers and vacations and even some school time with the Hatchers in Waynesboro, thirty miles from Augusta, where Evelyn began teaching hard-of-hearing children in the public school system after she had taken a lip-reading course.

The Hatchers had a summer house about fifty miles south of Savannah, near a community nestled along the connected creeks, canals, marshes, and sounds at the edge of the Atlantic Ocean. The area was full of romance, with a rich history of pirates and Indians, including Blackbeard and the Cherokee. Lonnie and his big brother would paddle a canoe out to Wolf Island, now a wildlife refuge and national wilderness area, at the mouth of the Altahama River, flowing from the heart of Georgia. Sometimes they would stay out for hours, returning under a pink sky after sunset.

Lonnie loved the water. He and his friends would swing from the vines and leap shrieking into the tidal pools and creeks, sometimes under a full Georgia moon. There was an old cabin on a piece of dry land surrounded by marsh, and some nights they would sleep on the floor, under a big mosquito net draped from the rafters.

Like his great-grandfather, grandfather, uncle, brother, and his grandfather's friend and baseball teammate Woodrow Wilson (who argued for the establishment of a strong merchant marine), Lonnie attended the Richmond Academy High School in Augusta, an all-male institution with ROTC training. Cliff Hatcher saw to his schooling. Lonnie had just begun his senior year when World War II broke out in Europe. He had to wait until he was eighteen to sign up for service, but then he wasted no time. Three days after his eighteenth birthday and one day before Pearl Harbor, he took the entrance exam for the U.S. Merchant Marine Cadet Corps. He completed the eight weeks of basic training at the cadet corps temporary base at Fort Schuyler, in the Bronx. The four-year program had been squeezed into an emergency cram course because the War Shipping Administration needed to feed more mariners to the ships, if not the sea.

Cadet-Midshipman Dales got his orders to the *Santa Elisa* on early graduation day, April 27, 1942. Sixteen days on the water between Brooklyn and Belfast were the sum of his seagoing experience. But at least he had a mentor in Fred Larsen. They were soul mates destined for battle at sea as a team.

PART II • • •

THE SECOND GREAT SIEGE

F or nearly three thousand years, because of her sheltered ports and strategic position as a natural stone fortress between Europe and Africa, Malta had been fought over by the world's most powerful navies. The island was discovered in about 800 B.C. by Phoenician traders, the ancient Mediterranean's best navigators, who came from Syria and Lebanon in galleys rowed by slaves and convicts. They named the island Malat, or "safe haven." Little did they know that the safety offered by the harbor would bring perpetual conflict over the centuries to come.

The Phoenicians were followed by the Greeks, who developed the Phoenicians' galleys into sleek trireme warships, 100 feet long and only 15 feet wide, powered by as many as 170 professional rowers who trained like athletes. A trireme could hit 12 knots and turn at full speed within its own length. It was designed for ramming an enemy's vessels broadside and sinking them, a tactic that would be used by destroyers against submarines in World War II.

The Carthaginians came from Africa in hundreds of ships and used Malta as a naval base during the Punic Wars from 264 to 146 B.C. Hannibal was born a Carthaginian on Malta in 247 B.C., and Maltese babies are still given his name.

According to the Book of Luke, the apostle Saint Paul was shipwrecked on Malta for three months in A.D. 60 and began the conversion of the island to Christianity.

Malta was part of the Roman Empire for seven hundred years, although Roman culture didn't leave much of a mark. Arabs later ruled for 220 years, and their influence remains, most heavily on the Maltese language and the physical features of the Maltese people, a beautiful blend of

Arabic and Italian. The Sicilian Normans had their hundred years with Malta next, followed by the Germans, French, and Spanish.

In 1530 the Maltese archipelago was given away by Spain's King Carlos I, who was also the Holy Roman Emperor Carlos V. For the price of one Maltese falcon per year, he turned Malta over to the Order of Knights of the Hospital of St. John of Jerusalem, a monastic order that had been founded in Jerusalem as a hospice for pilgrims at the beginning of the Crusades. But the Knights of St. John had turned toward militancy, as the Ottoman Turks threatened western Europe and Christianity with the expansion of their Islamic empire.

From Malta, the Knights sent their warships after the Muslim corsairs, the privateer pirates who roamed North Africa's Barbary Coast. Malta's first Great Siege occurred in 1565, when 40,000 Turks in 181 ships attacked the 9,000 Knights.

"If the Turks should prevail against the Isle of Malta, it is uncertain what further peril might follow to the rest of Christendom," said Queen Elizabeth I. It was an historical comment that Winston Churchill might have echoed, except four centuries later the threat came from the Nazis.

The Great Siege lasted 114 days. With Spanish reinforcements, the Knights prevailed, using their cannons to fire the Turks' severed heads back across the harbor.

Thousands died in the bloody fighting, but the duration and firepower of the first Great Siege was nothing compared to the assault by the Axis during World War II. The second siege of Malta lasted ten times as long, with one-ton bombs replacing the cannonballs.

Having saved the Christian world from Islam, the Knights' fame spread around the world. They became known as the Knights of Malta and ruled for 268 years. This was Malta's golden age, as the Knights built churches, gardens, cathedrals, and palaces. Cities rose out of the rock and dust, revealing a timeless architecture in their walls, bastions, battlements, and vaults.

By now the Knights had been warriors for five centuries, but they didn't abandon their roots, building one of Europe's best hospitals in Valletta, the city they created. Eventually, inevitably, they grew decadent, and the Maltese rebelled against their rule, feeling they owed the Knights nothing anyhow, as the Knights had been forced upon them. So when Napoleon arrived in 1798, the islanders supported his takeover. He rewarded them by declaring an end to the Inquisition and the use of judicial torture.

But the illusion of Napoleon as liberator died overnight, as he immediately looted the magnificent rococo churches and palaces in order to finance his next conquest, Cairo. France was at war with Britain, and Napoleon wanted Egypt for a base to drive the British out of India. He loaded his great three-decker flagship, *L'Orient*, with the Knights' gold and diamonds and other treasures, and within two weeks he was gone from Malta, leaving a garrison to govern the island with guns.

Enter the British Royal Navy. The young Admiral Horatio Nelson, commanding fourteen ships, sailed all over the Mediterranean that summer, searching for Napoleon's fleet, obsessed with finding Napoleon and frustrated by his elusiveness. He finally located seventeen French ships in Egypt's Aboukir Bay at the mouth of the Nile on August 1; attacking immediately and decisively, he destroyed them in the brutal Battle of the Nile, which lasted two nights and a day.

Napoleon himself was already gone, but the 120-gun *L'Orient* was there. Her magazine exploded when she was hit by British cannons, blowing blazing bits of wood, gold, jewels, and bodies high into the night sky and raining them down on the other ships. The burst was seen as a flash of orange light twenty miles away. A hunk of *L'Orient*'s mast landed on one of the British ships, and its captain had it carved into a coffin, which he gave to Nelson as a trophy to remind him of his victory, as well as his mortality. Nelson kept it propped open against the bulkhead in his cabin, to remind his officers of his humor.

Napoleon's garrison on Malta was later evicted by Nelson's fleet, with the help of the Maltese people, mostly illiterate peasants led by priests, who this time were the besiegers instead of the besieged. As the Knights had achieved glory by fighting the Turks, the Maltese were admired for their fortitude in rejecting Napoleon and standing up to his soldiers, those mighty conquerors of Europe. Showing that they could be revolutionaries when they needed to be, the Maltese barricaded the French garrison in Valletta until they surrendered and were sent home.

In 1800 the Union Jack flew for the first time over Malta, which accepted formal colonization in 1814. As a British officer said when Malta became part of the empire, "Brave Maltese, you have rendered yourselves interesting and conspicuous to the world. History affords no more striking example."

CHAPTER 7

GLADIATORS

One hundred and forty years of freedom from aggression had ended for Malta on June 11, 1940, as more than forty Savoia-Marchetti SM.79 trimotor bombers, escorted by about two dozen Macchi MC.200 fighters, appeared over the glistening Mediterranean at 6:49 A.M., coming from three airfields on Sicily. The bombing was somewhat surreal, as excited boys climbed onto rooftops to watch while old women cowered under their beds and prayed. Hot splinters of shrapnel rained down on the streets, whizzing softly as they fell, and the boys ran to retrieve them as if they were arrowheads, not knowing that they would have 3,340 more opportunities in the next 1,185 days to collect shrapnel souvenirs.

The sea breeze carried the acrid aroma of cordite from guns and bombs. Soldiers from the Royal Malta Regiment fired rifles with wild optimism at planes flying two miles high. Windows in Valletta rattled to booms from the big guns on the old monitor HMS *Terror*, moored in Grand Harbour to bolster the shore defense. Dirt roads leading away from Valletta were jammed until midnight with stunned families scurrying into the country with their belongings stacked in horse-drawn carts and teetering wheelbarrows, diving for cover from the bombs that fell during a second attack in the evening.

Many of the 369 bombs that fell that day—250 kilos, 100 kilos, and some 20-kilo incendiaries—fell at random, on a hospital, a convent, a school, a hotel, a cinema, a Turkish cemetery. Thirty civilians were killed and 130 wounded, and 17 more died the next day from their injuries. Among those killed in the morning were Antonia Furrugia, twenty-five, her children Ninu and Joe, five and four, her niece Josephine, three, and the baby she carried in her womb. Charles, eighteen months old, was the only one of the children to survive.

The Italian dictator, Benito Mussolini, had announced his declaration of war on Britain the previous evening, shouting it from the balcony of the Palazzo Venezia in Rome in a speech broadcast live by Italian state radio and heard all over Malta.

"We have only one watchword," he said. "This word is already in the air and is burning in Italian hearts from the Alps to the Indian ocean: Conquer!

"People of Italy! To arms! Show your tenacity, your courage, your worth!"

"Il Duce" was fond of calling the Maltese his "blood brothers" and had promised that he would free the Maltese from their yoke of British colonialism and return them to what he said was their rightful ethnic fold. He promised that if he bombed the island, it would be with flowers. Win their hearts and minds. He presumed he would be hailed as a liberator by the people of Malta and that the conquest would take mere weeks. But like Napoleon, he failed to account for the Maltese people's depth of fortitude, let alone their perception. Sixty percent of the Maltese might have been illiterate, but they weren't dumb.

They spat "blood brothers" back in his face. The Maltese could tell the difference between shrapnel and flower petals. They could see it in their dead and wounded children, beginning the first day of the siege that would last more than three years.

Malta had been worried about an attack or invasion from Sicily for five years. Civil defense brigades patrolled the streets, and Boy Scouts stood twenty-four-hour watch over the sea at the edges of the island. Because Mussolini had used mustard gas to speed up his conquest of Abyssinia (Ethiopia) in 1936, Maltese families learned how to suit up in gas masks and gloves, armed with buckets and brooms. There was even a special baby gas mask, designed to enclose the entire infant.

British ambivalence about the defensibility of Malta had slowed the plan for arming the island with antiaircraft guns. On the first day of the siege, there were less than half as many guns as there were supposed to be. Eleven months earlier, Prime Minister Neville Chamberlain had promised Malta 112 heavy and 60 light antiaircraft guns, but only 34 and 22 had been delivered, adding to the 24 old three-inch guns that had been installed during the Italian assault on Ethiopia. And none of the planes that had been earmarked for Malta was anywhere near the island.

"I think more fighters for Egypt and a fighter squadron for Malta are both urgent," Admiral Cunningham had told the Admiralty. "Malta is of immense value to us, and everything possible should be done to minimize the damage that Italian bombers may do to it."

Cunningham and Churchill believed that Malta should be held at all costs, but, said Cunningham, "The Army and Royal Air Force did not take the same view. Malta, they considered, could not be held and defended against continual air attack from Sicily, and possible invasion."

Since Churchill wasn't a dictator, he couldn't make all things happen by mandate, and he wasn't a magician, so he couldn't create materials out of thin air. He also had a lot on his mind, namely, other fronts to worry about. And when Malta was attacked, he had been prime minister for only a month.

Governor William Dobbie had been assigned to Malta on April 28, 1940, just six weeks before the bombing began. His belief in God's will was fatalistic and sometimes fanatic, although the devout Catholics of Malta might not have thought his faith was extreme. A Scottish Protestant, he led after-dinner prayer meetings and Bible readings, and was held in awe by the islanders for his striding through falling bombs as if he were protected by a divine shield. While others dived for shelter, Dobbie stood on walls to get a better view, secure that God was by his side.

"Through the goodness of God, I had learned to know something of His grace and power long before I reached Malta," he said. He offered evidence at his prayer meetings of how the Bible spoke to Malta; he saw himself like King Jehosaphat being attacked by the Ammonites and Moabites:

> Humanly speaking, the situation was desperate, and little hope appeared on his horizon. He, likewise, spoke to God, and implored His help. God's answer was one we may still take to heart today: 'Be not afraid, for the battle is not yours, but God's.
>
> These and many other instances recorded in the Bible were naturally a tremendous encouragement to me, and I believe, to many others in Malta. They so exactly fitted our case that we might have thought that they had been expressly written for us.

The antiaircraft fire on the first day of the siege was more abundant than accurate. No planes were shot down, but Italian pilots reported a "curtain of fire" around the island and said that some twenty British fighters had challenged them. But there were only three little Gloster Gladiator biplanes. For the first two weeks of war in the sky over Malta, the over-achieving Gladiators were the island's entire air force.

The RAF had sent a commanding air officer to Malta, without airplanes to command. The AOC, the New Zealander "Sammy" Maynard, had been a World War I flying ace and was a "quiet, able, thorough and determined man with none of the flashy trappings and film-star swagger of many high-ranking officers determined to blaze a meteoric career for themselves across the dark sky of war, according to *Faith, Hope and Charity*."

Ten crated Gladiators had been accidentally left behind on Malta in April, when the aircraft carrier *Glorious* had hurriedly left for Norway, after Germany invaded that country. Maynard asked Admiral Cunningham if he could save four of them for his newly formed Malta Fighter Flight, and it was done. The Admiralty wanted the planes for other fronts, but Cunningham persuaded the dubious First Sea Lord, Dudley Pound, that Malta was worth four obsolescent biplanes, at least. The Admiralty later sent instructions for the Gladiators to be crated back up and shipped to the Middle East. But, said their ace pilot George Burges, "The admiral more or less told them to take a running jump."

AOC Maynard kept one of the four Gladiators on the ground in reserve, and there were only six pilots in Malta Fighter Flight anyhow, with three on duty at one time. The three planes that took to the air against impossible odds became known as Faith, Hope, and Charity. The miracle-working mechanics who kept the planes airborne called them Blood, Sweat, and Tears.

But they were worth it. Sometimes the SM.79 bombers—known as "flying buffalos" for the humps over their fuselages—turned and ran when they saw the Gladiators coming. The sight of one of the little biplanes chasing a flying buffalo lifted Maltese spirits. With a top speed of just 250 miles per hour at 14,000 feet, the Gladiators were slightly slower than the SM.79s but chased them anyhow. And they were more than 100 mph slower than a diving MC.200—called Saetta, or "lightning bolt"—but they could virtually pivot in the sky and thus outmaneuver the fast Italian fighters.

There wasn't enough fuel for the Gladiators to patrol in the air, and because it took them nearly seven minutes to climb to 15,000 feet, the pilots sat in the cockpit on the ground waiting for the next raid, in order to save the two minutes it would take to run to their planes and strap in. Sometimes they sat for hours in triple-digit heat, until hemorrhoids became a problem for the pilots, who already suffered from the Malta Dog.

The pilots of Malta Fighter Flight were cheered wherever they went. They were the new Knights of Malta. All of them were volunteers from among the few flying RAF personnel on Malta in April. None of them had flown a Gladiator before.

Flight Lieutenant George Burges, who would score three kills and three probables to earn a Distinguished Flying Cross, had been AOC Maynard's personal assistant, performing clerical chores; he had gone from being a pencil pusher to "Il Ferocio," as the Maltese called him.

Peter Keeble drove his Fiat Topolino flat out from the Hal Far airfield to his apartment on the coast, where he went sailing with his pretty wife, Lorna. Timber Woods was the lone wolf, a superstitious Irishman who feared only the color green. Peter Hartley escaped the stress of combat on his farm with pigs and chickens. The baby of Malta Fighter Flight, Pete Alexander, was high-strung on the ground but indifferent to danger in the air, and was the first of a long line of Canadians who would fly fighters from Malta.

The commanding officer, Jock Martin, was stereotypical RAF, with a handlebar mustache growing over a pipe, a rowdy sense of humor, and a sidekick bull terrier (until the dog walked into a Gladiator prop). Long in the tooth and battle-scarred, he walked with a limp from a crash in a Fairey Gordon, a biplane bomber they called the "Beast" because it was so big and slow.

Amazingly—miraculously, the Maltese would say—all six pilots survived the impossible odds against Faith, Hope, and Charity; although Hartley was burned over most of his body when Charity's eighty-gallon gas tank was hit by machine-gun fire from a Fiat CR.42 biplane in July. He dived headlong out of the plane with his khakis on fire, and was rescued from the water.

On July 16, Flight Lieutenant Keeble was killed flying a Hurricane. That morning he had received a letter informing him that his brother, also an

RAF pilot, had been shot down and killed. His final words before climbing into his plane were "I want to get one of those bastards today."

Peter Keeble—handsome, fearless, and hotheaded—was the first RAF pilot to die over Malta. The pilot of the CR.42 that hit him followed him in, crashing within a hundred yards of the Hurricane. Keebler had gotten the "bastard" who had shot him down.

CHAPTER 8

FROM NELSON TO CUNNINGHAM

T hirteen days after Italy attacked Malta, France capitulated to Germany, an act that turned over 1,300 miles of North African coastline, including Tunisia and Algeria, from the Allies to the Axis. Overnight, allies became enemies. One day the French and British sailors were drinking pals in Alexandria bars; the next day their commanders, Cunningham and Vice Admiral R. E. Godfroy, were facing a battle between the fleets at point-blank range in the harbor. Admiral Cunningham dramatically and creatively solved the standoff in the desperate eleventh hour, ignoring impatient and demanding cables from Churchill; much to the relief of both fleets, Godfroy finally agreed to disarm, discharge fuel, and disembark 70 percent of his men.

A Scot raised in Ireland, Admiral Andrew B. Cunningham was called "ABC" or "Cutts" by his men. He drove a car as if he thought he were Tazio Nuvolari, the Italian Ferrari driver who raced at the ragged edge; and he was known to occasionally flick a butter ball across the table with his spoon. He was generally irascible and sometimes short-tempered, and at age fourteen had been called "Meatface" for his "love of a scrap," as he was reminded by a classmate in a congratulatory letter when he took command of the Mediterranean fleet, based in Alexandria.

Cunningham's warships were outgunned and his submarines vastly outnumbered by those of the Italian Navy. But, he said, "We never gave a thought to the strength of the Italian fleet. We were perfectly confident that the fleet we had at Alexandria could deal with them if they chose to give battle."

As Count Galeazzo Ciano, Mussolini's son-in-law and minister of foreign affairs, wrote in his diary on June 28, 1940, "The fighting spirit of His British Majesty's fleet is quite alive, and still has the aggressive ruthlessness of the captains and pirates of the seventeenth century."

Like Nelson looking all over the Mediterranean for Napoleon in the summer of 1798, "Meatface" was itching for a scrap with the Italians. On July 7 he sailed from Alexandria with three battleships, five cruisers, seventeen destroyers, and the venerable aircraft carrier *Eagle*, headed to Malta to escort four ships carrying noncombatants (including his wife and two nieces) back to Alexandria. But on the first morning at sea he received a report from the submarine *Phoenix*, which had spotted six Italian warships about two hundred miles east of Malta, so he went after them. By the time he found them the next afternoon, off the southern coast of the toe of Italy, the Italian fleet had grown to two battleships, twelve cruisers, and too many destroyers to count. But that didn't stop Cunningham from attacking. The encounter at Calabria was the first sea battle between British and Italian fleets in history.

Cunningham commanded the convoy from his flagship, the battleship *Warspite*, whose fifteen-inch guns scored a heavy hit on the battleship *Giulio Cesare*—"at the prodigious range of 13 miles"—and the Italian fleet retreated. "I suppose it was too much to expect the Italians to stake everything on a stand-up fight," he said, with a touch of disappointment.

Admiral Inigo Campioni, the Italian commander, had called for air support, but his bombers didn't arrive until after he had retreated, and then they attacked the Italian ships.

Churchill wasted no time in using the Battle of Calabria to push for more arms for Malta.

"A plan should be prepared to reinforce the air defenses of Malta in the strongest manner with AA guns of various types and with Air planes," he wrote on July 12 to General Lord Hastings "Pug" Ismay, his chief of staff and secretary of the imperial defence. When a foot-dragging reply came back from the First Sea Lord of the Admiralty, Dudley Pound, Churchill replied with a testy message: "We must take the offensive against Italy, and endeavor once again to make Malta a Fleet base for special occasions."

Admiral Pound, who was Cunningham's superior in the chain of command, wasn't convinced that Malta was worth saving. He asked Churchill to consider evacuating Malta and conceding the entire central and eastern Mediterranean, which would have meant abandoning whatever and whoever was left on the island to the Axis. Cunningham was told to start thinking about a withdrawal plan. "If it had come to pass it would have been a major disaster, nothing less," said Cunningham.

The nagging issue of aircraft for Malta was ongoing. When eight Hawker Hurricanes landed at Luqa airfield to refuel on their way to Egypt, Malta's commanding air officer, Sammy Maynard, snatched five of them, with their pilots—"impressed" was the word used to describe what might also be called "shanghaied." The pilots were trained to simply ferry the Hurricanes, not fly them in combat, but this was war. None of them liked it. Some survived, and some didn't.

Churchill knew the value of Hurricanes to Malta—their 324-mph top speed could match that of the fastest Italian fighters. Even with the Battle of Britain beginning at this time, he asked the Admiralty, "As we have a number of Hurricanes surplus at the moment, could not the Malta Gladiator pilots fly the Hurricanes themselves?"

Admiral Cunningham had been putting pressure on the First Sea Lord as well, and the Admiralty finally gave in. On August 2, 1940, a dozen Hurricanes were officially sent to Malta, flown off the ancient aircraft carrier *Argus* from 380 miles away. They buzzed Malta in two formations, with the roar of their 1,280-horsepower Rolls-Royce V-12 engines stopping hearts; but when people realized that the powerful planes were on their side, they danced in the streets. One Hurricane crashed when it hit a bomb crater on Hal Far airfield upon landing, and two more were destroyed on the ground in an air attack forty-eight hours later, but nine new arrivals were better than none.

The pilots thought they would be going back to England the next day, to fight the Luftwaffe over London in the Battle of Britain; but again, Sammy Maynard "impressed" them. They were angry about having to stay in that hot hellhole Malta, doomed to dust, hunger, and dysentery like the rest of the islanders. But they would get their chance with the Luftwaffe over Malta soon enough.

On August 30, 1940, a convoy with four merchant ships finally steamed toward Malta. Initiated and driven by Churchill, it was called Operation Hats—he liked to wear so many. The warship escort included the battleship *Valiant* and aircraft carrier *Illustrious*, the ships that introduced radar to the Mediterranean, enabling enemy planes to be located from fifty miles away. This convoy from Gibraltar rendezvoused with more warships, commanded by Cunningham and steaming from Alexandria.

The Italians saw them coming. From naval bases on Italy and Sicily, Regia Marina (the Italian Navy) sent out a fleet of warships.

The *Illustrious* carried twenty-four Fairey Swordfish biplanes, their forty-eight fabric wings fluttering in the breeze on the flight deck. Irreverently but affectionately called the "Stringbag," for its fabric-and-wire construction, the Swordfish could carry a 1,500-pound torpedo slung under its belly or a combination of 500-, 250-, and 20-pound bombs. An Italian reconnaissance plane spotted the *Illustrious*, so the Italian warships turned away. Supermarina, the Italian admiralty, based in Rome, was afraid of the potent old Stringbags.

Regia Aeronautica (the Italian Air Force) wasn't deterred, however, and bombers attacked Operation Hats. But *Illustrious* also carried a squadron of new two-seat Fairey Fulmar fighters, each with eight guns; they shot down six "flying buffalos" and more SM.79s were damaged, while others jettisoned their 2,750-pound payloads over the sea and turned for home.

The three freighters and one small tanker were escorted into Malta's harbor, with a tugboat towing one of the freighters, which had a hole in her hull and a smashed rudder from near misses—bombs that land in the water close enough for the concussion to cause damage. The merchant ships carried 40,000 tons of supplies and were greeted by cheering Maltese lining the bastions and barrancas, five deep in some places.

But the cheery mood lasted just three days. On the evening of September 5, as Churchill was announcing the success of his Operation Hats to the House of Commons (and as Minda Larsen was having her twenty-fourth birthday, without a cake because the Nazis took all the eggs), the Junkers Ju 87—the scary Stuka—made its debut over Malta. The Luftwaffe had sent fifteen Stukas to Sicily, and five of them went looking for the battleship *Valiant* in Grand Harbour. She was already gone, so the Italian pilots—rushed into the cockpit after taking only half of the twenty-five-hour German training course—bombed a fort instead. There was little damage, but the writing was in the sky, and it was as ugly as the plane.

In October 1940, Malta got its first big bombers. A dozen Wellingtons, called "flying cigars," landed at Luqa after being flown from England. There were no ground crews to prepare them, but they made a bombing run the next night anyhow, to Naples Harbor, barely getting airborne on the treacherously short and crater-filled Luqa strip. For the next mission the payload was decreased to lessen the weight, but that evening's heat and humidity robbed the engines of power, and two of four Wellingtons went down just after takeoff, killing five crewmen and making orphans of five children whose parents were killed when one of the bombers crashed and burned on their house.

Bombers were at least as important to the war in the Mediterranean as the Hurricanes and other fighters, because bombers could cripple the enemy, while the fighters' role was support and defense. But the fighters got the attention, because spectacular dogfights over Malta were like a spectator sport, watched by thousands. The Malta bombers rumbled away without fanfare, usually after dark, and destroyed targets in Italy and Sicily, as well as ships in convoys to North Africa that supplied the Axis' drive toward Egypt and Persian oil. With some bombers, Malta could now shift from a defensive to an offensive position. But big bombers needed many tons of aviation fuel, which could only come on ships.

Admiral Cunningham led another convoy into Malta: five freighters escorted by four battleships, five cruisers, one aircraft carrier, and thirteen destroyers. But it was just a stop along the way to Italy's Taranto Harbor for him.

There was also a new Photo Reconnaissance Unit on Malta, with three high-flying, American-made Martin Maryland bombers, whose range of 1,300 miles gave the Allies the ability to look down on every Italian port and airfield in the Mediterranean. Reconnaissance flights over Taranto, 350 miles northeast of Malta, had photographed six Italian battleships.

Under a nearly full moon on Sunday, November 11, twenty Swordfish flew off the *Illustrious*, 170 miles out to sea, toward Taranto Harbor. Eleven of the "Stringbags" carried 1,500-pound torpedoes, and the rest were armed with 250-pound bombs. Harbor defenses heard the slow, droning Stringbags coming and started firing before they even got there.

"The sky over the harbor looked like it sometimes does over Mount Etna in Sicily, when the great volcano erupts," said Charles Lamb, one of the Stringbag pilots. "The darkness was torn apart by a firework display which spat flame into the night to a height of nearly 5000 feet."

But the slow Stringbags flew under the barrage, skimming as low as five feet over the water. They dropped torpedoes that blew huge holes in three of the battleships, sinking them in the shallow water; the other three battleships ran from the harbor before morning. The sensational success of the Battle of Taranto was attributed to Malta's Photo Reconnaissance Unit, flying the camera-equipped bombers.

Early on the afternoon of December 20, Admiral Cunningham steamed again into Grand Harbour, bearing Christmas gifts: eight cargo ships full of food and supplies from Alexandria. "Our reception was touchingly overwhelming," he said. "I went all over the dockyard next morning with the Vice-Admiral, and was mobbed by crowds of excited workmen singing 'God Save the King' and 'Rule Britannia.' I had difficulty in preventing myself from being carried around."

Meanwhile, thousands of Luftwaffe personnel were traveling through Italy on trains, showered with candy and fruit at each stop. Comando Supremo had invited the Luftwaffe to Sicily to obliterate Malta.

Warplanes arrived by the dozens in daily flights, and soon there were more than a hundred German bombers on Sicily—Junkers 88s and 87s and Heinkel 111s—with hundreds more on the way, along with squadrons of Messerschmitt Bf 110 fighters.

The aircraft carrier *Illustrious* had enabled the Allies to rule the

Mediterranean for four months. Off the Sicilian shore, Germany's best pilots practiced on a floating mock-up of the *Illustrious*, with its 620-by-95-foot flight deck.

At high noon on January 10, 1941, the Luftwaffe made its Mediterranean debut, diving from 12,000 feet. Thirty Stuka dive-bombers screamed down on the *Illustrious* as she steamed toward Malta in a convoy. Another thirteen Stukas targeted the battleships *Warspite* and *Valiant*, on each side of *Illustrious*. The Luftwaffe had caught the Royal Navy unprepared for the attack, with only four Fulmar fighters in the air at the time, covering the convoy.

The Stukas dived in synchronized waves of three, from different heights and bearings, dividing and confusing the antiaircraft fire. At angles of 60 to 90 degrees—absolutely vertical—they fell to 800 feet and dropped 500-kilogram armor-piercing bombs with delayed fuses, to penetrate the carrier's flight deck and blow it up from the inside.

The *Warspite* was hit by one bomb that didn't explode. "One of the staff officers who watched it hurtling over the bridge from astern told me it looked about the size of the wardroom sofa," said Cunningham, commanding the convoy from *Warspite*.

Cunningham knew that the Luftwaffe had moved into Sicily, but he had taken the *Illustrious* into the highly exposed Sicilian Narrows anyhow. Air Marshal Arthur Tedder, commanding the RAF from Cairo, had told him that British fighters could easily handle the Ju 87 Stuka. But four Fulmars against forty-three Stukas in coordinated dives wasn't what either man had in mind. The convoy's fighters also had to deal with ten Messerschmitts and eighteen Heinkel He 111 torpedo bombers.

The *Illustrious* was hit seven times in six minutes, with one of the bombs falling into the open bay of the hangar, where some 50,000 gallons of aviation fuel were stored. As the burning behemoth listed toward Malta for the next nine hours, Captain Denis Boyd steered with the engines and the three screws, because the rudder was smashed. *Illustrious* entered the harbor just after nightfall, with hot spots glowing orange in the dark. One hundred twenty-six men were dead, with many more injured.

The convoy's sole freighter intended for Malta made it into the harbor, carrying forty-two more antiaircraft guns along with the necessary soldiers, 4,000 tons of ammunition buried under 3,000 tons of seed potatoes, and twelve crated Hurricanes.

Two nights later, ten Wellington bombers got some revenge. They dropped 127 bombs on Sicily's Catania airfield, destroying eleven MC.200s, nine Ju 87s, six He 111s, two Ju 52 cargo planes, one Ju 88, and one SM.79. Seven of the Wellingtons made it back. And three nights after that, nine Wellingtons repeated the attack, without loss; their crews estimated that they had put thirty-five dive-bombers—Stukas and Ju 88s—out of action.

The Luftwaffe had used up all its bombs, but a convoy to Sicily brought more. On the cloudless winter afternoon of January 16, with the sun shimmering off the still water of Grand Harbour, the sky fell in on Malta.

Forty-four Stukas escorted by ten MC.200s and ten CR.42s, and seventeen Ju 88s escorted by twenty Bf 110s, arrived over Grand Harbour, intending to finish off the *Illustrious*. The RAF sent up all the fighters it could: three Fulmars and four Hurricanes.

The fighters shot down five bombers and claimed another five probables, but the antiaircraft guns scored zero, because they couldn't aim low enough to hit the Stukas when they were vulnerable, flying level at 100 feet after their dives and racing out of the harbor at more than 200 mph. The gunners on the bastions were actually looking down at the Stukas. One antiaircraft gun missed a low-flying plane and blew off part of the lighthouse at the mouth of the harbor.

Malta's "box barrage" of antiaircraft fire appeared for the first time during this attack. The ack-ack guns raised rectangular walls of flak like beaded curtains in a sixties restaurant. The box barrage was intended to foil the attackers, not really shoot them down, and it succeeded too well in misdirecting the aim of the bombers. The Three Cities along the docks, Vittoriosa, Cospicua, and Senglea, were heavily hit.

"Our instructions were clear, to sink the carrier *Illustrious* only," said Johann Reiser, one of the 101 Luftwaffe pilots. "It is true we hit all round the harbor, houses, buildings, roads, and killed many civilians . . . but the murderous anti-aircraft fire all around, north, south, east and west, made it impossible for us to aim properly. It was like hell."

The day also featured the debut of a new Axis weapon, as a guided missile zoomed heavily through the box barrage. It was Fritz PC 1400, an experimental secret rocket that German scientists had been working on for two years. The huge bullet-nosed bomb had four stubby wings and a tail and was guided toward *Illustrious* by radio. It failed to explode or kill any-one when it landed on a nunnery in Vittoriosa. Another Malta miracle.

Most of the seventy-two people killed that day were crushed by rubble, with more dying trapped under blocks of limestone in the days that fol-lowed. The devastation looked so clean afterward. Where once there had been a building, afterward there were just big white chunks of stone. Thousands of them covered the Three Cities.

Five thousand people took shelter in the old railway tunnel in Valletta that night, and it remained packed with teeming humanity for months. Tunnels that had been dug by the Knights under the city were inhabited for the Second Great Siege. There were rows upon rows of triple-high bunk beds, each wooden rack big enough for three children. Some of the boards were scorched black from futile attempts to burn out the bedbugs, fleas, and lice. Hungry rats slinked in the shadows, terrifying the children.

The brave souls who left the shelters the next day were rewarded with some good meals. The sun rose on hundreds of dead fish floating in the harbor, which were quickly scooped up and sold out of carts, cooked for breakfast, lunch, and dinner over fires made from shattered furniture. The fish tasted like gunpowder, but the redolence created by their grilling helped deodorize the air, which was growing putrid with the stench of dead horses.

But the German bombers had failed: they had missed *Illustrious.* After nearly two weeks of round-the-clock welding of the worst holes, she sneaked away from Malta under the full moon of January 23, 1941, bound for Virginia for drydock repairs. Radio Berlin said she was at the bottom of the harbor.

The bombing of Malta by the Luftwaffe continued. The real siege had begun.

CHAPTER 10

SIEGE ON THE RAF

F or the first six months of 1941, no freighters got through to Malta. The "Magic Carpet," that trail of fast minelayers and minesweeping submarines from Alexandria, kept the island alive with foodstuffs and drums of fuel carried in their mine bays. A sub could carry eighty-eight tons of aviation fuel, enough to keep the RAF airborne for three days.

The RAF on Malta had a new commanding officer: Air Marshal Hugh Pughe Lloyd, whom everyone simply called Hew Pew (with a great deal of respect). He toured the island on his first day on the job.

"The trail of ruin was to be seen everywhere," he said.

The small size of the three aerodromes was sufficiently depressing a spectacle, but the air-raid shelters for the airmen were woefully inadequate, while underground operations rooms, in which there might be telephones, existed only in name.

There was not one single petrol pump even such as could be seen in any British village. Our stock was kept in bulk storage of very limited capacity away from the aerodromes, but by far the greater proportion of it was distributed in five-gallon tins in small dumps spread over the island—most of them open to the sky.

How the technical personnel maintained and operated the aircraft baffled my imagination. The humble spanner [wrench], hammer, and screwdriver were as scarce as hens' teeth; and the motor transport, had it been in Britain, would have been used for roadblocks. The engines and the airframes had to be repaired and overhauled, and if parts were unserviceable they had to be made to work, as there were no spares.

Similarly with the motor transport, the air-sea rescue launches and all the thousands of items of equipment. It was never-ending.

That summer of 1941, the quality of life on Malta was affected by events elsewhere in the Mediterranean and beyond. Mussolini had invaded Greece the previous fall, but by winter the Italians were driven out; Germany invaded in April, and, taking some pressure off Malta, most of the Luftwaffe on Sicily moved to Greece in June. (The Royal Navy rescued 16,500 soldiers during the evacuation of Greece, but three cruisers, six destroyers, and 1,828 men were lost to Axis bombers.) Hitler also attacked Russia in June, stealing more planes from the Mediterranean. With Axis airpower down, the time was ripe for a convoy to Malta, from the west.

A tough South African admiral, Neville Syfret, commanded Operation Substance, with six freighters carrying food, ammunition, troops, and thousands of tons of aviation fuel. Just before the convoy entered the Strait of Gibraltar, Syfret sent a note from one of his destroyers to the master of each merchant ship, via rocket line—a shotgun pistol that fired a canister on a rope for 250 yards, over the bow of each ship. Syfret wanted to make sure that none of his words were lost in the translation of semaphore signals.

For over 12 months Malta has resisted all attacks of the enemy. The gallantry displayed by the garrison and people of Malta has aroused admiration throughout the world. To enable their defence to be continued, it is essential that your ships, with valuable cargoes, should arrive safely in Grand Harbour. The Royal Navy will escort and assist you in this great mission: you and your part can assist the Royal Navy by giving strict attention to the following points: Don't make smoke. Don't show any lights at night. Keep good station. Don't straggle. If your ship is damaged, keep her going at the best possible speed. Provided every officer and man realizes it is up to him to do his duty to the very best of his ability, I feel sure that we shall succeed. Remember that the watchword is: THE CONVOY MUST GO THROUGH.

Admiral Cunningham sent a decoy convoy from Alexandria to lure any enemy aircraft away. Syfret's ships arrived in Grand Harbour on July 25, untouched.

Syfret came back in September with Operation Halberd. At the mouth of the Sicilian Narrows, Admiral Harold Burrough took over command and sneaked the merchantmen along the shore of the island of Pantelleria, Mussolini's own little Malta—he had been building it into a military base for twenty years. Burrough's boldness delivered eight of nine cargo ships, with one sunk by bombers. The Italian fleet had come out to intercept but again had returned to Naples. Some 60,000 tons of supplies reached Malta, enough to get the island through the winter.

During the time the Luftwaffe was away, Malta's bombers (including some new fast Bristol Blenheims) and submarines from the 10th Flotilla were also productive. Some forty freighters delivering supplies to North Africa were sunk in September and October, and 63 percent of Axis shipping was sunk in November.

It was all too much for Hitler. Germany's occupation of Greece no longer needed the full attention of the Luftwaffe, so he sent the air force back to Sicily. He brought in Field Marshal Albert Kesselring, giving him the title Commander in Chief, South, with control over Germany's land and air forces in the Mediterranean and North Africa.

"I lost no time in familiarizing myself with my new front," said Kesselring, a former fighter pilot—shot down five times, he said—who got around by flying his own light plane, a two-seat Fieseler Storch, which had gangly legs for landing on rough terrain. "The result of these informative flights was to confirm my view that the menace to our communication from Malta must be removed, and to bring home to me the decisive importance of the Mediterranean to the war.

"Over and over again, sometimes with the support of the Comando Supremo, I urged Göring and Hitler to stabilize our position in the Mediterranean by taking Malta."

Kesselring had a plan to invade Malta, beginning with two thousand Axis paratroopers dropped from two hundred gliders over the edge of the island in the dead of night, followed by ten thousand commandos brought in by sea, climbing rope ladders up the 120-foot-high cliffs on Malta's southeast coast. It was called Operation Hercules, and it had the enthusiastic support of Admiral Erich Raeder (C in C, Navy) and Admiral Eberhard Weichold (C in C, Mediterranean).

Mussolini figured it would be an easy conquest, but Count Ciano expressed realistic fears in his diary:

Malta's anti-aircraft defense is still very efficient, and their naval defense is entirely intact. The interior of the island is one solid nest of machine guns. The landing of paratroops would be very difficult; a great part of the planes are bound to be shot down before they can deposit their human cargo. The same must be said for landing by sea. It must be remembered that only two days of minor aerial bombardment by us was enough to make their defense more stubborn. In these last attacks we, as well as the Germans, have lost many feathers.

And then there were the Maltese farmers, who were known to skewer bailed-out Axis pilots to the earth with their pitchforks.

Churchill was aware that an invasion was in the wind, if not carried by it. It was a no-brainer. The War Cabinet studied and discussed the probabilities for a month, finally deciding that it would take the enemy three weeks to assemble the troops and equipment for such a large operation, so they would worry about it when reconnaissance saw some signs of preparation.

Hitler had once confided to Admiral Raeder, "I am a hero on land and a coward at sea." Operation Hercules was largely a naval operation—an Italian one, at that—and he never really liked it. And so he killed it.

"The German High Command failed altogether to understand the importance of the Mediterranean and the inherent difficulties of the war in Africa," said Raeder. "The calling off of this undertaking was a mortal blow to the whole North African undertaking."

"It was the greatest mistake of the Axis in the whole war in this theater," added Admiral Weichold.

Kesselring was disappointed that he wasn't allowed to take Malta—Rommel had eagerly offered to do the job—but he did the next best thing: he began to obliterate the island.

The Luftwaffe had a new weapon: the Messerschmitt Bf 109F. With its 1,350-horsepower Daimler-Benz engine, the 109 could fly much higher and faster than a Hurricane. In the first encounter between the two planes, twelve Hurricanes were attacked by an equal number of 109s; eight of the Hurricanes were shot down, with no loss to the enemy fighters.

With Bf 109F escorts, the Axis bombers over Malta were all but untouchable. Some eight hundred bombs were dropped on Hal Far, Luqa, and Takali airfields in January 1942, destroying fifty Hurricanes on the ground. Frantically, more pens for the aircraft were built. Every available body was drafted; thousands of soldiers, sailors, and Maltese volunteers worked around the clock filling empty petrol cans with dirt or limestone rubble, stacking them 14 feet high, into three walls each 90 feet long: that was one pen for a Wellington bomber, built by 200 men and women working eighteen hours.

"In January and February 1942," said Kesselring, "the tide had turned: Our shipping losses had been reduced from 70–80 percent to 20–30 percent."

Four British freighters were sent in a convoy from Alexandria in March, with three reaching the harbor. Hew Pew immediately sent scores of RAF men down to the docks to unload the aircraft materials, and they worked all that night, digging for the crates containing Hurricane engines and spare parts; by the next afternoon there were eighteen more serviceable fighters. Governor-General Dobbie didn't have the same sense of urgency; available troops were not used, and the stevedores didn't work around the clock. Two days later, all three freighters were sunk, with only about 5,000 of 25,000 tons unloaded. Without actually naming Dobbie, at least not on the record, Lloyd blamed the grievous loss on "sheer ineptitude, lack of resolution and bomb-stunned brains incapable of thought."

Dobbie believed it was God's will.

The prime minister could see that Dobbie was losing his grip and needed a rest. "The long strain had worn him down," said Churchill, who replaced him with General John Prendergast, 6th Viscount Gort, the heroic leader of Dunkirk. The new Governor Gort landed in a flying boat at Kalafrana seaplane base during a bombing raid, bringing the George Cross medal to the island. His Majesty the King had awarded the highest civilian honor to the 270,000 people of Malta, "to bear witness to a heroism and devotion that will long be famous in history."

It was finally time for the Supermarine Spitfire, which brought new levels of power, elegance, grace, and violence to the air over Malta on its distinctive elliptical wings. The new Spitfire Mark V boasted a 1,470-horsepower Rolls-Royce Merlin V12 supercharged engine, could hit 374 mph at 20,000 feet, and could usually take the Messerschmitt 109 in a dogfight. The trusty old aircraft carrier *Eagle* flew off thirty-one Spitfires in three runs into the Mediterranean in March, but adding just thirty-one planes was like adding teardrops to the sea. They were were lost as fast as they came in, often bombed on the ground.

"I now appealed to the President, who clearly saw that the island was the key to all our hopes in the Mediterranean," said Churchill.

On April 1, he cabled FDR:

1. Air attack on Malta is very heavy. There are now in Sicily about four hundred German and two hundred Italian fighters and bombers. Malta can only now muster twenty or thirty serviceable fighters.

2. It seems likely, from extraordinary enemy concentration on Malta, that they hope to exterminate our air defence in time to reinforce either Libya or their Russian offensive. This would mean that Malta would be at the best powerless to interfere with reinforcements of armour to Rommel, and our chances of resuming offensive against him at an early date ruined.

3. Would you be willing to allow your Carrier Wasp to do one of these trips? With her broad lifts, capacity and length, we estimate the Wasp could take 50 or more Spitfires.

4. Thus instead of not being able to give Malta any further Spitfires during April, a powerful Spitfire force could be flown into Malta at a stroke and give us a chance of inflicting a very severe and possible decisive check on enemy.

On April 20, forty-six Spitfires were flown off the USS *Wasp*. They were attacked by eighty-eight dive-bombers within twenty minutes of their landing on Malta. "Wave after wave dived down, until it was impossible to count any more in the failing light," said AOC Lloyd. "It was an unforgettable sight of holes, smoke, dust and fire. The newly arrived pilots were speechless. They had never seen anything like it."

When the dust cleared, only twenty-seven Spitfires could be mustered for battle the next morning.

Four days later Churchill was at it again with Roosevelt. He cabled:

I am deeply anxious about Malta under the unceasing bombardment of 450 1st line German aircraft. If the island fortress is to hold out till the June convoy, which is the earliest possible, it must have a continued flow of Spitfires. . . . I shall be grateful if you will allow Wasp to do a 2nd trip. . . . Without this aid I fear Malta will be pounded to bits.

FDR agreed again. Back at the Clyde, the *Wasp* was loaded with forty-six more Spitfires.

• • •

General Rommel had been brought into North Africa by Hitler, to push back the British Eighth Army, whose Western Desert Force of 30,000 soldiers—including many New Zealanders, Indians, and Australians—had destroyed the much larger but poorly equipped Italian Army.

"At long last we are going to throw off the intolerable shackles of the defensive!" cried a delighted Churchill when the British advance began. "Wars are won by superior willpower. Now we will wrest the initiative from the enemy and impose our will on him."

But Churchill had had to take most of the Western Desert Force out of Libya and send them to Greece. Unfortunately, the withdrawal had begun on the same day Rommel had arrived in North Africa. Since then, Rommel's Afrika Korps had been steadily pushing back what was left of the Eighth Army.

The Luftwaffe blitz over Malta continued, neutralizing the RAF and enabling an even higher percentage of supplies to reach Rommel, by both land and sea. Axis aircraft flew nearly nine thousand sorties in April, dropping 6,730 tons of bombs on the three airfields as well as the cities around the harbor.

The lack of fuel meant that the Hurricanes and Spitfires couldn't patrol; they had to wait for an enemy attack and then scramble up to meet it, which was a deadly disadvantage. Fighters were grounded for lack of rivets to repair their shot-up skins. Radio operators directed make-believe squadrons in the sky, hoping that the listening Axis would send their fighters to 20,000 feet to chase nonexistent planes.

Pilots with time on their hands manned the Bofors antiaircraft guns on the cliffs around Takali, but they still couldn't do much because ammunition was rationed to fifteen shells per day. Soldiers with Browning machine guns hid in the trees, to defend against raiding enemy aircraft.

The bombing was so focused that sailors with the 10th Submarine Flotilla at Lazzaretto were ordered not to wear their white caps during the day, because the caps could be targets. The five remaining submarines were spending their daylight hours at the bottom of Marsamxett Harbor, along with the skeletons of many dead warriors. But that wasn't safe either, because the water was shallow and a bomb on the surface would still be destructive.

But hiding was futile. With great despair, the last of the "Fighting

Tenth" was sent off to safe harbor in Alexandria, resulting in the cessation of its attacks on Axis convoys in the central Mediterranean. At least the submarine flotilla had run out of fuel oil anyhow. The submarine P-35 got in a parting shot off Pantelleria, sinking a 4,200-ton freighter with two torpedoes fired from 11,000 yards.

With little resistance from Malta, Rommel received 237,000 tons of supplies out of 244,000 tons shipped in April, tripling the March amount. That was 97 percent.

"Kesselring was setting a cruel pace," said AOC Lloyd. "By the end of April we were back to seven serviceable Spitfires. By July 1, we calculated, we should be out of business.

"For us, the siege of Malta had taken an ugly turn. The specter of famine stalked the island."

PART III

ALLIES

On the evening of June 11, 1942, exactly two years after the beginning of the siege on Malta, Fred Larsen made fast the *Santa Elisa* to the Newport pier. The ship had steamed down from Belfast in a small convoy protected by Spitfires, through the Irish Sea, and deep into the Bristol Channel to the busy and secure port of Newport, Wales.

She'd been sent there to load coal from the Welsh mines, much to the dismay of Captain Thomson, because the coal was so dirty and his ship so clean. But at least coal wasn't explosive, and it was a cargo often carried on the homeward journey, so the crew was happy to see it.

Then they heard that coal was usually taken to London, which burned some 30,000 tons a day. If the *Santa Elisa* were going to London, she'd have to curve around Land's End and run east into the English Channel through "E-boat Alley," where German torpedo boats could race out of French ports at 40 knots and blow them to smithereens; and if they got through E-boat Alley they'd have to pass Cape Gris-Nez, where the German shore batteries, twenty-two big guns that could fire all the bloody way across the channel to Dover, were waiting to blow them to smithereens; and if they got past Cape Gris-Nez they'd have to round Hellfire Corner and navigate the Goodwin Sands, 11 miles of shallow water and wide sandbars that had trapped some two thousand ships over centuries. More E-boats lurked in these shallows, along with Stukas diving out of the clouds to blow the merchantmen to smithereens.

Larsen listened to the gripes and fears of the men on his deck crew and said he didn't care where they were going, it was all the same to him. He just hoped that wherever it was, there would be Germans.

• • •

After meeting Minda and Jan at the Oslo train station, the Red Cross lawyer, Mr. Nansen, walked them through more paperwork and presented a travel itinerary to Lisbon. Minda learned that they weren't alone; they would be traveling to New York with seventy-six others, all of them with American roots or connections—like Minda and Jan, they were noncombatants being exchanged by the Red Cross for German prisoners of war.

The group was under the control of the Gestapo, watching at every turn. Minda wouldn't let go of Jan, in fear that he would be snatched away. A fellow exchangee named Erling Andersen offered to carry her two suitcases, and for the rest of the way he looked after the two of them, in addition to taking care of his own family, including a child about Jan's age. He was American-born, like Fred Larsen, but had been unlucky enough to be in Norway on the day Pearl Harbor was attacked, working as an engineer. When the Germans had declared war on the United States, they had arrested the Americans in Norway and put them in Grini, the concentration camp near Oslo. Andersen was used as a cook in the camp, so at least he didn't go hungry like the others. His wife, Johanna, had gotten him out after six months, using the same kind of perseverance that Larsen had used to get Minda and Jan out of Norway.

At least twenty thousand Norwegians were made prisoners at Grini during the war. It didn't take much to get arrested: a radio, a rumor, a glance, being Jewish. Grini was infamous for its high-voltage and barbed-wire fences. The camp's SS commander believed in "exercise" as punishment for offenses, such as failure to snap to attention with your hands clasping your thighs when an SS officer passed. Some died with their faces in the dirt. Some froze. They all starved.

"We tried to beat the pigs to their troughs," said Odd Westeng, a Resistance leader who was held in Grini. "We listened into the stillness of night, and heard heartbreaking screams coming from the interrogation chamber."

Westeng escaped through the fence and helped Norwegian Jews get out of the country before they were sent to Grini. It's not known how many Jews went to Grini, but about 750 were moved from Grini to Auschwitz, and 12 survived. Another 850 were led by the Resistance through the forest to Sweden. Children were hidden in carts and told to pretend that they were potatoes under a tarp. Jan might have been one of them, if Larsen had succeeded in joining the Resistance when he tried.

Minda Larsen and the other fleeing Norwegians took an all-night train from Oslo to Trelleborg, Sweden, with their Gestapo escort. There was only one of them on that train, at least only one that the Norwegians knew of, and he sat in the forward row while they ignored him. In the morning they looked out the windows; Minda remembers the vivid yellow flowers in the sweet Swedish sun.

From the Trelleborg station they were taken by bus to a ferry that crossed the Baltic Sea. The sky was blue and the water smooth, and the boat might have floated on the sighs of relief of its passengers, except they knew they were going to Germany. But it was an easy landing at the small port of Sassnitz, where there were no warships and few soldiers. The group was shuffled straight to a train to Berlin, 150 miles south. They arrived after dark, their blacked-out train squeaking spookily into the blacked-out city. For nearly four hours they were stuck at the station while bombs fell over Germany, as Britain had begun raids with hundreds of RAF planes at a time. When the bombers droned back to England, the train sped southwest across the dark heart of Germany, all that night.

Over the next two days, another train took them across France and Spain. At nine in the evening on June 11, at the same time that Fred Larsen made fast the *Santa Elisa* to the Newport pier, Minda arrived safely in neutral Lisbon with her son and their seventy-six new friends. The hard part of her journey was over. She'd had her two years of hell with Hitler.

CHAPTER 12 • • •

OPERATION HARPOON

On that same moonless night of June 11, about three hours after Fred Larsen had docked in Newport and Minda had arrived in Lisbon, the SS *Kentucky* steamed away from Gibraltar. She was the queen bee of a convoy called Operation Harpoon, which included one battleship, two aircraft carriers, four cruisers, seventeen destroyers, four minesweepers, an oiler, a minelayer, two corvettes, and six motor patrol boats, all to escort the *Kentucky* and five freighters 996 miles to Malta. Heavy enemy attack was predictable, and the mission was critical.

Admiral Cunningham had scanned the American merchant fleet looking for tankers, and the SS *Kentucky*, owned by the Texas Company (soon to become Texaco), was the clear choice. She was one of the biggest and fastest tankers in the world, and was state of the art—her hull was welded, rather than riveted. She had only recently been launched and had made just one brief run, Philadelphia to the Delaware Capes and back.

Britain had been getting some of the best freighters America could sacrifice, although not always willingly and too often to the sea. The *Kentucky* hadn't earned the Texas Company a dime before the U.S. government claimed her for the British, after the request from Cunningham came through channels. Some on the American side weren't happy about it—most notably Admiral Ernest King, commander in chief of the U.S. fleet—but it was understood that FDR wanted to do all he could for Churchill.

The *Kentucky* was the third welded-hull tanker built for the Texas Company by Sun Shipbuilding and Drydock Company, of Chester, Pennsylvania. The first was the SS *Ohio*, followed by the SS *Oklahoma*, which had recently been torpedoed and sunk off Savannah, Georgia. Kapitan Reinhard Hardegen, whose U-123 had claimed nine freighters off the U.S. coast in January, had returned for a second unchallenged raid in April.

The *Kentucky* was sent to Gibraltar with 103,000 barrels of aviation fuel, steaming across the Atlantic without an escort, an astonishing risk. She used her powerful new steam turbine engines to average 15.8 knots, despite a four-day gale. In Gibraltar she was unceremoniously transferred to the Ministry of War Transport. The Yanks were yanked and put on a tub back to New York, and a crew from the British Merchant Navy moved into the luxurious quarters on the new tanker.

The *Kentucky*'s aviation fuel was off-loaded in Gibraltar, and she took on 2,000 tons of diesel, needed for the generators that drove Malta's antiaircraft guns; 2,000 tons of kerosene, needed for heat and cooking by the suffering islanders; and 9,000 tons of fuel oil, most desperately needed so the 10th Submarine Flotilla might return to Malta and resume its attacks on the Axis convoys supplying Rommel in North Africa.

Governor Dobbie had cabled the War Department that there were 920 tons of black and white oils left, good enough for five weeks. That had been nine weeks earlier—before he had been replaced by Gort. Now Malta was down to the sludge in its storage tanks.

If the Axis didn't know that all it had to do to force the surrender of Malta was keep a tanker from delivering oil, it should have. Thanks to the American attaché in Cairo, Colonel Bonner Frank Fellers, Axis commanders sometimes knew as much as Churchill himself.

Fellers reported to General George C. Marshall, President Roosevelt's chief of staff, who was looking ahead toward American infantry combat in Europe and wanted to learn all he could. Because Churchill wanted to keep FDR and Marshall happy, the British Eighth Army was encouraged to open its gates for the diligent Fellers. He attended staff meetings; he drove to the front in a camouflaged van he called the Hearse and greeted British officers with bottles of Johnnie Walker; he moved in social circles in Cairo and milked contacts for information.

From the embassy in Cairo, using a secret code, Fellers sent radio messages with descriptions of military actions and plans in the Mediterranean, Egypt, and North Africa. He also sent details about Malta's dire straits to Marshall, indicating that surrender was imminent.

Unfortunately, the Axis had the code. It was called the Black Code, and had been stolen by an Italian spy. Eager to flaunt the coup, Mussolini had shared some of Fellers's early messages with the Germans, who used them to break the code themselves. For about nine critical months, everything Fellers told Marshall and FDR, he unwittingly told Rommel and Hitler as well.

Hitler appreciated the messages—"our good source," he called Fellers—but it was Rommel who studied each word. The information from Fellers was "stupefying in its openness," said one of Rommel's staff officers after the war, and it "contributed decisively to our victories in North Africa."

"Any friend of Bonner Fellers is no friend of mine," General Dwight D. Eisenhower later told a beautiful British socialite who was enamored with Fellers, before turning his back to her at a Cairo dinner party.

Thanks to Fellers's messages, the Axis knew that Operation Harpoon was coming, and that Malta needed the oil from the tanker to survive. Regia Aeronautica lined up eighty-one fighters, sixty-one bombers, and fifty torpedo bombers, and the Luftwaffe added another forty bombers.

In the first attack, at daybreak on Sunday, June 14, the *Kentucky* shot down one bomber. "One of the destroyers picked up three German airmen who stated that they knew all about the convoy sailing, and had been waiting for us," reported Captain Roberts, the *Kentucky*'s new master. "Personally, I had not known until two hours before sailing where or when my ship was to proceed."

In the second attack, a torpedo bomber came in at 200 feet, half a mile off the *Kentucky*'s port beam. "I saw three splashes in the water," said Roberts, "and could faintly see the wakes approaching the convoy. I immediately altered course hard to starboard and managed to avoid them. The cruiser HMS *Liverpool* and the Dutch merchant vessel *Tanimbar* were both struck by these torpedoes."

The *Tanimbar*, which was carrying ammunition and aviation fuel in five-gallon cans, sank in seven minutes, with thirty men killed. The second torpedo blew a huge hole in the new cruiser *Liverpool*, and she had to be towed back to Gibraltar. Volunteers were given an extra tot of rum for retrieving the bodies of the twelve men who were steamed to death in the engine room.

After the *Illustrious* disaster, the Admiralty had stopped sending its most valuable ships into the treacherous Sicilian Narrows, which pinch the Sicilian Channel between Tunisia and the island of Pantelleria. Stukas flew into the narrows from the nearby North African airfields that Rommel had taken back, U-boats gathered just inside the mouth of the narrows, and fast E-boats lurked in the dark shallows in the middle of the night.

At dusk, as planned, the battleship, both aircraft carriers, three of the four cruisers, and seven destroyers turned back to Gibraltar. The remaining ships maneuvered from two columns to one as they steamed into the narrows, with the *Kentucky* last in the line of five merchantmen, moving at 12 knots and zigzagging to dodge torpedoes.

As Operation Harpoon was steaming in blackness toward Malta, Admiral Cunningham was in London, packing for his new job behind a desk in Washington, and he wasn't happy about it. The First Sea Lord, Admiral Dudley Pound, had insisted to a reluctant Churchill that he needed Cunningham as head of the Admiralty delegation there. It didn't help that Cunningham felt that the man replacing him as C in C of the Mediterranean, Admiral Henry Harwood, was not up to the job.

"So as to free our naval forces if the convoy is cornered," Harwood had cabled Churchill before Operation Harpoon began, "I intend to arrange for the merchant ships to be scuttled, as by doing this they will release the warships for offensive purposes against the enemy, or, if this is impossible, for a rapid return through the bombing areas. What I particularly want to avoid is the loss of both escorts and convoy."

What Churchill wanted to avoid was the loss of Malta. The whole point of the warships was to protect the merchant ships, not attack the enemy. And how could a man like Churchill read the words "rapid return" without hearing "run from the fight" ring in his ears like the boom of a fifteen-inch gun?

The dark night in the Sicilian Narrows passed without any attacks on Operation Harpoon. But as the sun rose on the *Kentucky,* shells from six-inch guns started flying from the east, as if El Sol were spitting bullets at her bow. Admiral Alberto Da Zara had raced overnight from Palermo on the north side of Sicily, with two cruisers and five destroyers, to stand between the convoy and Malta.

Captain C. C. Hardy, commanding Operation Harpoon in the antiaircraft cruiser *Cairo*, sent his five largest destroyers ahead to fight off the Italian warships. The leading destroyer took twelve hits, and *Cairo* was hit twice as she tried to hide the merchant ships behind a smoke screen.

Then, in perfect coordination with the shelling from the warships, the Italian bombers arrived.

A Stuka dive-bombed the MS *Chant*, a 5,600-ton Danish freighter with an American crew carrying aviation gas, ammunition, and coal. All but three men jumped overboard before her superstructure collapsed from the explosions, and she quickly sank. Another merchantman, the *Burdwan*, was disabled and abandoned.

From "Monkey Island," the platform over the bridge, Captain Roberts watched a Ju 88 dive at the *Kentucky* and drop two bombs that "straddled the poop," said the third mate. Giant columns of water crashed on deck.

The chief engineer reported that the main generator steam pipe was fractured and that without electricity, he could neither fill the boilers nor raise steam. He was overwhelmed by the complexity of the *Kentucky*'s engine room, having had just three days in Gibraltar to learn the Westinghouse steam turbine engines, the Brown-Curtiss water tube boilers, and the elaborate electrical system. The fracture in the steam pipe was repairable, but he didn't have the know-how. He desperately needed the help of the Texas Company's American engineer, who had been with the *Kentucky* for nearly a year, all during its construction and trials, and had wanted to stay with the ship to Malta. But when the Ministry of War Transport took over a ship, it became an all-British affair. Politics and protocol doomed the *Kentucky* and threatened the survival of Malta.

The minesweeper *Hebe* began to tow *Kentucky* but could make only 5 knots, so Captain Hardy sent back a destroyer to help. Then, he reported, "I reconsidered and cancelled this order as I came to the conclusion that I could not afford to immobilise one of the three remaining fleet destroyers for this purpose, while the threat from enemy surface vessels was considerable."

True to Admiral Harwood's intentions, the convoy left the disabled *Kentucky* behind, "like a stranded whale," said the third mate.

It appears from Captain Hardy's report, a rambling jumble of sixty items full of contradictions and impossibilities, that he changed his mind about orders to the convoy three times in three hours. He finally took a page out of Harwood's manual and ordered the *Kentucky*'s master, Captain Roberts, to scuttle his ship.

But there were no explosive charges in any spaces for scuttling, because there hadn't been time in Gibraltar to install them. The *Kentucky* had a strong honeycomb structure with welded seams. The minesweepers *Badsworth* and *Hebe*, sent by Captain Hardy to sink her, didn't have the firepower for the job.

Meanwhile, Admiral Da Zara had sent a cruiser and two destroyers around to the rear of the convoy, where the *Kentucky* drifted, abandoned. The British minesweepers cut out when the mast of the Italian cruiser *Montecuccoli* appeared on the horizon, leaving the *Kentucky* and her load of precious fuel to the enemy. Except for a few scorches, a broken steam line, and some destroyed wiring, there wasn't a scratch on her. All Da Zara needed to do was hook up the two destroyers to *Kentucky* and tow her back to Pantelleria. Captain Hardy had effectively handed Malta to the Axis.

But Admiral Da Zara dropped it. "Arriving at the scene, the Italians saw the sea strewn with debris, and all over the horizon were the burning ships and those left behind to help them," reveals the official Italian history. "The tanker *Kentucky* had only a small fire aboard, but several shells from the *Montecuccoli* and then a torpedo from the *Oriani* caused her to explode in flames like a huge funeral pyre, and shortly thereafter she sank."

The irony was "most convenient," said Hardy. Admiral Da Zara was given a medal by Mussolini.

The remains of the convoy reached Malta in the middle of the night. Just outside the harbor, four ships struck mines; one destroyer sank, two were damaged, and the fourth and biggest of the five freighters, the 10,400-ton *Orari*, was holed and lost much of her cargo just outside the breakwater. Glistening waves of oil lapped ashore in the morning sun.

The Admiralty said that Captain Hardy's decision to scuttle the *Kentucky* had been justified by the safe arrival of one and a half freighters. The Royal Navy said that he had "acted throughout with conspicuous courage and resource in the handling of his force for the protection of the convoy."

There's no record of what Churchill might have said about the abandonment, botched scuttling, and ultimate loss of the *Kentucky* to Italian guns. He must have believed the sorry story would have been different if Cunningham had been there, but at this point he didn't care who was at fault. He knew one thing: a tanker had to get through to Malta or the island was lost. There was one more moonless period before Malta would have to be evacuated.

On June 16, the day after *Kentucky* went down, he wrote a "Most Secret" message to the First Lord, the First Sea Lord, and his chief of staff, General Lord Ismay.

"It will be necessary to make another attempt to run a convoy into Malta," began the memo. "The fate of the island is at stake, and if the effort to relieve it is worth making, it is worth making on a great scale. Strong battleship escort capable of fighting the Italian battle squadron and strong Aircraft Carrier support would seem to be required. Also at least a dozen fast supply ships, for which super-priority over all civil requirements must be given."

The memo ended, "I shall be glad to know in the course of the day what proposals can be made, as it will be right to telegraph to Lord Gort, thus preventing despair in the population. He must be able to tell them: 'The Navy will never abandon Malta.' "

CHAPTER 13

MALTA'S LAST HOPE

F ive days had passed since the *Santa Elisa* had arrived in Newport and been loaded with coal. On June 16, the day that Winston Churchill told the Admiralty that there would be another convoy to Malta under the next dark moon, the *Santa Elisa*'s coal was off-loaded, "without a word of explanation," said Captain Thomson.

The next morning, before leaving 10 Downing Street and boarding his special train, Churchill dictated a note to the king that began, "In case of my death in the journey I am about to undertake . . ." He was bound for the Firth of Clyde, where there was a Yankee Clipper flying boat waiting to take him to Washington.

Churchill's death on such a strenuous journey in time of war was always a possibility. On this trip there was the added risk of attack by enemy fighters, especially since the Germans would have intercepted any messages from Colonel Fellers about the trip. The British had finally figured out that intelligence was being stolen from Fellers, so they had ordered him back to Washington, but that had occurred only on the previous day.

Churchill wrote another note, to Deputy Prime Minister Clement Attlee:

The First Sea Lord has given me four alternative schemes for a further attempt to victual Malta from the West. You should obtain this paper from him. Of these schemes the first is the most satisfactory, but it depends upon American help for which I will ask the President. Meanwhile I have told the First Sea Lord to begin loading the ten supply ships.

We are absolutely bound to save Malta in one way or the other. I am relying upon you to treat the whole question of the relief of Malta as vitally urgent, and to keep at it with the Admiralty till a solution is reached. Keep me advised so that I can do my best with the President.

The message reveals that it had been Churchill's order to load the *Santa Elisa*. These words were Captain Thomson's missing explanation.

Churchill feared that President Roosevelt was "getting a little off the rails," meaning that FDR was clinging to the idea that the United States should enter the war in Europe with an invasion of France from the English Channel, instead of North Africa from the Mediterranean. Churchill believed that a premature invasion of France was "the only way in which we could possibly lose this war" and that the trip to Washington to advance this argument was necessary.

While he was flying across the Atlantic, messages were sent ahead for him. On June 18, the Chiefs of Staff wrote to General Ismay:

1. We have considered the means of getting oil to Malta in the next convoy. The only really satisfactory solution is to ask the President to lend a 15 knot American oiler for this purpose. The "OHIO" is due in the Clyde on the 20th June, which would give time for her to be fitted with paravanes, A.A. armament, confidential books etc. British gun crews would be provided but it is highly desirable to retain American crew who are trained to work the Diesel engines.

The final item:

5. We attach greatest importance to obtaining "OHIO" with crew and request that Prime Minister approaches President as soon as possible.

The SS *Ohio*, Kentucky's faster big sister, was Malta's last hope.

The prime minister's entourage included his doctor, Sir Charles Wilson; his secretary, his clerk, his valet, Frank Sawyers (finder and keeper of the Turkish cigars), a bodyguard from Scotland Yard, and stewards. The seventy-four seats in the spacious Clipper cabin had been replaced by a dining saloon and bunks, so everyone got a good night's sleep during the twenty-seven-hour flight. There was also a galley serving delicious meals washed down by brandy and champagne. Shortly before landing, Churchill asked, "Where's dinner?" He was told that meals were now being served on "sun time," and the prime minister replied, "I go by tummy time, and I want my dinner!" He got it—they all did—and he ate a second dinner at the British Embassy that evening, after the pilot passed near the Washington Monument so Churchill could get a good look, before landing on the Potomac.

The next morning Churchill flew up to Roosevelt's estate, in Hyde Park, New York, on the steep banks of the Hudson River, where the president immediately took him on a tour. They had planned to talk that afternoon about how to cooperate on the research and building of the atom bomb, but Roosevelt needed more information from Washington, so it was postponed until the next day.

Churchill got along famously with Harry Hopkins, FDR's curious right-hand man. "I told Harry Hopkins about the different points on which I wanted decisions, and he talked them over with the President, so that the ground was prepared and the President's mind armed upon each subject."

Churchill's mind was armed with Malta, in particular the next convoy, for which the *Ohio* was needed. They met after lunch on Saturday the twentieth and settled the main issues of development of the atom bomb, basically conceiving the Manhattan Project; so they didn't get to many of Churchill's subjects. They had planned to take the president's train to Washington the next day, but they didn't have the day to lose, so they left that night.

When Roosevelt and Churchill wanted to use code names, they called themselves "Colonel Warden" and "Admiral Q," like little boys playing soldier, as Eleanor Roosevelt once observed uncomfortably. Maybe they sat up late on the train and talked, in which case it would have been a good time for Admiral Q to raise the subject of the SS *Ohio*. A master of manipulation and sweet talk when he needed to be, Churchill would have started with a compliment: there was certainly no tanker in the British fleet with the speed, strength, and majesty of the *Ohio*. Maybe the fate of Malta was decided then and there, over cigars and brandy, on a railroad car rumbling through the night.

Or maybe it wasn't decided until the next day. There was a whirlwind of meetings at the White House that Sunday—Father's Day, 1942. The father generals were all called at home and told to come to work. The day blurred, especially after the red-eye train. There was a meeting in the president's office. A telegram was handed to FDR. He handed it to Churchill without a word. Tobruk, the symbol of British will, had fallen. The land battle in the Mediterranean was now on Egypt's doorstep.

"This was a hideous and totally unexpected shock, and for the first time in my life, I saw the Prime Minister wince," said General Ismay.

Another cable arrived from Admiral Harwood in Alexandria, announcing that he was sending the Royal Navy fleet through the Suez Canal and south into the Red Sea, because the Alexandria Harbor was within range of Luftwaffe bombers that would soon be in Tobruk. Harwood's move would trigger a civilian exodus, with Egyptians and others jamming the trains for Palestine.

The prime minister was not happy with Admiral Harwood. One of the messages that had been waiting for him when his Clipper had landed in Washington was a postmortem on Operation Harpoon from Harwood, and Churchill must have winced—and raged—at these defeatist words: "Everybody naturally has the desire to help Malta, but the trouble is the feeling of impossibility."

As the news of the fall of Tobruk ricocheted around the White House like machine-gun bullets on the bridge of a destroyer, Churchill retreated to his room, blown away. But, said Sir Charles Wilson, "In a man of Winston's temperament, defeat is never final. There is never any danger of his folding up in dirty weather."

Impromptu meetings were held late into the night, as the Allies' warrior chiefs moved into and out of rooms in the White House, discussing and debating how to defeat Hitler. General Eisenhower was called, and he was introduced to Churchill, who would come to call Ike "my prairie prince." But it was Admiral King, commander in chief of the U.S. fleet, whom Churchill had to persuade on this night, even though he likely already had FDR's permission to borrow the SS *Ohio.*

King was a first-generation Irishman who didn't like either the British or the Royal Navy. He was tall and hard, with intense brown eyes, a sharp nose, and a cleft in his chin under teeth that were usually clenched. His daughter said he was even-tempered: always in a rage. President Roosevelt said he shaved with a blowtorch. "Not content with fighting the enemy, he was usually fighting someone on his own side as well," said Admiral Cunningham, who would soon arrive in Washington to deal with him.

King wasn't impressed by Churchill's argument that the war would be won or lost in the Mediterranean, and that Malta was the crux. But Churchill needed King's support for another convoy to Malta. Directly or indirectly, King had to sign off on the transfer of the SS *Ohio* from the Texas Company to the Ministry of War Transport. Churchill couldn't go running back to FDR over King's head, especially not after the *Kentucky* loss.

King had just received a memo from General Marshall that began, "The losses by submarines off our Atlantic seaboard and in the Caribbean now threaten our entire war effort." It ended, "I am fearful that another month or two of this will so cripple our means of transport that we will be unable to bring sufficient men and planes to bear against the enemy in critical theaters to exercise a determining influence on the war."

This had been Churchill's relentless theme since before the war began—in fact, his opening act when he was made First Sea Lord in 1939 was to begin arming Britain's merchant fleet. But in the United States, Admiral King had been slow to do the same, with tragic results. Now, with King being so freshly chastised by Marshall, he wasn't inclined to resist Churchill. After the war, General Ismay would write Churchill, reminding him that on this day in the White House, "You successfully pressed King to start the convoy system."

They debated in the president's room, long into the night. When FDR suggested sending American troops to Egypt to assist the British Eighth Army, Marshall got so mad he walked out. He might have echoed what another general had complained: "The Limeys have his ear, while we have the hind tit."

Churchill was sixty-seven years old. He was on his fourth day of travel and meetings, with the world in the balance. The trip had begun with a twenty-seven-hour flight in a thundering flying boat, followed by long hours of eating, drinking, and debating. Add ten cigars a day, and don't forget the minor heart attack he'd had in the White House six months earlier, and one might think only God was propping him up. Or maybe it was the brandy. Or the opportunity, or maybe just the adrenaline.

The prime minister was in his element. He had the floor in the president's smoke-filled room. Everyone there knew about the loss of the *Kentucky*, if not the lapses that had led to its shameful sinking. It would have taken a great deal of cheek to argue that the British now had to have the best U.S. tanker, the SS *Ohio*, which was even faster than the *Kentucky*, for another convoy to Malta—and it must be right away, in the next moonless period, or Malta would fall, right on top of Tobruk.

The next morning, as the British Eighth Army streamed back toward Alexandria in disarray, Admiral King signed the order that led to the release of the *Ohio* for Operation Pedestal.

On June 23, the day Hitler promoted Rommel to field marshal for taking Tobruk, British Army stevedores began loading the *Santa Elisa* with high explosives.

The freighter's five holds were accessed through wide hatches that ran down the center of the main deck, three forward of the superstructure and two aft. The biggest booms were located at the forward corners of the hatch over hold number three, the largest and most stable, being nearest the center of the ship. These big booms lowered the heavy bombs and mines down into hold number three, as well as into number four, located just aft of the superstructure. The stevedores stacked the antiaircraft shells on top of the bombs and mines, the crated aircraft parts on top of the shells, and finally the tons of sacked flour and grain on top of the crates.

Smaller booms were located at the base of fifty-foot-tall king posts, forward and aft of the hatch over number two hold. Pallets of coal, needed by Malta's power plant, were swung into that hold.

Hold number five was near the stern, just forward and under the platform for the four-inch gun. One thousand tons of kerosene in 55-gallon drums were loaded in there.

But it was hold number one that scared the crew. It was the deepest hold, located just aft of the forepeak. It was being loaded with 1,300 tons of 104-octane aviation fuel, in five-gallon cans made of tin. They were called "flimsies," and there were 90,000 of them. They were crated in cardboard and stacked on a pallet, swung from the pier to the hold by the ship's forward boom, and lowered into the hold through the gaping hatch, 25 feet wide and 50 feet long.

The seals around the spouts of the cans were made of cork, and they leaked. Men working in the hold tied bandannas over their faces to filter the fumes, and they wrapped their shoes in cotton rags to stifle sparks from hobnails on the steel deck. "Those cans made perfect Molotov cocktails," said Larsen.

The crew of the *Santa Elisa* was told by the Ministry of War Transport that they could get off the ship while it was still in Newport if they wanted to, although they weren't exactly free to. If they chose not to volunteer for the upcoming dangerous secret mission, they would be confined to an army barracks until after it was over, six weeks without pay, maybe more if the *Santa Elisa* didn't make it back. So everyone stayed aboard.

The ship's Royal Navy liaison officer boarded, and luckily he got on well with Captain Thomson, but not even he knew where the ship was going. The crew was betting in dread on Murmansk, until a man from the Ministry of War Transport gave Captain Thomson a top secret packet, containing an envelope addressed to the RAF commander in South Africa. Thomson hinted to the crew that it didn't look as though they were headed to the Arctic.

But then the ministry dropped off some boxes in his cabin. He showed them to the purser, Jack Follansbee.

"Jesus, that's suicide!" cried Follansbee, his eyes bugging in fear at the fur hats and long underwear.

"Two days ago they gave me a Russian flag," said Thomson. He had thought it was a joke, but now he wasn't so sure.

Thomson and Follansbee had sailed together on the *Santa Lucia* and were good mates. The captain allowed his purser to buy whiskey, as long as he kept it under control, so for the next six weeks Follansbee ordered two cases of Johnnie Walker per week, one Red and one Black; at $12 and $12.50 a case it was so cheap he could hardly turn it down.

A taxi driver told them that the *Santa Elisa* was the first American ship to dock at Newport in three years; there were Yank soldiers up north, but American sailors in Newport were something new. The whole crew was invited to a church dance where they were greeted with red, white, and blue flowers—roses, delphiniums, and gladioli. Two girls teamed on the piano and accordion for a few rounds of "Deep in the Heart of Texas." The Yanks taught the Welsh girls how to jitterbug, and the girls taught them the hokey cokey, which at least one of the salty dogs turned lascivious.

Larsen himself was not the kind of man to do much dancing. He was Norwegian. When the father of one of the church girls asked him what ailed him, he stuttered that he just hadn't found the right girl yet. "Blimey, aren't these Yanks particular?" the man declared. But he and Larsen had a good talk. Mr. Jones had lived in Swansea during the Blitz, and his family had been bombed out twice. There were no days like that in Newport, but he still had to hang black curtains over the windows each night and wait in long queues for half a dozen plums. He'd been living like that for three years now, and he was sick of it.

Ensign Gerhart Suppiger, Jr., twenty-three years old and a skinny six feet four, with no experience at sea but boasting a college degree in business administration, commanded the U.S. Navy Armed Guard on the *Santa Elisa,* and he didn't like some of the things he'd seen so far. The new chief mate and the second mate had staggered home drunk together the previous night and then behaved badly after they found the purser's scotch. In particular, they had thrown a seabag full of Suppiger's laundry out a porthole. "The chief mate and second mate were drunk very much of the time we were in Newport," said Suppiger.

Now Suppiger was watching the loading of the aviation fuel into hold number one, and it smelled pretty sloppy to him. Too many flimsies were leaking too much fuel. When he sent two of his navy men down into the hold to catch the leaking flimsies, things got a little touchy. The chief mate, a salty old Swede, wasn't inclined to take orders from the ninety-day wonder with a diploma. This wasn't the navy. He told Suppiger to get his skinny ass off the deck; loading cargo was the chief mate's job, not the clueless new ensign's.

Suppiger told him that keeping the ship from exploding was precisely his job.

Larsen was helping with the loading of the drums of kerosene in hold number five. He too had an interest in the ship not exploding. He didn't have an interest in drinking, or in Swedes. Sweden had allowed the Nazis in the back door of Norway during the German invasion. His three-year-old son was in the grip of the Nazis thanks to help from the Swedes.

The spark that now threatened to set off the *Santa Elisa* wasn't going to come from hobnails. Resentment flew in all directions among the three men. But Larsen was a leader. "He had that old seamanship about him," said Peter Forcanser, the junior engineer. "He had that boss instinct. He'd say jump, and you'd ask how high."

Larsen knew that the volatile atmosphere could be bled only by solving the mechanical problem. An electrical fan to ventilate the hold was out of the question, because of the possibility of sparks. But Larsen told Suppiger and the chief mate that he could rig up a mechanical ventilation system with a fan and a crank, and that defused their anger. He also volunteered to run the steam ejectors. "Twice a day for an hour I pumped the gas out," he said.

After the hatch cover was bolted down on the 90,000 leaking cans of gasoline, more coal was stacked in hundredweight sacks on the deck over the hold, to protect it from penetration by shrapnel. A 500-pound armor-piercing bomb dropped from a Stuka would be another matter, to say nothing of torpedoes punching into the hold through the ship's hull.

Ensign Suppiger found flaws in other places. He and his crew of nine young enlisted men had come to the *Santa Elisa* straight from basic training together, and on the first day there were no life jackets for them—and none of Suppy's new shipmates seemed to be worried about it. Then a gunnery chief came to provide instruction in the firing and maintenance of the Oerlikons, but he didn't know anything about them.

The Oerlikons hadn't been covered in Officer Candidate School, so Suppy signed up his crew for the two-day antiaircraft gunnery school in Cardiff, to learn how to tear down, repair, maintain, and fire the Swiss-made 20 mm close-range Oerlikons, as well as the longer-range Swedish 40 mm Bofors. Larsen and his young protégé, the cadet-midshipman Lonnie Dales, joined them, even though both of them had already been to the British Merchant Navy antiaircraft gunnery school in Belfast.

They learned how to identify enemy aircraft, and they practiced simulated shooting. There was a darkened room called the "Dome," like an IMAX theater six decades ahead of its time. A Bofors simulator was bolted to the floor in the center of the room, and it rocked and rolled as if it were on the deck of a ship at sea, while firing a beam of tracers at a Stuka dive-bomber falling from a movie screen on the ceiling. The scene included sound effects: the thrump of the Bofors cannon at 120 rounds per minute and the scream of the Stukas that terrorized civilians all over Europe.

They moved to a shooting range in a deep green pasture along the Cardiff coast and manned a Marlin machine gun. A Spitfire zoomed from over the water and buzzed them, as they fired blanks from their Marlins at him. "He was a crazy Polish pilot," said Larsen.

Lonnie Dales had the highest score in the drill, better than Suppiger or any of his nine navy-trained gunners. Lonnie was always quick. The British instructor had never come across any boys from the Deep South before, and he went home wondering if they were all natural shooters like that.

While others chased Newport nightlife—and there wasn't much until the Yanks started coming—Larsen and Dales pursued learning. They took practical courses such as firefighting, although Larsen already knew something about fires from his experience with the fire in number one hold off Atlantic City in January.

Larsen and Dales also went to navigation school. Larsen was already doing much of the navigating on the *Santa Elisa.* He had brought his own sextant onto the ship, and always said that if the ship ever went down, the one thing he'd grab (after the photo of Minda and Jan) would be the sextant. It looked like a small crossbow, and he kept it safely stored in its walnut case. He had found it at a secondhand shop in San Pedro in the winter of 1938, before he had gone back to Farsund to go to the Norwegian academy. He was between ships at the time, working as a stevedore on the docks, so he had free nights to study navigation and practice using the sextant by sighting the stars over the dark ocean.

Navigation was usually one of the second mate's duties on a merchant ship, but Larsen had the task on the *Santa Elisa.* He was good at it, and Captain Thomson trusted him. It was a gift for a captain to have a third mate like Larsen, with his versatility, reliability, sobriety, and self-discipline.

The third mate was in charge of one of the four lifeboats. Larsen had worked with his twenty-two-man lifeboat in Belfast, when he and Lonnie Dales had rowed across the lough to visit Dales's relatives, but now there was more time for drills with the men assigned to the boat. They raced to lower it and learned to maneuver it; some of the men were British soldiers, nonswimmers who didn't even know how to row a boat. Dales was assigned to another boat, but he helped Larsen. There wasn't much about rowing a boat that the eighteen-year-old didn't know.

They rode the train together to London, where they met a couple of Royal Australian Air Force pilots, who flew Sunderland flying boats on

U-boat patrols out of Plymouth Harbour. The Aussies invited Larsen and Dales along one night, and although they didn't spot any enemy submarines, the Aussies showed them the drill. They cut their engines and glided the big plane, then shined the spotlights on the water. "If there were a U-boat down there," said one of the Aussies, "I'd pull on this cable and release those depth charges under the wings, and hope to straddle it with the splashes. A perfect shot would crush the sub like a tin of peaches."

Larsen also visited the American consul in Cardiff and got some good news. Five hundred and twenty-five dollars had been deducted from the account he had established for the purpose of getting Minda and Jan out of Norway; a ticket had been purchased for the passage of one adult and one child on a ship to New York. That was all he could find out. It didn't mean they were really on their way, but it was reason for hope, at least.

At the Newport pier, workers were all over the *Santa Elisa*, hammering, riveting, and welding. Two more 20 mm Oerlikons were added on a new platform on the bow—now there were six, counting the four on the bridge wings. The Oerlikons could fire 450 rounds per minute, with the quarter-pound shells exploding upon impact. It was most effective against airplanes at close range, but it could send a shell for more than two miles with the barrel elevated at 35 degrees, and it could bring down an enemy plane at 8,000 feet, with a lucky shot.

Ensign Suppiger made them move the .30-caliber Browning machine guns farther aft, on each side of the four-inch gun. Two Marlins were mounted on the forward resistor house, and extra ammo lockers were installed at every gun position. Three thousand rounds of 20 mm Oerlikon ammo were brought aboard, along with 6,000 rounds of .30-caliber and 1,000 rounds for the 40 mm Bofors, the bread-and-butter antiaircraft cannon. Fourteen British Royal Marine gunners came with the Bofors, fourteen more nonswimmers in combat boots.

Sixteen snowflake rockets were brought aboard. They burst in the night sky like white fireworks, and their luminescence lingered as they floated under a parachute. They could be used to see E-boats lurking in the dark shallows, although it was pretty hard to light up the enemy without lighting up yourself. Snowflakes were better for spotting survivors from blown-up merchant ships.

A depth charge launcher was bolted to the stern near the four-inch gun, along with a rack for the depth charges, big black drums containing

300 pounds of TNT. But it was the destroyers that usually took care of the depth charging during a convoy, as well as the rescue of survivors. Merchant ships had orders to keep moving.

Depth charges with fuses were strapped to bulkheads in the engine room, to be used if the ship needed to be scuttled.

Minesweeping paravane rigs were attached to the bows. A big steel A-frame extended beyond the forepeak, lowered into dangerous waters like a cowcatcher to trap the cables of floating mines anchored to the bottom. A trapped cable would slide off to one side of the ship and be sliced by a sharp slot at the end of the paravane. Then the drifting mine would be exploded by machine-gun fire from the decks of the ship. Gunners on other ships kept their guns at the ready, because if the first ship missed, the mine could be deadly to the other ships in the convoy.

Two FAMs, or fast aerial mines, were mounted port and starboard near the funnel. The FAMs were shot high into the sky by a rocket, which popped open to release 1,000 feet of piano wire, with a big parachute on top and a smaller one on the bottom, just above the small mine. The wire was meant to catch the wings of dive-bombers, and the mine would be yanked upward until it contacted the plane and blew it out of the sky. It was a top secret British weapon, but its effectiveness soon blew its cover. Ironically, it wasn't the mine that downed the planes, it was the piano wire, which tangled in propellers and snarled engines to a standstill, followed by a splash into the sea.

A pneumatic launcher for four PACs, or parachute and cables, was bolted onto Monkey Island, the thrilling open platform on top of the bridge. The PACs were a lot like barrage balloons around a harbor. The launcher shot a floating parachute four hundred feet up, trailing a steel cable attached to Monkey Island. It could slice the gull wing of a Stuka clean off.

Finally, a DEMS officer attached a buoy with a long coiled rope to Monkey Island.

"What's that for?" asked Follansbee.

"That's so we'll know where you're at when you get sunk," replied the officer.

It was better than what the *Melbourne Star* had. She carried a hundred pigeons to fly off desperate messages to Malta. There was a rating they called "Sergeant in Charge of the Pigeons."

Captain Thomson, lacking a master's experience, went to wartime navigation school while the ship was in Newport and learned "tricks like zigzagging and so on," he said. But he still hadn't been told where they would be going.

"From the look of the guns, the crew and I had a pretty good idea that we might expect some excitement," he said. "But the only thing I knew for sure was that if a bomb or torpedo came anywhere near that number one hold, the ship was done for."

On June 23, as the *Santa Elisa* was being loaded with bombs and aviation fuel, Prime Minister Churchill was riding the rails into the wilds of South Carolina. They were screaming for his head over the fall of Tobruk, in the House of Commons at home, but he had accepted an invitation from General Marshall to inspect the troops at Fort Jackson, and he wasn't going to let political attacks or military defeats change his plans. He wouldn't give his enemies the satisfaction. Damn the crises, full speed ahead on the Southern Express.

As the train rolled to a stop at the army camp, Churchill and his entourage were greeted by a military band and a mass of reporters. There was an empty seat in the back of one of the convertibles, and General Marshall invited along Churchill's valet, Sawyers, a character remembered for his missing teeth and the way he fussed over the prime minister. "His gestures combined with his lisp made him very funny indeed," wrote Churchill's secretary Elizabeth Layton Nel, in a sweet memoir.

All day they watched the army do its thing in the blazing sun, stirring up steamy red dust. There were hundreds of tanks, thousands of soldiers, and field exercises with live howitzers. Fat airplanes flew overhead, leaving a trail of parachutes filling the blue sky like snowflakes. "I had never seen a thousand men leap into the air at once," said Churchill, proving he was able to see the glass half full when he wanted to. "Only three casualties, one leg broken, one sprain, and one suspected skull fracture," added General Alan Brooke, chief of the Imperial General Staff and Churchill's top military adviser.

Twice, Roosevelt had cautioned Churchill's doctor—FDR correctly called him "Sir Charles"—to keep a close eye on his friend the prime minister, under the summer sun. This was not June in England. The doctor was glad that the prime minister had brought his Panama hat. The heat, dust, and terrain reminded Churchill of the plains of India, where he had fought as a young man and played polo when he wasn't fighting.

It's a wonder that he didn't have another heart attack. "All the long morning, we stood in the open, enveloped in dust, sweating in the sun, which beat down on the sandy stretch, as devoid of shelter as Salisbury Plain," said Sir Charles. "All afternoon, still standing, we watched a battle between two mechanized forces until my eyes watered with the glare and my feet seemed too big for my shoes.

"Winston, so easily bored by most things, can spend hours, apparently with profit, inspecting troops," he marveled.

They flew back to Washington that evening. The prime minister was quite pink by now and was still wearing the Panama hat as they landed.

"The brim of the Panama was turned up all round and he looked just like a small boy in a suit of rompers going down to the beach to dig in the sand," said Brooke.

His valet, Sawyers, blocked him in the aisle and wouldn't let him get off the plane. "The brim of your hat is turned up, and it does not look well," he scolded. "Turn it down, turn it down!"

On June 23, as the prime minister was happily sweltering in the South Carolina sun, the SS *Ohio* was moored in Stobross Quay along the River Clyde. She had just arrived from Port Arthur, Texas, with a quick stop at Key West, where she had picked up an escort from the navy base there, a single destroyer that had followed her for twenty-four hours. After that she had been insanely all alone, out on an ocean full of U-boats, carrying 107,000 barrels of 104-octane Texas Company gas for the RAF. That was 3,745,000 gallons.

Her arrival in the Clyde was celebrated. She was the first American tanker to bring fuel across the Atlantic to Britain since the war began. There was a letter of appreciation waiting for Captain Sverre Petersen from Lord Leathers, the all-powerful minister of war transport.

The Master
U.S.A. Tanker "Ohio"
Clyde Anchorages

Dear Sir,

It is with great pleasure that I have been requested by Lord Leathers, Chief of the Ministry of War Transport, to send you from his Lordship his personal message of welcome at your safe arrival in the Clyde with the first cargo of oil carried in a United States Tanker. This special United States assistance in the rebuilding of United Kingdom oil stocks is greatly appreciated and valued. I have, on his Lordship's behalf, to thank you and your Officers and Crew for the safe carriage of this first cargo.

In sending you this, his Lordship's personal welcome, I trust your stay on this side may be a pleasurable one. I can assure you all at the ministry here and elsewhere will gladly lend you any assistance which you may call on them to give.

I remain, Sir,
Yours faithfully

The *Ohio* was big, fast, and sweet. She could carry more fuel than any other tanker on the water. Long and lean, at 514 feet and 9,264 gross tons, she had the bow of a schooner and the stern of a cruiser, with an elegant sheer and bold prow. She was fitted with the latest Westinghouse steam turbine engines that churned out 9,000 shaft horsepower, spinning a single screw of solid bronze whose four blades spanned 20 feet. During her standardization trials off the Delaware Capes, four days before she was delivered to the Texas Company, she had hit a fantastic top speed of 19.23 knots in the measured mile, fully loaded with seawater ballast.

When she was launched by Sun Shipbuilding and Drydock Company of Chester, Pennsylvania, there was no ship like her. She was built like a battleship. Her sisters, the *Oklahoma* and *Kentucky*, had come along since then, but they had been sunk; so now she was again the only tanker on the high seas with a welded hull. Neat wide seams bonded her bulkheads and hull, where hundreds of thousands of rivets were used on lesser ships. Two thick bulkheads made up her backbone, and twenty-three transverse bulkheads, strengthened by girders, sectioned her into thirty-three honeycombed cargo tanks. There were nine fat tanks down the middle and twenty-four smaller wing tanks, with a sophisticated pumping system that discharged oils from each tank quickly and cleanly.

Inside the living quarters, she was like a luxury liner. The cabins of the master, chief mate, and chief engineer cascaded with mahogany, and even the ordinary seamen had single cabins. There were a large smoking room on the upper deck and separate mess rooms for the officers and men. The pantries were full and the coolers huge, and a sailor could get everything from grapefruit to ice cream. Best of all, there were big percolators that brewed rich coffee twenty-four hours a day.

The *Ohio* had been conceived by Torkild "Cap" Rieber, the Norwegian-American chairman of the Texas Company, soon to become Texaco. Sun Shipbuilding had given him a four-foot-long model of the new tanker, which he displayed on a table outside his office in the Chrysler Building in New York and proudly showed off to visitors. He'd been a tanker man all his seafaring life. He had sailed from Oslo at fifteen and by twenty-two was an American citizen and captain of his own tanker, carrying crude away from Spindletop, the oil field that changed the shape of Texas.

Rieber went to work for the Texas Company, and for the next thirty years he punched and cursed his way to the top like a pirate captain, wheeling and dealing in tankers. When he became chairman in 1935, President Roosevelt encouraged him to build more tankers. He bought oil fields around the world the way he collected tankers, including a place for the Texas Company in the Persian Gulf.

He sold oil to anyone who could pay for it, including the Fascists building up for the Spanish Civil War. When FDR found out and threatened to charge him with treason, Rieber began smuggling the oil through Italian ports, discharging it there for Spain to get later. Sometimes the orders to Rieber's tankers were so secret that their masters didn't even know where they were going until they were at sea.

"We have the clearest possible evidence that T. Rieber, Chairman of the Texas Company, has himself made arrangements with the manager of his Italian company to do everything possible to assist Spain to charter neutral tonnage and accumulate stocks of oil, part of which from information received seems to be intended for Italian account," said an internal memo at Britain's Foreign Office dated June 14, 1940, three days after Italy attacked Malta.

So the Axis bombers over Malta might have had Texas Company fuel in their tanks. But that wasn't all.

U.S. Exports of Oil to Spain Increase
Fear Expressed in Washington Diplomatic Circles That It May Be Going to Hitler

WASHINGTON, July 19, 1940—Fear that oil being sent by American companies to Spain may seep through to feed Chancellor Hitler's war machine was expressed in diplomatic circles here today. Gasoline and oil have been going to Spain not only from Texas but from fields in Venezuela and Colombia. . . . Much of this oil, it is claimed, went to Italy directly and indirectly from the United States and American-owned fields in Latin America before Italy entered the war. . . . Diplomatic sources assert that the Texas Corporation, of which Torkild Rieber is chairman of the board, has a contract to supply the Spanish oil monopoly with most of its gasoline and petroleum products.

And it wasn't just Spain. Rieber was accused of assisting in the smuggling of arms and oil in 1940 to the Fascist-backed Mexican revolutionary Juan Andre Almazán. The Mexican government had claimed the oil fields of American companies, which were not above secretly supporting a revolution to get them back.

When Fred Larsen left Norway after graduating from the Farsund Mates and Masters College and marrying Minda, his first job was as bosun on the Texas Company tanker MS *Louisiana.* He had heard of Torkild Rieber—every sailor had heard of this larger-than-life sea captain/executive—and admired the accomplishments of his fellow Norwegian American. The *Louisiana* sailed out of Wilmington, Delaware, mostly to the depots in Port Arthur, Texas, but sometimes she delivered fuel deeper into the Gulf of Mexico and the Caribbean.

Scuttlebutt moves around the decks of ships at sea as quickly as mice. Larsen listened a lot more than he talked, and as bosun on the *Louisiana,* he heard it all. And he didn't like what he heard. He heard about tankers being sent from Port Arthur with fuel for Fascists in Mexico or Spain. He hadn't become a merchant mariner in order to run guns to revolutionaries, in Mexico or anywhere else. The *Louisiana* hadn't been sent on such a mission yet, but she was operating in the area, and it appeared to be just a matter of time. So in the spring of 1940, after about eight months as bosun on the *Louisiana,* he left the ship.

He was lucky to get off when he did. She was later torpedoed off the coast of South America by U-108, which chased the wounded tanker for seven hours before finishing her off with two more torpedoes. There were no survivors among the forty-nine men who were swallowed by the flames from 92,514 ignited barrels of gasoline.

If the *Ohio* had been built much sooner, she might have been caught up in these midnight missions. She might even have carried oil to the German Navy. Maybe that's what she had been intended for. Rieber had twice traveled to Germany to cut oil-trading deals. During his second trip he had met with Hermann Göring, second in command of the Third Reich, chief of the Luftwaffe, and creator of the Gestapo. Göring introduced Rieber to Admiral Raeder, commander in chief of the German Navy.

Torkild Rieber was in far deeper than he realized—and FDR told him so when they talked in the White House in January 1940, after Rieber's meeting with Göring. Rieber had placed a high-profile German lobbyist on the Texas Company payroll, giving him an office in the Chrysler Building, an apartment in the Waldorf-Astoria, a house in Scarsdale, and a new Buick for his flashy blond wife. The Texas Company also retained a German patent attorney who turned out to be a spy, using patent numbers to send secrets to Germany. The tip of this iceberg was exposed in the *New York Herald Tribune* that August, and public outcry forced Rieber's resignation.

But he had squeezed in a final larger-than-life act, one last blast to end his seafaring career. On July 24, he had put on his master's cap and pushed his old buddy Sverre "Snowy" Petersen aside at the helm of the *Ohio*, which had just discharged a load of Sky Chief at the Bayonne, New Jersey, terminal. Rieber had received his letter of instruction as an internal memo within the Chrysler Building: "As arranged verbally, the Enrollment of the S.S. 'Ohio' should be taken by you to the Custom House during the forenoon of July 24th, and you should be endorsed as Master, replacing Captain Sverre Petersen . . . who will proceed with ship to Port Arthur as passenger."

Rieber had followed the *Ohio*'s standardization trials, and he had charted the progress of Petersen's fast run delivering the ship from Sun shipyards to Port Arthur, so he knew what the big tanker could do. His final turn as master wasn't a farewell cruise, it was a flat-out record run. If Howard Hughes could do it—he had set a speed record for airplanes of 352 mph in 1935—so could Cap Rieber.

The Ohio's thirty-three empty tanks could take seawater ballast on the run back to Texas, so she could be tuned for speed. A perfect balance could be found, using the ship's sophisticated pumping system to shift seawater around.

Rieber and Petersen were both on the bridge, and they had more than 10,000 steam turbine horsepower in the engine room. No tanker captains had ever been blessed with so much power to play with, let alone a mission to use it all.

In his final run as a sea captain, Rieber wound the big tanker out and broke all records, covering 1,882 nautical miles in four days and twelve hours. The *Ohio* averaged 17.4 knots, arriving at 1 A.M. on July 29, 1940, nearly a day early, with Cap Rieber laughing at the helm all the way.

Twenty-three months later, at daybreak on June 27, 1942, the prime minister's flying boat splashed down in the mouth of the River Clyde. Churchill called the return flight from Washington uneventful, although he had especially enjoyed a "tummy time" breakfast of fresh lobster and champagne while the big Boeing was refueling in Newfoundland in the wee hours. He was less pleased by the foiled apparent assassination attempt, the previous night in Baltimore, by one of the agents hired by the U.S. government to guard him—"turned out to be a lunatic," he said.

The flying boat landed just downriver from where the *Ohio* was moored in Stobross Quay. Churchill rushed off to catch his waiting train, in a hurry to get back to London and go straight to work, but he should have asked for a motorboat to take him to the *Ohio* so he could plant a good-luck kiss on her sweet, shapely bow. The fate of Malta, and maybe the free world, was riding on the American tanker.

PART IV

OPERATION PEDESTAL

CHAPTER 16

MASTER DUDLEY MASON

On the Fourth of July, Fred Larsen and Lonnie Dales were sent by Captain Thomson down to the Newport police station to bail some of the crew of the *Santa Elisa* out of jail. After an excellent lunch of filet mignon and blazing plum pudding on the ship, a few of the men had been led to believe by a flammable mix of patriotism and pub hopping that it would be a good idea to replace the Union Jack with the Stars and Stripes on the mast of a destroyer that had once been American and was now British. Not surprisingly, the bout between the Royal Navy and the drunken American merchant mariners on the Welsh pier did not end with a win for the Yankees.

As Larsen and Dales were dealing with the delicate details of the release, Larsen's sister, Christina, was waiting on the South Street Pier in New York City for Minda and Jan to come down the gangway of the SS *Drottningholm*, which had just berthed. But they didn't get off the ship.

In the Clyde, the SS *Ohio* had been taken by tugboats up the narrow river into Glasgow, where she was berthed at the King George VI dock, in a state of political limbo. FDR had agreed to loan the *Ohio* to the British, and Churchill had successfully persuaded Admiral King to go along with the deal, but the issue of whether the *Ohio* would sail under a U.S. or U.K. flag had not been addressed in the haste of that weekend in Washington. The crux of the matter was that the American crew knew how to operate the tanker's sophisticated systems, and if a British crew were to take over, they would have precious few days to learn. The Americans were housed in Glasgow hotels while diplomats dickered and officials of the U.S. War Shipping Administration and British Ministry of War Transport exchanged cables.

The Texas Company's top operating executive, T. E. Buchanan, wrote a memo to company president Rodgers saying, "I am sure the War Shipping Administration agent feels the same as we do about changing flag, but it is the Navy's wish that the British handle this particular problem for which the S.S. 'Ohio' is needed." Meaning that both the Texas Company and the British preferred the experienced American crew to stay with the ship but Admiral King wouldn't go along with it: if the goddam Brits wanted the *Ohio* so badly, let them crew it.

Meanwhile, the *Ohio*'s Norwegian-American master, Snowy Petersen, was clinging to the helm. He had been at sea for nearly half a century, since the day he had left Norway on a square-rigged sailing vessel in 1896, and had been with the Texas Company for thirty-two years, most of them as a master. He'd been waiting for a ship like the *Ohio* all his seafaring life, and he wasn't going to give her up without a fight. He told the Brits they'd have to pry his cold dead hands off the wheel, as only a man who'd been washed overboard by a hurricane and swum three miles to shore can. It didn't matter where she was going—Murmansk, Malta, wherever—he insisted on commanding her. He demanded to know upon whose authority the *Ohio* was being turned over to the Brits.

"I'm afraid it's the highest authority possible, Captain," replied the agent for Lord Leathers, adding that a deal had been made between the president and the prime minister, so changes to the scheme were not bloody likely.

The controversy was finally settled after three weeks, on July 10. The disappointed American crew was told to pack up and board the SS *Monterey*, a troop transport ship bound for New York.

"There was quite a scramble, considering the amount of gear a person can collect in two years on board ship," said the second assistant engineer, J. T. Murphy. "Not having enough bags, the chief mate turned the deck department to making canvas seabags. There was no formal ceremony in turning the ship over to the British. The American flag was hauled down and replaced with a British flag."

On July 15, a "Hush Most Secret" message from the Admiralty made it official: "It is intended to run a convoy of 13 merchant ships and one tanker to Malta from the U.K., leaving about the 2nd August, arriving about the 13th August."

The convoy would be called Operation Pedestal. The merchant ships were to be escorted by two Royal Navy battleships, four aircraft carriers, seven cruisers, and twenty-five destroyers, along with support ships such as oilers, corvettes, and minesweepers. The thirteen freighters would carry aviation fuel, and the tanker *Ohio* would carry fuel oil, diesel, and kerosene. Operation Pedestal must succeed at all costs. Malta might be lost to the Axis if Pedestal failed, and if Malta were lost, the Persian Gulf oil would be within Hitler's reach.

"As you know we live a hand-to-mouth existence and our future, indeed our fate, depends on the success of the next convoy," Governor Gort wrote to General Ismay in late July. "Aviation spirit remains our Achilles' Heel and the Middle East Defence Committee consider it *vital* that aircraft operating from Malta should attack ships crossing the Mediterranean. . . . If we run out of aviation spirit and can no longer operate fighters, the chances of getting another convoy into Malta will be very doubtful."

Dudley William Mason, age forty, the new master of the SS *Ohio*, carefully cocked his master's cap at a jaunty angle over his right eyebrow, like a listing ship. He often wore a bemused little smile, tilted up toward the brim of his hat, like an accessory to balance the look. His dry sense of humor kept his children in stitches. Nothing about him was dark except his eyes, shadowed as if something kept him up at night. He was shy but firm and was said to have a quick and instinctive decisiveness, sharp attention to detail, and a record for making the right calls.

Mason had been a merchant seaman for twenty-two years, all of them with the Eagle Oil and Shipping Company, whose fleet included about thirty tankers; the Ministry of War Transport had assigned the *Ohio* to Eagle, on a what was called a "bareback charter." But Mason didn't have much experience as a master. He was listed in the ship's records as "First Mate (master)," as if it were a pending or temporary thing, until he proved himself.

He had fallen for the sea as a teenager living on the north Devon coast, at the edge of the Atlantic. He had joined the British Merchant Navy at eighteen, with enough education thanks to night school to be an officer apprentice. He had risen to first mate by age thirty, but his career had stalled at that rank for ten years, until he was made acting master of the *Empire Pearl*, being built at the Sunderland shipyard on the North Sea. His humor had been challenged by his debut as a master. After the champagne bottle smashed against the *Pearl*'s bow at her launch, she slipped off the cradles as she slid down the ways and was wedged for three weeks.

The *Empire Pearl* was nearly as big as the *Ohio*, but she could do only 12 knots. On her second run, from Edinburgh to Aruba for a load of fuel, Mason had gotten mixed up in the middle of Operation Drumbeat. Off Cape Hatteras on January 24, 1942, he had heard the distress call of *Empire Gem*, a sister ship carrying 10,600 tons of gasoline. A torpedo from U-66 had set off an inferno that only two crew members survived.

The *Empire Pearl*'s owners had sold her to Nortraship, the Norwegian Shipping and Trade Mission—the government in exile in London, more or less—so Mason had been sitting at home in Surrey since spring, waiting for his next assignment. A more experienced master had been scheduled to take the *Ohio*, but something had happened, and at the last minute Mason was called.

"Captain Mason was specially selected for this job, despite the fact that he is our most junior master, on account of his proven initiative and efficiency, and splendid fortitude," said Eagle Oil and Shipping.

Mason was told to hurry up to Glasgow, but nothing more. He left on a train from London that afternoon, having no idea of the importance of the mission awaiting him.

J. T. "Jimmy" Murphy, a young American and former second assistant engineer of the *Ohio*, had volunteered to stay behind in Glasgow to orient the new chief engineer, James Wyld. For three days, Murphy gave Wyld a crash course on the operation and maintenance of the steam turbines and boilers, with all their pipes, pumps, gauges, and controls. Wyld had been an engineer with Eagle Oil and Shipping for more than half his forty years, but he'd never seen anything so complex and dazzling as the vast engine rooms of the *Ohio*.

The Royal Navy had studied all the things that had broken on the *Kentucky* but shouldn't have, and a senior engineer came aboard *Ohio* to make modifications. Both of the steam turbine engines—a 6,000-rpm high-pressure and a 4,500-rpm low-pressure engine—were mounted on rubber bushings to absorb the blow of a near-miss bomb. The steam lines were supported by lumber and cushioned with springs, and their brittle cast-iron fittings were replaced by softer steel ones. Another generator was installed to provide emergency lights and power to the engine room.

"It was a bloody monster," said Allan Shaw, at the time a wiry nine-teen-year-old ordinary seaman. "It was mounted in the middle of a pas-sageway in the crew's quarters aft, just over the engine room, so we always cracked our shins on it when we scrambled to battle stations."

Sixty-three years later, Shaw would be one of the last two living sur-vivors of the *Ohio*'s crew. The other would be in a mental institution, to which he was committed soon after the horrors of Operation Pedestal.

The ship's most radical upgrade, designed by Eagle Oil's chief engineer, was a life support system intended to keep the big tanker afloat even if she had holes in her hull. Using the two big compressors in the engine room, plus a new four-cylinder diesel compressor mounted in a forward hold, air could be fed at 120 pounds per square inch into a 1.5-inch line that ran along the ship's backbone. Branching off this main line were .75-inch flex-ible hoses with quick fittings, which could be connected to feed com-pressed air into the holds. Seawater could be forced by air pressure back out the bomb or torpedo hole it had gushed through. The engineer had in-vented the system as a salvage technique, to be installed by divers in sunken ships to float them up like a big steel balloon, but using it proac-tively in the *Ohio* was a new idea.

After the modifications in the engine rooms were complete, more guns were added to the existing Oerlikons on each of the two bridge wings: a three-inch, high-angle antiaircraft gun on the bow and a five-inch low-angle gun on the stern. Another pair of Oerlikons was bolted to the port and starboard sides of the poop deck, just forward of the funnel. Two Browning machine-gun placements were put on the foredeck, and a pneumatic launcher for four parachute-and-cable rockets was installed on Monkey Island, a third level welded over the bridge.

Finally, a big new Bofors 40 mm antiaircraft cannon was placed on a steel platform over the poop deck, aft the funnel. Dive-bombers always at-tacked from the rear, so the Bofors was the most important gun.

For nearly a month, as her identity changed conspicuously, speculation over *Ohio*'s mission stirred debates over pints in pubs all over Glasgow. On the sunny summer afternoon of Friday, July 24, as thousands of people were getting off work and heading for the pubs, tugboats came for the *Ohio* at the King George VI pier and towed her to the Bowling oil wharf. Half the city of Glasgow was watching as she moved down the River Clyde.

On July 25, Admiral Weichold, the German commander in chief of the Mediterranean, received an intelligence report that said "A large-scale Allied operation is about to break into the Mediterranean. Large merchant-ships and fleet units are being fetched from far and wide in preparation."

And in London, the Admiralty received a secret message from its spy in Tangier: "Reliable contact reports Germans know about convoy Glasgow to Malta and have detailed aircraft and warships for interception in Mediterranean."

None of the captains of Operation Pedestal ships had been informed yet. There were probably more Germans than British who knew about Operation Pedestal to Malta.

On July 31, as the *Santa Elisa* steamed out of the Irish Sea and into the Firth of Clyde, Fred Larsen and Lonnie Dales watched the hills of Scotland roll past the pink summer sky, in shades of green and gray. The ship slowed to a stop in Loch Long, and as they let go the anchor, they could see the *Ohio* moored off the *Santa Elisa*'s port bow.

"I know that ship," Larsen told Dales. "She's the *Ohio*. I was on a Texas Company tanker a lot like her, the *Louisiana*, when she was launched. They made a big deal about her. She's got a welded hull and big steam turbine engines. That's a fast, beautiful tanker. I wonder if she's going to be in a convoy with us."

The *Ohio* lay long and low in the water, silhouetted by the setting sun. Splashed with battleship gray paint and bedecked with guns, she looked little like the shapely, colorful tanker she once had been. Her dull sides slowly got lost in the long dusk and she was soon swallowed by night. But the sweet shape of her bow came back as a full moon rose over the water.

No one on the *Santa Elisa* had ever seen a tanker so conspicuously armed. Sailors came on deck for a smoke and a look and wondered aloud what the *Ohio* might mean to them. They were certain she was there for the same reason they were, whatever that might be. Between the moonlight and flashes from Cloch Point Lighthouse, which had been guiding ships through the Clyde since 1797, they could see other armed freighters anchored nearby, as a dozen more merchantmen had come from Newport, Belfast, and Liverpool.

Dudley Mason had been master of the *Ohio* for two weeks now. He had taken care of some details that evening, chores that he believed needed his attention and that he duly entered into the ship's log:

6 PM

A. Byrne (Messman), when questioned concerning not returning dishes to the Galley, freely admitted he intentionally threw those aluminum dishes over the ships side because he did not want to wash them. He stated he was willing to pay for them. The cost of these dishes was 21 shillings each. The Eagle Oil Shipping Co. reserve the right to take any legal proceeding they think justified at a future date in the civil court.

8 PM

The entry concerning A. Byrne (Messman) was read over to him & he had no reply to make except he questioned the price of these dishes.

On the *Santa Elisa*, Ensign Suppiger was still having trouble with the ammunition. He'd been given the wrong kind of shells for the Oerlikons in Newport, so he had to try to straighten it out while the ship was in the Clyde. The next day a DEMS officer came aboard to inspect the guns, and when Suppiger complained about the ammo, the DEMS officer suggested he go ashore and tell the U.S. Navy liaison officer his problem. When Suppy found the liaison office, he felt compelled to take notes:

Office consisted of: 1 Lieutenant Commander, 1 Ensign, 3 CPO's, 1 station wagon, 3 Lt. JG's, 2 motor launchers, 15 ratings, 1 convertible Packard, and Lots of women and liquor.

The lieutenant commander was in Edinburgh that Saturday afternoon, but the ensign told Suppiger they could find him at a party later that night, so after a few hours hanging around in the office with Lots of women and liquor, they piled in the station wagon with the three petty officers and went to the party, where they found the lieutenant commander with a girl, and he wasn't exactly interested in hearing about ammunition problems.

But on Sunday morning a small barge came alongside the *Santa Elisa* and loaded 500 rounds of 40 mm shells for the Bofors, 6,000 rounds of .30-caliber for the Browning machine guns, and 3,000 more rounds of the wrong kind of 20 mm shells for the Oerlikons.

The Royal Navy crew of eight boarded next, led by the ship's new liaison officer, Lieutenant Commander Barnes. A fifty-foot-long RAF rescue boat came alongside and was lifted out of the water by a boom and loaded onto the forward cargo deck. Otherwise known as a "crash boat," it would be needed in Malta to pluck shot-down pilots from the sea.

At 1600 hours that Sunday afternoon, the masters, Royal Navy liaison officers, and radio officers of Operation Pedestal's fourteen merchantmen were summoned to a meeting on the heavy cruiser HMS *Nigeria*, the flagship of Admiral Harold M. Burrough. Burrough had planned Operation Pedestal with Admirals Neville Syfret and A. L. Lyster at the Admiralty, after studying Operation Harpoon and attempting to solve each of the problems that had led to the loss of the *Kentucky*.

The masters and officers climbed the *Nigeria*'s ladders and took seats in the empty aircraft hangar, a big steel box located high amidships that stored the cruiser's antisubmarine patrol plane. The craggy Burrough introduced himself, tossed a stack of papers on a table with a thump that rang in the metal room, and said, "Gentlemen, it is our great privilege to be chosen to go to the aid of Malta."

"For a moment, none of us said a word," said Captain Thomson. "We knew Malta was at the end of its endurance, and this was the last, desperate attempt to get through. The Admiral might as well have said it was our great privilege to commit suicide. But we all nodded our heads, accepted our orders, and said, 'Thank you, sir.' "

For the next two hours, Burrough explained the mission. The thirteen freighters and one tanker would leave the Clyde at 2000 hours that evening, August 2, escorted by a few destroyers, and on the way to Gibraltar they would be joined by about fifty more warships, plus four oilers, two tugboats, and eleven fast minesweepers and motor launches coming from Malta to meet them. It was every fast ship the Royal Navy could scare up, he said, and they had come from the North Atlantic to the Indian Ocean, to see that the merchantmen made it to Malta. The destroyers would rescue the survivors of sinkings, which should be expected. No merchant ship was permitted to slow down for survivors.

Each of the freighters was loaded with about 1,500 tons of aviation gas, carried in cans so it could be poured directly into the airplanes' tanks on Malta's airfields. Admiral Burrough acknowledged that each freighter was a giant floating Molotov cocktail, but this was war. The aviation gas was divided among the freighters because it was assumed that some of them wouldn't get through, and it was too great a risk to put all the gas in the tanker because it would be the primary Axis target. The *Ohio* carried all the oils because they could be pumped out and transferred into the island's storage tanks—especially those tanks used by the 10th Submarine Flotilla, still exiled in Alexandria and waiting to return to Malta. Her thirty-three tanks contained about 8,900 tons of fuel oil, 2,000 tons of diesel, and 2,000 tons of kerosene.

That's it, said Burrough. It's up to us to keep Malta fighting. The Royal Navy submarines and RAF fighters and bombers need us to deliver the fuel, and the Maltese need us to bring the food. If we go down, Malta goes down. If Malta goes down, Hitler takes over the Mediterranean. May God help us in our mission.

The rigid Royal Navy tended to regard the merchant navy as an outfit full of free spirits, and Burrough was concerned about laying it on the line like that to civilians, telling them point-blank that some of them should expect to be blown up. He didn't doubt their courage, just their discipline. He reminded the masters that orders must be followed without challenge or question.

The continuous evasive maneuvering would be especially difficult. Radical movements, coordinated or solo, were often needed to dodge bombs and torpedoes. The ships had been chosen for their speed, and never in the history of naval warfare had a fleet of seventy warships and freighters and one tanker attempted to travel together at 16 knots, let alone try to change formations and execute emergency turns.

The convoy would have to practice on the way down to Gibraltar, said Burrough. The exercises would be called Operation Berserk. Some of the officers rolled their eyes at each other, but none of them laughed.

"The operation was discussed down to the smallest detail and models were used to demonstrate exactly what action each ship was to take when changing from one cruising disposition to another," Burrough reported. "I was quite satisfied by the time the conference came to a close that all concerned knew exactly what to do under all circumstances, and was most impressed with the cheerful and determined manner in which the Masters went out to make this operation a success."

At precisely 2000 hours on Sunday evening, August 2, the fourteen merchantmen quietly slipped out of the Clyde, escorted by the destroyers

Amazon and *Zetland.* They formed a column led by the 7,500-ton *Deucalion,* spread out over fifty-two minutes to the 7,800-ton *Almeria Lykes,* the only other all-American ship besides the *Santa Elisa.* They passed through the North Channel and steamed north of Ireland, out into the open sea. The masters all carried thick manila envelopes with detailed instructions, marked "Not To Be Opened Until 0800/10th August," which was when the convoy was scheduled to enter the Mediterranean to meet its fate.

As the Operation Pedestal convoy steamed away from the Clyde at dusk on August 2, Winston Churchill took off from a Gibraltar airfield in the "Commando," a converted Liberator bomber with a couple of mattresses thrown into the back on shelves where the bomb racks had once been. He had spent the day in Gibraltar after leaving from London the previous midnight and flying all night, sitting for the first couple of hours in the copilot's seat as the plane flew low over the south of England, with its young American pilot hoping that word had reached the antiaircraft guns not to shoot them down.

Now they were headed off over enemy territory in Africa toward Cairo, with Churchill again riding shotgun, his oxygen mask modified so a cigar could fit between the nosepiece and chin rest. "He looked exactly as though he was in a Christmas party disguise," said the officer in charge of oxygen.

General Brooke had left England one day earlier, so he could stop in Malta and visit Governor Gort. His Liberator took a more dangerous route over the Mediterranean, risking the nearly full moon, and landed before dawn between the bomb craters on Hal Far airfield. Brooke was concerned about Gort, who insisted on living on reduced food rations, "in spite of the fact that he was doing twice as much physical and mental work as any other member of the garrison. Owing to the shortage of petrol he was using a bicycle in that sweltering heat, and frequently had to carry his bicycle over demolished houses."

"The conditions prevailing in Malta at that time were distinctly depressing, to put it mildly," said Brooke. "Shortage of rations, shortage of petrol, a hungry population that rubbed their tummies looking at Gort as he went by, destruction and ruin of docks, loss of convoys just as they approached the island, and the continual possibility of an attack . . . without much hope of help or reinforcements."

The next morning at sunrise, Churchill and Brooke landed in their separate Liberators on an airfield near the Egyptian pyramids. Churchill had flown to Cairo to find out what was wrong with the Eighth Army and fix it.

He thought he already knew the problem: General Claude Auchinleck. Rommel was stalled without supplies outside El Alamein, and Churchill wanted Auchinleck to begin moving west again. More immediately, he wanted the Axis airfields between Alamein and Tobruk neutralized for Operation Pedestal, and he wanted Auchinleck to stage some sort of diversionary attack so the Axis bombers would be drawn away from the convoy's ships.

Auchinleck, "the Auk," was a tall, rugged Scot, red-headed, square-jawed, and stubborn. He didn't believe his Western Desert Force could resume the offensive for another six weeks, and he was resistant to having his soldiers used as decoys for bombs for the sake of a distant merchant convoy.

"The bloody man does not seem to care about the fate of Malta!" Churchill shouted to Sir Charles Wilson about Auchinleck.

"The plight of Malta had become an obsession with him," said Sir Charles of Churchill.

"Rommel, Rommel, Rommel! What else matters but beating Rommel!?" Churchill ranted, pacing the floor of his air-conditioned room at the British Embassy in Cairo.

Churchill felt that Auchinleck couldn't see the direct connection between the strength of Malta and the success of the Eighth Army. Couldn't he see that Operation Pedestal was critical to the defeat of Rommel? Where did the Auk think the attacks on Rommel's supply lines and convoys were coming from, if not from the RAF bombers and Royal Navy submarines, which were needed so badly back on Malta?

"We're going to lick Rommel!" Churchill told everybody he met in Egypt, so often that "Lick Rommel" soon became the slogan of the visit. The prime minister wore a Bombay bowler that looked like a pith helmet, brandished a big black horsehair fly swatter, and was never without a cigar despite the heat. He had taken a new code name for this trip, Mr.

Bullfinch, and those around him spoke mysteriously and reverentially about how Bullfinch had done this, gone there, or said that.

He climbed into a new Dakota, the RAF version of the Douglas DC-3 airliner, and flew over the North African desert to the front, El Alamein, to research the situation and have a word with Auchinleck. Upon his return to Cairo, he fired the Auk and replaced him with Lieutenant General Bernard Montgomery, who was "quick as a ferret and almost as likeable," said Brooke. But, said Churchill, "If he is disagreeable to those about him, he is also disagreeable to the enemy."

The prime minister ended his trip with a directive intended for Montgomery that couldn't have been more clear:

I. Your prime and main duty will be to take or destroy at the earliest opportunity the German-Italian Army commanded by Field-Marshal Rommel, together with all its supplies and establishments in Egypt and Libya.

CHAPTER 19

ADMIRAL NEVILLE SYFRET

At sunrise on August 3, as Winston Churchill and General Brooke were landing in separate Liberators on an airfield near the pyramids, the incipient Operation Pedestal convoy was steaming south off the coast of Ireland. The merchant ships were formed in four columns separated by six cables, about 3,650 feet, or six-tenths of a nautical mile, long. The *Santa Elisa* was in position 42, fourth column and second in line; and the *Ohio* was off the *Santa Elisa*'s port beam in position 32. Larsen was at the helm of the *Santa Elisa*, standing the watch from 0400 to 0800. "Our course took us about 300 miles out into the Atlantic, seemingly to pretend that we were not going into the Mediterranean," he said.

Captain Thomson had told Larsen and a few others that they were headed to Malta, but he hadn't announced it to the crew. "A knot of us starts debating our destination," said the chief engineer, Ed Randall. " 'Dakar,' says somebody. 'A second front,' says another, pointing to the warships all around us. Others argue for Alexandria, East Africa, and Madagascar, and some of them put cash on the line to back up their theories."

Admiral Burrough had left the Clyde in the cruiser *Nigeria* at midnight, and by steaming at 33 knots had now caught up. He commanded the convoy to merge from four columns into two, just for practice. The complicated maneuver would need to be rehearsed many times on the way to Gibraltar, because there would be no time or room for error at the entrance to the Sicilian Narrows, when it would need to be done for survival.

"Practicing zigzag courses on the way down to Gibraltar was pretty easy," said Allan Shaw, the ordinary seaman on the *Ohio*. "Ships doing sixteen knots are easier to handle and quicker to maneuver than slow-moving ones."

But not everyone found it so simple; some of the freighters had trouble staying in position and staying out of the way of other ships. "Station keeping at this stage was naturally very poor, but I was confident that these fine ships could with training be moulded into a well disciplined team," reported Admiral Burrough.

At 0845, Captain Mason called the crew of the *Ohio* into the petty officer's mess and told them where they were going. He opened the envelope labeled "Not to be opened until 0800/August 10" and read them a letter from the First Lord of the Admiralty wishing them Godspeed and good luck.

"I addressed the whole crew, explaining the object of the voyage, nature of the escort, and what was expected during the voyage," he reported to Eagle Oil and Shipping. "A considerable amount of what had passed at the Conference the previous day was told, and I advised them I would be only too pleased to answer any questions they might like to ask."

"You men have been specially chosen for this voyage," he told them. "Just remember that. You are chosen men. I want no dodgers, no questions asked when an order is given. If you're called upon to do extra duties, remember that this is a special voyage, and one of enormous importance. I don't expect it's going to be a picnic. But we will have a massive escort. There might be a raid or two, but we're not going to have any trouble getting there. We will get to Malta."

"I concluded my remarks by telling them that I had no doubt whatever that they would all do their utmost as and when the occasion demanded, and that I had absolute faith in them all. The loud cheers that followed were spontaneous, and it seemed to start the voyage in a friendly atmosphere which existed throughout the whole operation."

At 0930 the heavy metal arrived, steaming up on the convoy at 23 knots. "I was on watch, and I was able to see what looked like a battle fleet approaching us from the north," said Frank Pike, a British Army corporal on the *Santa Elisa* being taken to Malta to work on the radar. "Two battleships were clearly visible, along with several more cruisers, two aircraft carriers and a lot more destroyers. Fortunately, they turned out to be on our side."

Acting vice admiral Neville Syfret, a lean and hungry South African, squinted into the sun from the bridge of the battleship *Nelson*, his flagship.

His teeth gripped the tip of the stem of his pipe, which smoked like the barrel of a rapid-fire cannon and dangled dangerously toward the armor-plated deck of his battleship, much like the way he lived. He liked to hang it out there. He was the right man for a ship with so many guns, because guns were in his blood. He'd been a young gunnery officer on a cruiser in World War I, roaming the vicious North Sea. After the war he had been fleet gunnery officer for the Mediterranean Fleet and later had commanded the Naval Gunnery School at Devonport.

Admiral Cunningham said Syfret was "a tower of strength, a man of great ability and of quick and sound decision with a brilliant war record. His great knowledge and charm of manner made him a delightful comrade."

Churchill had made Syfret an admiral when Syfret was secretary to the First Lord of the Admiralty, and Churchill was that lord. He fit the prime minister's mold, with the right stuff in his résumé for a mission like Operation Pedestal. He knew a lot about running to Malta, having commanded the cruiser *Edinburgh* on two previous convoys. He had taken six out of six freighters to Malta with Operation Substance; and, working with Admiral Burrough on Operation Halberd, had charted a daring course along the island of Pantelleria to deliver eight of nine.

Syfret was fresh from victory in Operation Ironclad, the invasion of Madagascar, the first major amphibious assault of the war. Lying just off the southeast coast of Africa, Madagascar was a steaming 900-mile-long island with strange wildlife living in the mountains and rain forests and a beautiful mix of French-speaking Afro-Asians walking the streets. In Napoleon's time, those streets were roamed by more than a thousand pirates of English, French, Portuguese, Dutch, and American bloods.

At the northern tip of the island lay the port of Diégo-Suarez, which the Vichy French had controlled, the Japanese coveted, and the Allies needed, because of its position along shipping lanes flowing around the Cape of Good Hope, up the east coast of Africa, through the Red Sea, and into the Suez Canal. The French hadn't been attacking Allied merchant shipping, but if the Japanese were to take Madagascar they would use Diégo-Suarez as a submarine base. An invasion was deemed necessary by Churchill.

Syfret had planned Operation Ironclad in a matter of days and commanded the mission from his flagship, the battleship *Ramillies*. He had sent in two decoy invasions, with planes dropping dummies from parachutes on one side of the island and a cruiser firing dummy shells on the other. The merchant navy had carried in soldiers and Royal Marines to the dark west side of the island, which the French had mined and considered impenetrable. The marines had transferred to a destroyer that dropped them at a jetty, and, with air support from two aircraft carriers, had fought their way to the harbor and captured it in two days.

Immediately after Ironclad, Syfret had put on his civilian clothes to travel incognito and hopped a train west across the southern tip of Africa, from Durban to Cape Town. From there he had boarded the armed merchantman *Canton* to get back up to Freetown, 3,500 miles from the Cape of Good Hope. He had been lounging on the deck of the freighter reading a book in the tropical sun when the message had come from the Admiralty that he was needed in London to plan and lead another top secret mission. The *Canton* had dropped him at the Takoradi base, and he had flown the rest of the way, a grueling trek on available military aircraft.

The battleships *Nelson* and *Rodney*, now steaming within sight of the *Santa Elisa*, were close sisters like the cruisers *Nigeria* and *Kenya*, though not nearly so young and quite a bit heavier. They were the biggest warships in the Royal Navy: 710 feet long, 106 feet wide, and displacing 34,000 tons. A camouflage paint scheme floated like gray clouds over each hull, and forty-five gun barrels stuck out like hedgehog quills. They carried nine sixteen-inch guns in three triple turrets mounted forward of the bridge tower and twelve six-inch guns in six double turrets aft. There were also six five-inch guns, eight two-pounders (so called for the weight of the projectile), two 20 mm Oerlikons, and eight .50-caliber machine guns.

The battleships, aircraft carriers, and cruisers were escorted by the destroyers *Ashanti, Pathfinder, Eskimo, Somali, Tartar,* and *Quentin*, making a dozen destroyers in the convoy so far, with many more to come.

Jack Follansbee came onto the bridge of the *Santa Elisa* and said to Captain Thomson, "What an escort!"

"You haven't seen anything yet," replied Thomson.

"It looked to me as if the whole British fleet was escorting us," said Larsen.

"Maybe that escort should have made us feel better, but in a way it made us feel worse," said Thomson. "It was so terribly big that the crew realized, for the first time, that we were heading into something deadly."

CHAPTER 20

LIEUTENANT COMMANDER ROGER HILL

Before he left Scapa Flow to join up with Operation Pedestal, Lieutenant Commander Roger Hill, commanding officer of the destroyer *Ledbury*, got drunk one night and stole a chicken on his way back to the ship. At thirty-two, he was one of the youngest destroyer captains in the war, although he was not inexperienced, having been in the Royal Navy for fifteen years. He had a scraggly black beard and wore a striped rugby shirt at sea, so he looked a bit like a pirate, but he also played the piano and could be quite high-strung, so his crew never knew what to think about him.

"The *Ledbury* had been adopted by an American heiress, who sent them lots of goodies," said a jealous sailor from another ship. "They did nothing but play Glenn Miller and Harry James records, which this heiress had sent. She got Captain Hill his little piano, too, which he somehow squeezed into his quarters."

On the night of the stolen chicken, Hill and the ship's doctor had been pub hopping on his motorcycle, a thumping 500 cc single-cylinder Norton whose rear tire was squashed flat against the cobblestone streets—Hill had stuffed grass into it, for want of a rubber patch. The doctor boasted he could sneak up on a chicken and wring its neck before it squawked. And he succeeded—until they staggered up the gangway and the chicken got a second wind under the captain's coat and squawked like only a half-strangled chicken can, said Hill.

Hill had been assigned to command the *Ledbury* while she was being completed at the Southampton shipyard. He rode up on the Norton on an ugly January night and climbed to the unfinished bridge, where he imagined he was shooting down Stukas: ack-ack-acking with an invisible Oerlikon at the drizzly sky. He also had the capture of a U-boat and its crew all worked out in his mind. After forcing it to the surface with depth charges, the *Ledbury*'s gunners would hold down the sub's hatch with tracer fire while a boarding party would scramble onto its deck, open the hatch, and herd the surrendering Germans with machine guns. Hill would climb down into the sub himself and claim its Enigma decoding machine, the ultimate trophy. "I peopled the *Ledbury* with lusty, happy sailors ripping out the shells at an unprecedented rate of fire," he said.

Hill's third fantasy was ramming a German battleship. It was an especially daring dream because the little *Ledbury* was only a 1,010-ton *Hunt*-class destroyer, although she was being used for the work of a larger *Tribal* class, because so many *Tribals* had been sunk.

"He wasn't very popular with the ship's company, you know," said the doctor, John Nixon. "The crew called him 'Phyllis.' It wasn't a term of endearment, and I'm not going to say any more than that. But that was in Scapa Flow, a very dreary place. He used to get very worked up, as many a captain did, trying to maneuver a small destroyer in that place. He used to get tantrums, swearing at the ship's company and the gunnery officer, Musham. That doesn't go down very well. It's better for a ship's captain to keep his cool, if he can."

"Still, he possessed the element of luck in full measure, and the men knew it," said Robin Owen, his cadet.

It may have been true that there were times when Hill's heart flopped onto the sleeve of his woolen peacoat, but that's because it was like a lion's and it needed some room. As the *Ledbury* steamed to meet Operation Pedestal, he was both depressed and angry.

One month earlier, the *Ledbury* had been part of the infamous PQ17 convoy to Murmansk. Tracking the convoy from London, First Sea Lord Dudley Pound had incorrectly and singularly believed it was about to be attacked by the German battleship *Tirpitz*—he had seen phantoms, possibly a symptom of the brain tumor that would kill him. So he ordered the Royal Navy escorts to scatter, leaving the merchantmen to be slaughtered by German bombers and U-boats that the warships could have fought off.

"The dismal tale of each ship or little group of ships, some of them accompanied by one or more of the smaller escort vessels, became a saga in itself," said Churchill. "Of the 34 ships which left Iceland, 23 were sunk, and their crews perished in the icy sea or suffered incredible hardships and mutilation by frostbite. Fourteen American ships in all were sunk. This was one of the most melancholy naval episodes in the whole of the war."

The disaster of PQ17 made Operation Pedestal all the more important to Churchill. His use of the word "melancholy" is suggestive—and profound. He was plagued by bouts of depression he called "marauders" or the "Black Dog"; the main reason he kept Dr. Sir Charles Wilson by his side was to keep the demons away. After the consecutive devastating defeats of Operation Harpoon, Tobruk, and PQ17, Churchill knew that one more loss might mean a vote of "no confidence" from the House of Commons. The prime ministership was riding on Operation Pedestal.

When the warships returned to Scapa Flow after PQ17, the Royal Navy sailors were met with hostility. Some of the *Ledbury*'s men got drunk and had a fight with some Yanks from a cruiser who called them yellow Limeys. "The feelings of the Americans from the cruisers and destroyers which had been on PQ17 ran high, and there were some serious fights ashore," said Hill. "In fact, there were some deaths, I heard."

Before the *Ledbury* left Scapa Flow to join Operation Pedestal, Hill had told his men that he intended to disobey any order to leave the survivors of a sunken merchant ship in the water. But he doubted that such an order would come, this time. He knew that Admiral Syfret was a fighter, having years earlier served under Syfret's command on the cruiser *Caradoc*, based in China, eight hundred miles up the Yangtze River.

But PQ17 wasn't the only reason Hill's emotions were raw. His kid brother, a twenty-one-year-old Royal Marine officer, had been killed in November when the battleship *Barham* was torpedoed in the Mediterranean; she had capsized within five minutes and been on her side when she blew up, killing 862 men.

It was easy for a man of Hill's emotion and imagination to program himself to leap into the ocean to rescue survivors, as if the seawater would get the bitter taste of PQ17 out of his mouth. That's what he did when a Sunderland flying boat crashed into the water near the *Ledbury* out in the Atlantic.

The *Ledbury* was one day ahead of Operation Pedestal, escorting another convoy. The pilot of the antisub Sunderland had made the rookie mistake of flying low over the convoy in a fog; three of the merchantmen had failed to recognize the friendly aircraft and opened fire. The Sunderland passed over the *Ledbury* with one engine on fire, diving toward the sea. Hill raced through the fog and found the crashed plane on the water with the crew sitting on one wing. The Sunderland sank, and there was an underwater explosion.

The Sunderland's depth charges had been set to explode at fifty feet, and the pilot had failed to eject them before the plane hit the water.

"When the spray from the explosion had settled, leaving a bubbling circle of foam, the crew of the plane were scattered all over the place. I thought the quickest way would be for me to fetch the most distant man, since I was a fast swimmer," said Hill.

He turned to his cadet and declared, "Take the helm, pilot, I am going after that man!" And he leaped off the bridge, thirty or more feet into the water, furiously stroking toward the man, whom he saved.

Eight of the nine Sunderland airmen died from the concussion of the depth charges. "It looked like their buttons had been pressed in by a thumb," said Don Allen, a radar operator on the *Ledbury* bridge. The dead airmen were sewn up in hammocks, weighted down with boiler bricks, and buried at sea.

Captain Hill knew that his superiors wouldn't approve of his diving overboard and leaving his ship in the hands of a cadet. The words "Take the helm, pilot, I am going after that man!" sounded more foolish than gallant to the Royal Navy.

Charles Henry Walker, still built like a bull at age ninety, was the cook on *Ledbury* and captain of its water polo team. He dived into the water behind Hill to make sure his captain didn't drown. "Afterward, the captain looked me close in the eye and said, 'Walker, you didn't see nothing, did you?' and I replied, 'No sir.'

"The navy never did like Roger Hill's ways," he adds. "He was still a lieutenant commander when he got out. They should have made him a 'Sir.' "

CHAPTER 21

OPERATION BERSERK

Day and night, warships joined the convoy and took their place in the formation, until there were about sixty ships of all kinds. Each day at high noon, from the bridge of the *Santa Elisa*, Fred Larsen took a reading of the sun with his sextant, plotting the convoy's course just for practice. He read the stars from the bridge during his watch from 0400 to 0800 and plotted the course again.

The master of each merchant ship had been given a thick book of twenty-four cruising dispositions, with instructions on how to merge from one to another, but only a few of the formations applied to the merchantmen, and the masters were thankful for it. The basic freighter formation was four columns, with the two big battleships, *Nelson* and *Rodney*, leading a fifth center column made up of the aircraft carriers, none of which was planning to go all the way to Malta. The carriers were the convoy's wide backbone, with freighters on each side. The seven cruisers covered the freighter columns, port and starboard, and a wedge-shaped ring of destroyers screened the outside against U-boats and enemy aircraft.

For days, the ships practiced zigging, zagging, merging, turning, shooting, signaling, and more, sometimes at top speed and often in darkness. Admiral Syfret was pleased by how the merchantmen learned the moves. They would make a total of twenty-seven emergency evasive turns, many of them actual U-boat alerts, with destroyers dropping depth charges in the direction of unseen submarines.

"Bump-bump-bump, they went," wrote a young merchant sailor named Desmond "Dag" Dickens, the son of a cousin of Charles Dickens, "and for every bump a colossal fountain of white spray would heave itself out of the calm blue water."

"They're dropping them at random," said Captain Thomson. "The idea is that the depth charges will keep the U-boats at a distance. Everybody knows they're out there, waiting for a chance."

Late in the afternoon of August 5, Admiral Burrough broke away from the convoy in his swift cruiser, *Nigeria.* Her ungainly Walrus antisubmarine patrol plane was launched from the steam-powered catapult in the aircraft hangar high amidships, and it flew ahead of the cruisers in slow circles, looking for subs. Burrough ordered the *Nigeria* cranked up to 30 knots and disappeared toward the pink sunset, skipping over the sun-kissed waves like an offshore powerboat racer at Key West. He was in a hurry to get down to Gibraltar, to work out the logistics for the final day of Operation Berserk, as the ongoing exercises on the way down to Gibraltar were so aptly named.

There were now five aircraft carriers with the convoy. "When *Indomitable* joined my flag it is believed to have been the first occasion when five of Her Majesty's aircraft carriers have ever operated in company at sea simultaneously," said Admiral Syfret. The *Indomitable* had steamed around Africa from Madagascar, where Syfret had used her in Operation Ironclad. But because she had been a day late leaving Freetown, she had had to race to rendezvous with Pedestal and needed fuel when she got there.

The oiler *Abbeydale* was there for that purpose but had never refueled an aircraft carrier before, so the attempt didn't go well, and *Indomitable* would have to go ahead into Gibraltar to refuel and then back out into the Atlantic to rejoin the convoy. In fact, none of the warships in the previous Malta convoys had ever needed refueling at sea, because Malta had always had enough to get them back home.

"In this case Malta had no oil to spare," said Syfret. "The problem of oiling three cruisers and 26 destroyers at sea, under enemy observation and in U-boat-infested waters, was an anxious one, failure of which could have seriously upset the whole plan."

On Saturday night, August 8, there were seven ships from Operation Pedestal refueling in Gibraltar, enough that Admiral Burrough called a midnight meeting of their captains. In the nearby neutral Spanish town of Algeciras, two Royal Navy officers finished their late dinner and on their way out passed a German sitting at a table.

"Today we see you," the German told the officers with a knowing smile.

"You sail out and you sail back, you sail out and you sail back. Then you will sail out and don't come back. Then we go out and get you."

On the blistering hot Sunday afternoon of August 9, as Winston Churchill was firing General Auchinleck in Cairo, the convoy was still out in the Atlantic Ocean just west of Gibraltar, preparing for the closing exercise of Operation Berserk. It was time for the war games.

On the *Santa Elisa*, Captain Thomson posted the signal from Admiral Syfret.

To all ships:

Commencing at 1700 this evening mock warfare exercises will be held. One half of the carrier-based aircraft will take off at 1700 and will simulate an air attack on the convoy. The attack will be performed in the following order: 1715 dive bombing, 1730 torpedo bombing, 1745 strafing, 1800 high and medium level bombing, 1815 combination all types of attack. At 1830 all planes will return to their carriers. During these exercises unloaded anti-aircraft weapons may be trained on the aircraft.

It was a thrilling hour and a half, especially the final fifteen minutes, "combination all types of attack." Larsen and Dales each manned an Oerlikon, at their battle stations on the forward and after port bridge wings. Planes screamed over the ships' bows and masts as gunners tried to keep them in their sights, with their fingers held away from the triggers. Men on the monkey decks dodged imaginary strafing from Hurricanes and practiced imaginary launching of the parachute-and-cable rockets. They all tried to memorize the features of their own Spitfires, Hurricanes, Martlets, Fulmars, and Albacores. Larsen and Dales had already been to the school, so that part was just review for them.

Admiral Syfret had attempted to coordinate this grand finale while maintaining wireless and radio silence, because they were within reach of German electronic ears in Morocco and Tangier, but he soon saw it was hopeless. The exercise "did entail a great volume of W/T [wireless] and R/T [radio] traffic which must have been very apparent to enemy or enemy-controlled listening stations," he reported, but added, "This risk to security was considered acceptable when balanced against the benefit to be derived from the practices."

The sun sank into the sea like a flaming red beach ball. Darkness exposed the glittering lights of two shores, Spain to the north and Morocco to the south, divided by the Strait of Gibraltar, narrowing to eight miles wide. A fog fell on the moonless night, and the Rock of Gibraltar rose from a ghostly mist, as the convoy slipped through the strait as invisibly as sixty ships can. Only the greenest or most optimistic believed that they were still unseen by the enemy, even in the foggy night. There was a German observation post in Algeciras, and on the African side, at Spanish Cueta, an Italian agent lived in an apartment with a view over the strait.

The ships squeezed between the continents in two very long columns, somehow missing the fishing boats. "I think the whole Spanish fishing fleet was out there, lit up like Christmas trees," said Larsen. He was still on the bridge when the fog lifted, later in the night. The *Santa Elisa*'s radio was picking up Spanish communication.

"Much to our horror, signal lights from North Africa and Spain were lighting up the convoy, sending messages back and forth about our arrival," said Dales. His jaw dropped when he heard what he thought were the words "Santa Elisa."

By sunrise, the convoy was clear of the Strait of Gibraltar and the Spanish and African coasts and was steaming at 15 knots. The shadows of Spanish mountains rose out of the morning mist. Admiral Syfret sent out a final signal in the calm before the storm:

> You may be sure that the enemy will do all in his power to prevent the convoy getting through, and it will require every exertion on our part to see that he fails. When you are on watch, be especially vigilant and alert, and when you are off duty, get all the sleep you can. Every one of us must give of his best. The garrison and people of Malta have been defending their island so gallantly against incessant attacks by the German and Italian air forces. Malta looks to us for help. We shall not fail them.

CHAPTER 22

OPERATION BELLOWS

W hen this war is a misty memory in the minds of old men, they will still talk of the convoy for Malta which entered the Mediterranean early in August 1942," wrote Norman Smart, the war correspondent for the London *Daily Express,* on board the cruiser *Cairo* and carrying a pen and a crystal ball. "With its vast escort it was ten miles across. It was more than 50 ships. Almost to the blue bowl of the horizon stretched this armada, hurrying to succor Malta."

The pilot of an Air France flying boat, on a flight from Paris to Algiers, looked down at the wide armada. The unwritten rule for noncombatant commercial pilots from neutral countries was simple: stay out of it, and you won't be shot down. But the Vichy pilot was unable to sit on the astonishing sight and radioed home that he could see thirty-two ships. Within minutes, Comando Supremo and the Luftwaffe had the information.

The *Indomitable* picked up the Air France pilot's message, and sent up a Hurricane, which flew alongside the airliner. Larsen listened in as the *Santa Elisa*'s radio received the Hurricane pilot's voice. "The passengers are looking very uncomfortable," he told *Indomitable.* "Shall I shoot the bastard down?"

The answer, this time, was no.

If the convoy's presence and location were now known, its intentions remained a mystery to the Italians. It seemed too big to be merely taking supplies to Malta. General Ugo Cavallero, commander in chief of the Italian High Command (Comando Supremo), thought this might be an invasion of North Africa, and he canceled a trip to Africa because he believed there would be a huge air and naval battle in the days ahead. Admiral Luigi Sansonetti argued that with five aircraft carriers, it had to be a massive flying-off of aircraft to Malta, and if so it must be stopped at all costs, as an RAF offensive from Malta would ruin them. Others thought that some of the convoy must be headed for Alexandria, to build up the fleet there. Admiral Arturo Riccardi ordered reconnaissance aircraft from Sardinia to snoop around when the convoy got within range.

There were five Italian and three German submarines waiting in the western Mediterranean, patrolling between Algiers and the island of Formentera off the east coast of Spain, a distance of about 120 miles. A dozen destroyers ran interference for the convoy, in a bending row that was nine miles wide. They kept the subs at bay that night, but just before dawn on August 11, 60 miles south of Ibiza, the Italian *Uarscieck* launched three torpedoes at the aircraft carrier *Furious*. They missed by a mile, but a destroyer saw the torpedo tracks and dropped some depth charges. The submarine captain heard the exploding depth charges and reported back that the *Furious* was sunk. The news was on Italian state radio that night, mentioning *Furious* by name, which gave the convoy sailors a good snort, but Syfret had to send a message to London asking the Admiralty to notify the families of the *Furious* sailors that their men were still alive and well.

So far things were going well, but there was one big logistical problem that upset Admiral Syfret. Just before the convoy had left the Clyde, the Admiralty had informed Syfret that Operation Bellows, the flying-off of more Spitfires to Malta from *Furious*, had been added to his carefully laid Pedestal plans. Syfret had nearly snapped the stem of his pipe between his clenched teeth. He cited the trouble it caused in his report, including the "general unsettling effect on all, which last minute changes always cause."

His restrained words were a discreet way of calling the situation a "balzup," which was a favorite British expression during the war, akin to the American "snafu" (situation normal, all fouled up). Syfret knew Malta needed the thirty-eight Spitfires carried by *Furious*, but he told the Admiralty he wished they had thought of it sooner.

There were a number of problems with Operation Bellows. Spitfires had never flown off the ancient *Furious* before—not once. She had been the first aircraft carrier in history to land a plane while under way, in 1917, and since then her flight deck had been extended to fly off more powerful planes, leaving a sharp hump in the middle. The thirty-eight Spitfires for Malta were fitted with older propellers that spun at a lazy 2,650 rpm, making barely enough speed for the planes to get airborne.

Back in the Clyde, the Spitfires' RAF group captain had made a test takeoff. He had twisted the boost of his supercharged V-12 Rolls-Royce Merlin engine up to an eye-popping 18 psi ("pulling the tit of the Spit"), and even with 30 knots of wind over the deck and his plane backed all the way to the far edge of the flight deck, he avoided by only feet what the pilots called a "splash over the sharp end."

So the Air Ministry combed the country for forty new airscrews, or propellers, which were delivered to Glasgow; but it took three days, and in the meantime, Operation Pedestal had left without the *Furious*. Airplane mechanics worked around the clock for ten days to install the new airscrews, as *Furious* raced to catch up. They also adjusted and tested the engines, radio transmitters, cannons, machine guns, hydraulics, electrical and compressed air systems, oxygen, and instruments, any one or more of which the Spitfire pilots knew might still malfunction.

A pilot might climb into his cockpit on the flight deck, give his mechanic a final serious look, and ask, "Are you sure everything will work?" And the petty officer might cheerfully reply, "Maybe, sir!"

The Spitfires were painted desert camouflage and fitted with a huge tropical air filter under the sharp nose, giving the plane a strong chin. They carried long-distance fuel tanks, aerodynamic 100-gallon cans strapped under the fuselage between the wheels, to be dropped into the sea when empty, like a beer can tossed off a redneck's fishing boat. Later in the war, the auxiliary fuel tanks were actually filled with beer for the troops fighting in France. The delivery system evolved until finally wooden beer kegs were attached under the wings in place of depth charges.

There wasn't much room for error in the 550 or 600 miles between the *Furious* and Malta. Pilots carried only a scroll map, compass, and watch, and radio silence had to be maintained. They were told to point the plane east at an economical 165 mph for three and a half hours, and look for a twelve-mile-wide limestone strip that looked like a golden leaf floating on a big blue lake. Hug the North African coast, and fly at 20,000 feet in the areas where Messerschmitt 109s were known to roam. Watch your back around the Hobgoblin—the island of Pantelleria. And if you wander toward Sicily, you're dead.

Some of the pilots were the best in the RAF, because after the Battle of Britain they wanted to go where the action was. But most of them were fresh meat and very young. They were told that if their plane didn't lift off the flight deck, suffered a splash over the sharp end, and didn't immediately sink, they were not to climb out of the cockpit and try to swim away, because the ship would run over them. It's better to sink with your plane, hold your breath while the aircraft carrier passes above, and then swim out of the cockpit to the surface. The advice was delivered with a straight face and met with a combination of awe and appropriate irreverence.

In the Clyde, there was one successful takeoff with a Spitfire using one of the new 3,100-rpm airscrews, and that was a relief, but no one had taken off with the extra 750 pounds that the full belly tank added. So the Spitfires' ammunition was removed to lighten the load, which Lieutenant Geoffrey Wellum, age twenty-one, discovered when he was in the hangar with his plane, carefully packing his parachute for the next day's flight to Malta.

Whilst absorbing this, a voice from behind me says: "Everything all right, Geoffrey?"

I look round to see Group Captain Walter Churchill, who is obviously generally keeping his eye on things.

"Yes thank you, sir. I'm still learning. As you can see, I'm watching my guns being loaded with cigarettes."

"Bloody marvellous, isn't it? To make absolutely sure of this take-off, it has been decided to take all the ammunition out so as to save considerable weight. I agreed because fags don't weigh very much and things on Malta have been pretty tough. It'll do the troops' morale a power of good to get some cheap smokes."

"That's very kind and considerate of us, sir. I hope the Germans and Italians don't know."

"What if they do? You couldn't hit any of them even if you did have ammunition, Geoffrey."

"I know you to be right, sir, but it would be nice to be in a position to keep on trying."

Operation Pedestal was 584 miles from Malta when the first Spitfires flew off *Furious*, at 1230 hours on August 11. At 1508 a final group of seven planes took off, and with the landing of thirty-six Spitfires at Takali and Luqa airfields, Operation Bellows was complete. Only one was lost, without a trace.

At 1830 *Furious* began steaming at high speed back to Gibraltar, with an escort of six destroyers: *Amazon, Wrestler,* and *Venomous* on the port wing and *Keppel, Wolverine,* and *Malcolm* on the starboard wing. That night the small convoy was steaming with no lights when *Wolverine's* radar picked up a submarine on the surface.

"0054½, dark night, no moon, bright stars, speed 21 knots, on port leg of zig-zag No. 12, R.D./F Type 271 contact was obtained, range 5,000 yds," reported its young captain, Lieutenant Commander Peter Gretton.

He didn't hesitate. The crew of the 700-ton Italian sub *Dagabur* never saw the snarling jaws of the *Wolverine* coming at them broadside at 26 knots. "We climbed all over the sub's conning tower and cut her in half," said Gretton. "We lost thirty feet of our bow, but by miracle the forepeak was bent over to the waterline and it sealed most of the damage."

The destroyer *Malcolm* said they heard survivors yelling in the water but didn't pick them up. They thought it was a German U-boat.

Furious wasted no time taking on twenty-three more Spitfires in Gibraltar and going back into the Mediterranean to fly them off. Malta was going to need them.

CHAPTER 23

DIVE OF THE *EAGLE*

German intelligence had seen Operation Pedestal coming a week earlier. On August 4, U-73 had been undergoing repairs at its cave in La Spezia, Italy, when urgent orders came from Admiral Karl Dönitz to go after the convoy: find an aircraft carrier and sink it.

Kapitanleutnant Helmut Rosenbaum of U-73 knew the *Eagle*. Nine years earlier, in the Chinese port of Tsingtau, when he had been a cadet on the cruiser *Königsberg*, he had been invited aboard the *Eagle* for cocktails and dinner by some of the British officers. Now he was trying to kill them.

As he lay in wait sixty miles off the coast of North Africa, he heard the propellers of the British ships on his hydrophones. The convoy was right on schedule. When he raised the periscope of U-73, he saw five destroyers and knew their sonar would locate his boat if he allowed them to come much closer. But beyond the destroyers he could see the *Eagle*, about four miles away, which he recognized by her unique high pilothouse on a tall tripod mast.

As he peered through the U-73's leaking periscope—he had rushed out of La Spezia before the repairs were finished—he ordered a brandy to calm himself down. "This is the first time I've ever seen him like this," said the first mate, Helmut Spieler.

He submerged to 100 feet and sped away. *Eagle* was at the tail end of the starboard column, and he stalked her for two and a half hours. When a destroyer dashed past U-73 at a distance of 200 feet, Rosenbaum made his move. He boldly slipped between two destroyers and passed in front of the battleship *Nelson*, at a depth of about 100 feet. He fully expected the destroyers to discover U-73 and start dropping depth charges. He was prepared to die for the fatherland, although maybe not for the Führer; like so many German officers, he separated the two.

He gulped a second brandy.

But the destroyers' sonar failed to pick up the 750-ton U-boat, because of the layered density in the water from currents of different temperatures. U-73 passed under the fourth column of the convoy, under the cruiser *Charybdis,* and sneaked down between the third and fourth columns, splitting the *Ohio* and the *Santa Elisa.*

Rosenbaum raised the periscope very slowly, because the water was calm and lookouts on the ships could see the slightest ripple. The *Eagle* was right before his eyes, a mere 500 meters away. He said it looked like a giant matchbox floating on a pond.

Eagle was zigging and zagging at 13 knots. She zigged away from him, hard to starboard. He knew she would come back. He tossed down a third brandy.

Finally the *Eagle* zagged toward him, hard to port, perfectly exposing all 667 feet of her port beam. He instructed four torpedoes to be set in a fan pattern and gave the command to fire. They were kissed good-bye and shot from the bow tubes of U-73 by a nineteen-year-old, the youngest man on the boat. U-73 was so close to the *Eagle* that only about 40 feet separated the torpedoes when they hit, sending rivers of oily brown water laced with debris and shards of metal hundreds of feet into the air.

The instant the teenager fired the torpedoes from the bow of U-73, Kapitan Rosenbaum took her down to 500 feet, a dangerous depth, nearly 200 feet more than the boat's textbook maximum, and ordered silence. Icy water squirted from unfixed leaks. The *Eagle*'s last gasps and creaks and spooky moans carried underwater to the U-boat, whose crew listened in amazement, awe, and fear. Soon depth charges shook their ship. Three hours would pass before Rosenbaum could creep back to the surface. He raised the periscope, saw an empty sea, and sent a signal to Berlin announcing his success.

Convoy—15 destroyers and escort ships, 2 cruisers, 9 to 10 freighters, one aircraft carrier, probably one battleship. Fan shot against aircraft carrier. 4 hits from 500 meters distance. Strongly audible sinking noises.

—All clear!—

Rosenbaum

The morning after the sinking of the *Eagle*, Kapitan Rosenbaum of U-73 was a national hero in Germany and was called back to Berlin, where Hitler decorated him with the Iron Cross.

Two images have been fixed for more than six decades in the fading memories of the dwindling numbers of veterans of Operation Pedestal, from that still summer afternoon in the middle of the Mediterranean Sea. One of them is surreal, a vivid and unbelievable picture of an aircraft carrier suddenly on its port side, with scores of men and a dozen airplanes sliding down the big flat deck like matchsticks and toys, pitching over the edge and tumbling into the sea.

The veterans say they can close their eyes and see it clearly, as if it were happening at this very moment. Their minds can't erase the image of hundreds of shouting heads in the oily water, along with the dead bodies. The men and the flotsam and the ugly black slick, glistening under the midday sun on the dead flat sea. That was all that was left, eight minutes after the torpedoes hit.

Few of the ships in the convoy saw much of the sinking because they were far ahead, but both the *Santa Elisa* and *Ohio* were nearby. *Santa Elisa*'s liaison officer reported that the *Eagle* was 10 cables (1.15 land miles) off his ship's starboard quarter, and Captain Mason said the *Eagle* was 1.5 miles off the starboard quarter of the *Ohio*.

Just before the torpedoes hit, said Lonnie Dales, "The weather was beautiful and the Mediterranean was flat calm. Right after lunch, we had a general alarm. We all dashed for our gun stations. This was the real thing!"

The general alarm was three long blasts, three shorts, three longs, three shorts. On the bridge, Captain Thomson shouted, "Keep your eyes peeled out there! One of the ships just spotted a torpedo wake!"

"I had been assigned a 20 mm Oerlikon on the port side of the bridge," said Dales. "Upon coming out of the wardroom to run to the gun station, I witnessed the HMS Eagle being hit by three torpedoes, before turning over and sinking immediately. It was a very, very sad and pathetic sight to see the sailors and planes all sliding off the deck as she rolled over and went under. In a matter of minutes she was gone. There wasn't even enough time to lower the lifeboats."

"Eagle was turning hard to port, and I could see her planes warming up on her flight deck," added the purser, Follansbee. "She was probably about to send off a patrol squadron, I thought. One of her planes had just started down her deck. Suddenly a huge geyser of water rose from the carrier's port quarter. Then a second geyser rose amidships and a third rose from her bow. Three muffled explosions then came across the water. Automatically I looked at my watch. It was quarter past one. No one spoke as we stood hypnotized by the sight before us.

"The carrier was listing heavily to port, and the plane which had started to take off was roaring down the crazily sloping flight deck in a desperate effort to leave the stricken ship. I watched breathlessly as the plane approached the end of the flight deck. Then the carrier's list increased and the plane slipped off the port side of the flight deck and plunged into the sea with a sickening splash. It was like a bad dream."

Captain Lachlan Donald Mackintosh had been skipper of the *Eagle* for only a couple of months, but he had already endeared himself to the crew by wearing his kilt and playing his bagpipe when the *Eagle* entered port. He was the chief of Scotland's Clan Mackintosh, fierce fighters whose Inverness roots reached back nearly eight hundred years. His great-grandfather, General Lachlan Mackintosh, had fought with George Washington against the hated redcoats after being driven out of the clan's Highlands.

Now, as his ship listed, he clung to a bulkhead on the starboard gun deck, shouting commands to lower some ropes so the men could climb down to the antitorpedo bulge on the hull and drop into the sea. Captain Mackintosh finally climbed down the rope himself and held on to his gold-braided cap as he leaped into the water, because he was still the captain of the men, if no longer of a ship. He swam to a Carley raft, about four by six feet and made of canvas and wood, with a bottom of meshed rope stiffened by battens. The men who were crammed on the raft greeted him with the ship's war cry, "Up the *Eagle*'s!," before they pulled him aboard and paddled away as fast as they could.

"I jumped from the gun deck, where Captain Mackintosh was," said petty officer George Amyes, now eighty-four, living in Hull on the North Sea, the town where he grew up and where his parents were killed by German bombs during the war. "When the first torpedo hit, I hadn't the faintest idea what the thump was—I thought we hit a whale or something like that. Then the ship began to list, and I saw Marines jumping from the flight deck, hurtling past the gun deck, and I figured it out.

"There were two nonswimmers sitting on the antitorpedo blister who were too petrified to jump. An officer came along and told them, 'Now's your chance to learn,' and he grabbed them by the hands and the three of them leaped together about thirty feet into the water."

The flight deck of the *Eagle*, just above the gun deck, was more than 50 feet above water when the ship was level, and its starboard edge got higher and higher as the nineteen-year-old Les Goodenough found himself perched there. "It had never entered 'me head that we'd get sunk," he said from his home in Reading, outside London. He'd been manning the starboard quarter Oerlikon when the torpedoes hit, and he struggled to release a Carley raft. But just below him a sailor was sitting in another Carley raft that was dangling from a ring bolt, and he was yelling for someone to release it, so Goodenough climbed down and joined him.

They cut the raft loose and glided 90 feet down a slope that was nearly 45 degrees by now. The port edge of the flight deck was already submerged, and the raft splashed into the thick oil on top of the water. Goodenough shouted, "Paddle!" as the suction from the sinking ship pulled them back, but they got away. They became known as the "toboggan team" in the stories they shared with their mates afterward.

Two hundred and thirty-one men were lost. Many of the victims were nonswimmers who were afraid to leap; they clung to the ship and went down with her. Others were trapped inside. The *Eagle* was no bigger inside than a battleship, having been built as one in 1914, so there wasn't a lot of room—sailors slung their hammocks wherever they could and competed for space with cockroaches and rats, which scurried along the beams in the hangars, staring defiantly down at them. When the ship began listing and the lights went out and the water rushed in, new sailors were frantically disoriented and prayed in the darkness for someone to lead them. The *Eagle* had four boiler rooms and three engine rooms, and all of the stokers in the B boiler room were lost, along with all of the greasers in the port engine room. There were other desperately lonely deaths. One sailor died behind bars in the brig. Compartments became steel coffins, which today hold skeletons on the floor of the sea, a thousand feet down.

No one will know how many were killed by the depth charges dropped by the warship escorts, aimlessly if not pointlessly—the navy had no idea where U-73 had come from or where she had gone. Immediately after the hits, the cruiser *Charybdis*, *Eagle*'s protector and partner for so long, angrily raced around and blindly launched depth charges. Destroyers followed. "Two destroyers were charging up and down dropping depth charges, and their obvious priority was killing submarines, not saving us," said one survivor.

"It happened a lot in the war," said Dr. Nixon of the destroyer *Ledbury.* "The destroyer captains didn't understand. I think I was the only one who really understood the effect of a depth charge on a man in the water."

There were men in the water everywhere. George Amyes had been swimming for some time, clinging to a bit of wood, when he recognized his buddy Stripey, the oldest sailor on the *Eagle.* "I grabbed him around the shoulders, thinking he was unconscious, but what I felt at his waist was mush. There was only half a man there."

Newspaper readers in London got an account filled with exclamation points, including the tales of heroism they wanted to hear and knew they could count on from their lads, before and after the ship "turned turtle." *The Daily Telegraph* of London told about the valiant ship's doctor, who rowed around to the rafts shooting morphine into the injured sailors.

The reporter Arthur Thorpe was picked up by a destroyer. "I was feeling half-dead and was brown from head to foot in the fuel oil," he wrote. "Many of us were sick through swallowing fuel oil, but tots of rum put our greasy stomachs right," meaning that the rum made the sailors heave up the oil.

Captain Mackintosh was picked up by the same destroyer as Thorpe. "How marvelously the officers and men behaved," he said. "I saw no sign of panic in the last few minutes in the life of the ship."

"There was a marked unwillingness on the part of the ship's company to abandon ship until a superior officer actually gave the order," he added in his own report to the Royal Navy, "and I was very impressed by the coolness, morale and discipline of all officers and men."

Mackintosh and Thorpe's rescuing destroyer, *Lookout,* was loaded with 536 survivors lining the rails; it came alongside *Laforey,* with 195. Another 198 sailors were picked up by the small tugboat *Jaunty,* and they swarmed over the decks like ants on a sugar cube, climbing the rigging to find space. All the survivors were happy to be alive, and as they recognized shipmates they cheered. "It reminded me of trains in a London station crowded with happy schoolchildren bound for a day out in the country," said Thorpe.

Twenty years after the loss of HMS *Eagle,* George Amyes traveled to Germany to meet the men who had been his enemies that day. Some had been killed when U-73 was sunk in the Mediterranean by American destroyers in 1943. Amyes's trips to Germany achieved more than personal closure, they rewarded his soul; he made friends.

Kapitan Rosenbaum died in the war in a plane crash. His widow gave Amyes a handmade book that a journalist had put together on her husband's naval career; it included the U-73 log and heretofore unknown details on the sinking of the *Eagle*. Amyes met also Rosenbaum's daughter, who was five when her father was killed. "I'm so sick and tired of hearing what a hero my father was," she told him. "I just wish, one time, somebody would tell me something bad about him, so that I could know he was human."

He met the man who as a teenager had sent the four torpedoes on their way. "I remember he called them 'my torpedoes,' not Kapitan Rosenbaum's or the U-73's, but 'my torpedoes,' " said Amyes. "He asked me, 'How much damage did my torpedoes do, how many men were killed?' When I told him upwards of two hundred, he went pale. He gasped, 'Oh my God,' and crushed his heart with his hand. I thought he was going to collapse. He never knew until then. It was the first time he had come in contact with anyone who had actually experienced the situation."

The story in *The Daily Telegraph* ended, "Then came a mighty rumbling as the sea poured relentlessly into the Eagle, forcing out the air. The water threshed above her in a fury of white foam and then subsided. She had gone."

"It was as simple as that," said Captain Thomson, who watched from the bridge of the *Santa Elisa*. "No fuss, no excitement, not even much noise. The carrier just sank. It was hard to believe then, and it's harder to believe now, but we saw it happen. And we had to keep on going, zigzagging back and forth and wondering if we would be next."

CHAPTER 24

DIVE-BOMBERS AT DUSK

E very sailor in the convoy was stunned by the sudden sinking of the *Eagle.* U-boats were not supposed to be able to penetrate the defense at all, let alone strike at the heart of the convoy. In Admiral Syfret's two previous convoys to Malta, none of his warships had been lost, but now he could see that he'd been lucky. The Axis was paying attention this time. He tightened the destroyer screen and sent out a message saying that the standard of vigilance had bloody well improve.

Five Italian and two other German submarines had missed the convoy when it passed between Algiers and Majorca, and they now began chasing it down. There were another eleven Italian submarines ahead, strategically divided into three zones off the coast of Algeria. The zigzagging convoy was like a roaming herd of wildebeest, and the subs were stalking lions, hidden by tall grass.

"During the next few hours several vessels reported submarines in the vicinity, and I sighted the periscope of a submarine on our starboard beam," said Captain Mason of the *Ohio.* "It appeared to be on the point of surfacing, but several ships opened fire and the submarine immediately dived. We could not use our own guns owing to other ships being in the line of fire."

The convoy was also being followed in the air. Four Junkers Ju 88s, flying from Sardinia and carrying cameras as big as garbage cans, tracked the ships with near impunity, because the Sea Hurricanes couldn't climb to the 32,480-foot ceiling of the Ju 88 spy planes. The supercharged engines of the Hurricanes were tuned for power at sea level, to lift off the aircraft carriers, and as a result were weak in the thin air of high altitude.

"Our fighters competed manfully at great height against the snoopers, but the speed and height of the Ju 88s made their task a hopeless one," said Syfret.

Malta was sending out spy planes too, from its Photo Reconnaissance Unit. "A heavy call was made on P.R.U. Spitfires, in order to determine the position and strength of enemy air forces, and of enemy surface forces," said Malta's RAF commander, Air Marshal Keith Park. Malta never stopped looking for the Italian battleships and heavy cruisers—or worrying about them.

There were some 540 operational Axis aircraft on Sardinia and Sicily, not counting those that British intelligence believed had been brought in from Greece and Crete. Altogether there might have been 1,000 planes intended for the obliteration of Operation Pedestal.

Syfret sent a message from his battleship, Nelson, to the ships in the convoy: Prepare for an air attack at dusk. It should be considered a certainty.

On the Santa Elisa, Fred Larsen checked his Oerlikon and made sure there were plenty of ammunition magazines, each holding sixty cartridges and loaded by two British soldiers. Lonnie Dales tested the red light pinned to his life jacket. Jack Follansbee asked the captain if he could fill four empty Scotch bottles with Jamaican rum from the keg and hide one in each lifeboat.

"Make sure no one sees you," said Thomson, knowing that if anyone did, the rum would disappear as fast as a tracer from the barrel of an Oerlikon.

Lookouts squinted into the hot pink sun on the western horizon, knowing that dive-bombers attacked from the rear, because there were fewer guns that could be trained aft. At 2045, radar detected Axis aircraft. A flag was raised from the stern of the Nelson that told the ships to expect the attack in seven minutes.

Thirty Junkers Ju 88 bombers came out of the clouds at 2056, while six twin-engine Heinkel 111s, each carrying two torpedoes under the fuselage, came skimming low over the water.

"By the time the attack developed, the sun was setting in a big red glow," Anthony Kimmins told his BBC radio audience. Kimmins had been a Royal Navy officer before the war and would become an actor, playwright, and filmmaker during and after it; Operation Pedestal was one of his early dramatic performances. He described the scene from the bridge of the cruiser *Nigeria*, where he had been standing alongside Admiral Burrough and trying to stay out of his way.

"The barrage put up by our ships was one of the most staggering things I have ever seen," he said. "Tracers screaming across the sky in all directions, and overhead literally thousands of black puffs of bursting shells. The din was terrific, but through it all you could hear the wail of sirens for an emergency alteration of course to avoid torpedoes, and the answering deep-throated hoots of the merchantmen as they turned in perfect formation. Then suddenly, a cheer from a gun's crew, and away on the port bow a Ju 88 spinning vertically downwards with both wings on fire and looking like a giant Catherine Wheel [fireworks pinwheel]. More cheers, and over to starboard another 88 was diving headlong for the sea, with smoke pouring out behind. At about 500 feet the automatic pullout came into action, and she flattened out and crashed on her belly with a great splash of water. Against the sunset you could see the parachutes of her crew as they drifted slowly downwards."

"It is impossible to describe the massive antiaircraft barrage that was put up by fourteen well-armed merchant ships and about fifty major warships, and it is equally impossible to understand how the enemy were able to survive," said Frank Pike in 2005. At the time of Operation Pedestal, he was a nineteen-year-old British Army corporal being transported to Malta on the *Santa Elisa*. Because he had artillery experience, Captain Thomson assigned him a battle station at the Oerlikon on the forward starboard bridge wing.

"In asking some of the soldiers to help man the Oerlikons," said Pike, "I think that the captain was probably trying to find a useful employment for us and at the same time give his crew some assistance. It was a service that we took on most willingly. The third officer, Mr. Larsen, spent some time instructing us in the loading of magazines, as well as the loading and operating of the gun, and dealing with stoppages."

The battleships and aircraft carriers had water-cooled, eight-barreled pom-pom guns, which recoiled with each shot; each barrel could fire 90 rounds per minute, and the gun spat out empty shells as if it were drooling brass. With 720 pumping strokes per minute, the pom-pom got the name "Chicago piano" because the barrels bounced like the keys of a boogie-woogie piano. There were at least ten of them in the convoy, sending thousands of pretty white puffs of shrapnel high into the sky.

"Crump-crump-crump-crump-crump they went, belching forth flame, death and destruction all over the sky," wrote Dag Dickens. It was a "picturesque barrage," reported the liaison officer on *Brisbane Star*.

If the pom-poms sounded like the rhythmic fast beat of a drum, the battleships' sixteen-inch guns were like hand grenades going off in the orchestra pit. It was the *Rodney*'s guns that had sunk the German battleship *Bismarck*, killing 1,946 out of 2,065 men. Now they were loaded with special shrapnel shells, for the first-ever attempt to use the big guns to shoot down airplanes.

"*Nelson*'s and *Rodney*'s main armament were spectacular morale boosters to have in company," said Hector Mackenzie, a Fleet Air Arm officer on the aircraft carrier *Indomitable*. "Our fighter pilots reported that even thousands of feet above these shell bursts, they were lifted about 500 feet, if over one when it burst."

The shrapnel shells made the guns louder than ever, and the barrels puked huge clouds of brown smoke when they burst, as pieces of hot metal scattered over any nearby ship. "It was unnerving, to say the least," said Lonnie Dales. "And, believe me, those guns were deafening."

"The din was unholy," said Ed Randall, chief engineer on the *Santa Elisa*.

"That was the most noise I've ever heard, and I've just come from Dunkirk," said a British gunner on the *Santa Elisa*, loading the Oerlikon on the after port bridge wing for Dales.

Ensign Suppiger, who led the U.S. Navy Armed Guard on the *Santa Elisa*, assigned himself to the four-inch low-angle gun on the stern, which wasn't used against aircraft. This gave him time to watch as the bravest of the Ju 88 pilots twisted through the flak and dived on the ships from about 8,000 feet.

"A tiny spot would appear high overhead, then it would start to dive," he said. "Thousands of tracers would be seen going in that direction. The plane would maneuver from side to side to avoid the gunfire, but would keep on coming and not break out of its dive until it had released its stick of bombs at about 700 yards.

"I noticed that it seemed as if most of the bombers were aiming at our ship. Bombs were falling uncomfortably close, with some sticks straddling the ship. I thought they were sighting on the black-and-yellow checkerboard deck of the RAF crash boat we were carrying as cargo. At my suggestion, Chief Mate Englund instructed some of his deck hands to cover this launch with a tarpaulin and thereafter our ship was not singled out."

"Circling maybe 5000 feet above us, the dive bombers look casual, almost contemptuous," said Ed Randall. "Then, two or three of them peel off and dive, usually toward the carriers and other warships. They figure they can wait around like vultures and pick off the cargo ships at leisure. As they roar down, you can make out the swastikas on their wings, and you can see the sticks of bombs drop out. At first they look as if they're floating down, distant, impersonal, harmless. Then they start zooming right at you, and you realize they're 500-pounders. Down in the engine-room, every near miss sends tools crashing to the floor as the ship lurches. And you keep your ears cocked for the telephone order from the bridge to abandon ship, because you don't want to get caught like a rat in a sewer. But up above there are ships sinking and men dying, and you're powerless to do a damned thing about it."

"Those babies were not easy to discourage," said Captain Thomson. "They came over us 15 or 20 at a time, paying no attention to the ack-ack barrage the convoy was sending up. They had all the guts in the world, and they seemed to be able to do what they liked with their planes. Maybe it sounds wrong to say I admired them, but that's the only word that will fit. I mean, I wasn't only afraid of them. I could see they were doing a beautiful job, the way our gunners were doing a beautiful job. As far as we were able to judge in the sweat and confusion of the attack, our gunners brought down three German planes. One plane, before we shot it down, dropped a string of bombs athwart our ship, two bombs falling on the port side and three on the starboard side. Thank God none of them landed anywhere near the Number 1 hatch."

"I was constantly on watch with the captain on the flying bridge, or on my gun station, port forward flying bridge wing," said Fred Larsen. "Whenever we had close misses, the generators would temporarily conk out. This would knock out our gyro compass which was located on the lower deck practically in engine-room one. The repeaters which were essential to our station were on the flying bridge. Since I was also in charge of the gyro compass, I would go down and reset the master gyro and balance it off to the correct heading.

"I was on my way up to my station when I heard the phone ringing on the lower bridge wheelhouse. I answered the phone and it was my friend the chief engineer Ed Randall, calling from the engine room wanting to know what was going on, since his tools were falling from the peg board. I told him it was just a near miss, and to put the tools back on the board and to switch the engine-room phone to the flying bridge so that I could keep him informed."

Three of the aircraft carriers had left the convoy: *Argus* had been along just for Operation Berserk, *Furious* was on her way back to Gibraltar after flying off the Spitfires, and *Eagle* was now on the bottom. That left *Indomitable* and *Victorious*.

Indomitable carried twenty-four Sea Hurricanes, fourteen Albacore biplane bombers, and ten new Grumman Martlet fighters, the American answer to the Japanese Zero, enjoyed by pilots for its steep climb rate. *Victorious* carried six Sea Hurricanes, fourteen Albacores, and sixteen two-seat Fairey Fulmars, which weren't much faster than the Gladiator biplanes they replaced but carried eight .30-caliber machine guns in the folding wings. *Victorious* was also the flagship of the Fleet Air Arm commander, Admiral A. L. Lyster, the Fifth Sea Lord, who had planned Operation Pedestal with Admirals Syfret and Burrough in London.

The Fleet Air Arm fighters had a difficult time seeing the gray bombers in the gray sky. Worse, the convoy gunners couldn't tell the friendly fighters from the enemy bombers. "They were firing at anything that flew," cursed one Hurricane pilot, landing after dark.

"It is evident that the dusk attack must be met with either Anti-Aircraft guns or fighters," reported Admiral Lyster. "Both cannot operate together.

"I am particularly impressed by the failure to hit by the Anti-Aircraft guns, both long range and short range, high and low," he added. "That the gunfire is a deterrent to the attacking torpedo aircraft is evident, and perhaps it may deter some of the more timid bombers and dive bombers. The fact remains, however, that the dividend paid for a tremendous expenditure of ammunition is remarkably low. I have the strong impression that not only is it inaccurate, but also undisciplined."

On the *Indomitable*, the premature explosion of a shell from one of the guns had blown out the flight deck landing lights and killed the flight deck's first officer, so the second officer brought the planes in with a flashlight in each hand and one in his mouth. Few of the pilots had any night landing experience. One crash-landed on *Victorious* while she was in the middle of a zigzag. "I saw a great sheet of flame rise from the flight deck," said Captain Thomson.

"So it went on, right up to darkness, the gunfire never easing up for a moment, the great columns of water as bombs dropped between the ships," continued Anthony Kimmins on the radio. "My last impression of that evening was a Ju 88 who made an attack astern of us. He found himself committed to making a getaway over the fleet, and he started making steep turns this way and that in a frantic effort to avoid the tracers which were screaming up at him from all directions. For a short time, by some miracle, he got away with it, but before long we were steaming past a burning patch in the water, where he had crashed in. As the terrific gunfire suddenly subsided, the comparative silence of the night was almost uncanny. There had been no damage to any of our ships from this attack."

At midnight on the *Santa Elisa*, they listened to the German news broadcast:

This is Berlin calling. Now here is the news in English:

The German High Command has just announced a naval victory in the Mediterranean. Here is the report. At 1 p.m. today, Central European time, one of our U-boats successfully torpedoed and sank a large British aircraft carrier. This carrier was part of an exceptionally heavily escorted convoy which is heading eastward toward Malta. Operations against this convoy will continue.

CHAPTER 25

BAD DAY FOR SECRET WEAPONS

As the men on the *Santa Elisa* were listening to the news from Berlin at midnight on August 11, two Liberator bombers and nine Bristol Beaufighters from Malta were raiding the Elmas and Decimomannu airfields on Sardinia. The Beaufighter had four 20 mm cannons in its thimble-shaped nose and six .30-caliber machine guns in the wings, and was excellent at night. Malta's commanding air officer, Keith Park, loved that capability in the Beaufighter and used it whenever he could. But he was furious because more Liberators were supposed to have been sent by the RAF command in Egypt, to cover for Operation Pedestal. It was the same old story: Malta gets the hind tit.

"It is felt that a very considerable effort could have been given to the success of this operation [Pedestal], had sufficient night bombers been able to operate over the enemy aerodromes on the required days," he reported. "Had the hoped-for total of 30 sorties been achieved, the story of this convoy might have had a happier ending."

But Park was pleased with the performance of his pilots. "Added to the success of this 'shoot-up' was the fact that the Beaufighters were able to report the vital information that two Italian cruisers were just leaving Cagliari harbor," he said.

The Italian cruisers were commanded by Admiral Da Zara, gunning for the total wipeout that had escaped him after the Battle of Pantelleria, as the Italians called Operation Harpoon. Two light cruisers with six-inch guns were steaming toward a rendezvous with more warships coming from Sicily. They planned to descend on the convoy below Pantelleria at first light on August 13, to annihilate whatever was left of the merchantmen as they staggered through the Sicilian Narrows after the bombers, submarines, and fast E-boats were through with them.

The convoy sailors never left their battle stations that night. Extra lookouts tensely searched for U-boats on the black water in the moonless night, knowing their chances of spotting a periscope were naught. Mostly they just held their breath and hoped their ship wouldn't be seen. Some men dozed fearfully on the steel decks under their guns, using their life belts for pillows. They listened to the swish of swells against the hulls of their ships cutting giant Zs in the sea at 15 knots, and wondered when the peaceful sounds would end with a bang that might kill them.

The thunder of a V-12 engine broke the stillness before sunrise on August 12. Admiral Lyster sent up eight planes at first pink light, and another four later in the morning to patrol in wide patterns around the convoy.

Just after 0900, nineteen Luftwaffe Ju 88s approached, and sixteen Fleet Air Arm fighters intercepted them 20 miles from the convoy. The fighters swooped down out of the sun from behind and shot down four of the Junkers. The rest were met with an inspired antiaircraft barrage that caused some of the attackers to drop their bombs early and bank northeast, back to Sardinia. Two more were shot down, one of them by the U.S. Navy gunner at the 40 mm Bofors on the bow of the *Santa Elisa*.

"Four Junkers 88s flew across our bow from port to starboard," reported Ensign Suppiger. "Our Bofors commenced firing and hit one plane at about 1500 yards range; this aircraft was hit in the tail and began smoking. One minute later it crashed into the sea about five miles off our starboard quarter."

"The Bofors was a great antiaircraft weapon," said Larsen. "I was glad I had the chance to go to school on the gun in Belfast. I liked the Oerlikons, but the Bofors had more range and power. Sometimes I wished I was shooting it, but I needed to stay on the bridge."

Some of the ships tuned their radios to the traffic between the fighters and aircraft carriers, and they broadcast the dialogue over the ships' speakers. Everybody's favorite pilot was Red Leader, a dry wit whose parodied Yankee drawl kept the sailors in stitches and caused the enemy to wonder if the U.S. carrier *Wasp* were along.

"We were listening to our old friend Red Leader going for some bandits," said Captain Hill on the destroyer *Ledbury*. "Then control called him: 'Red Leader, Red Leader . . .' and our hearts sank at the silence. Control called again, and then Red Two came up: 'Red Leader has just been shot down.' "

A parachute drifted into the sea, and Ledbury raced to rescue the pilot, hoping it would be Red Leader.

"I put the ship alongside, and they hauled him up in the nets," said Hill. "I leaned over the bridge. 'What is he, Jimmy?'

" 'A Hun, sir,' he called back."

Three more parachutes drifted down together. Jimmy asked the captain if they were going to rescue them, too.

"They're a bomber's crew," replied Hill. "Let them go to hell."

The German prisoner was handed a jug of lime juice and a stack of sandwiches and told to go around and feed the men at their battle stations. "The most interesting thing about him was that the nails of his boots were made of wood," said Hill, adding that Germany must have been using all of its steel for bombs.

The straightforward air attacks weren't working for the Luftwaffe, so the Italians took over in the afternoon, bringing *motobombe.* As described by *Warship International* magazine, the 900-pound *motobomba* might have been designed by Rube Goldberg. "These were self-propelled mines which were dropped by parachute, and, upon contact with the water, an automatic mercury device activated an electric motor which turned a propeller that drove the missile in an erratic circular path of about 15 km radius."

Admiral Syfret saw the *motobomba* parachutes about two miles ahead of the convoy, and sounded the siren to steer his five dozen ships hard to port. They made a gorgeous high-speed 90-degree turn to the north, swung wide of the *motobombe,* and left them spinning aimlessly and harmlessly around in the water, like a swarm of fat bugs.

The planes that dropped the *motobombe* were escorted by new long-nosed Macchi MC.202 Folgore fighters, replacing the MC.200 Saetta that had appeared over Malta in 1940. The MC.202 was powered by an inverted V-12 Alfa Romeo engine, and it could match the 372-mph top speed of a Spitfire, while its rate of climb was faster by 700 feet per minute. But the morning's second debut by an Italian weapon failed as badly as the first, as antiaircraft fire knocked down two of the new Folgores and damaged eight more.

Eight Fiat CR.42 Falco fighters, a small flock of Falcons, sneaked inside the Hurricane screen. *Indomitable* sent some Grumman Martlets after them, and five of the Falcons either spiraled or nose-dived into the sea.

Next came forty-three Italian torpedo bombers, escorted by thirteen Reggianne Re.2001 fighters, which also used the Alfa Romeo V-12 engine. The convoy fighters scattered the SM.79 and SM.84 torpedo bombers but couldn't keep them away from their designated targets, the cargo ships. They skimmed over the water like dragonflies, coming at the convoy from the port bow, starboard bow, and starboard quarter. One flew so close along the *Santa Elisa* that Lonnie Dales casually waved at the pilot from his Oerlikon on the bridge. The pilot waved back, knowing that the *Santa Elisa* couldn't fire, because there was another merchant ship on the other side of the plane. It was a daring maneuver that enemy pilots often used.

"The sky seemed to be full of planes," said Allan Shaw on the *Ohio*. "How the hell they ever got through the spider's web of tracers being fired at them, I'll never know."

At least three bombers and one fighter bit the waves during this attack. The battleship *Rodney* got into the act, firing her sixteen-inch guns in an attempt to bring down a bunch of aircraft all at once.

"About fourteen torpedo planes flew down our side, well out of range, and then turned towards us and seemed to be trying to come in from the quarter," said Captain Hill. "The Rodney trained her sixteen-inch guns and loosed off a few broadsides. There was an eruption of huge shell splashes on the horizon, and when this had cleared there was no sign of the planes. I cannot believe they were all blown to bits, but they all had certainly veered off to find an easier gap in the defenses."

Eleven bombers and six fighters had been shot down that morning, and not one ship in the convoy was seriously damaged. "Cow shits," the sailors sneered at the little bombs, even with six dead, when a 100-kilo fragmentation bomb landed on the flight deck of the *Victorious*.

In an afternoon broadcast by Italian state radio, Comando Supremo claimed that Axis bombers had sunk one destroyer and two merchant ships, while damaging two more merchantmen, a battleship, and three cruisers.

As the false boasts from Rome flew out over the airwaves, General Rino Corso Fougier, the commander of Regia Aeronautica, was sending off the next secret weapon from Sardinia. He had come up with the idea himself. A three-engined SM.79 "flying buffalo" was loaded with two 1,000-

kilogram megabombs, plus another 1,000 kilos of extra fuel, and a brave pilot took off in the bulging beast. At 13,000 feet he set a course due south for the convoy and bailed out over the sea.

From there, an escort plane guided the big buffalo by radio, with a General Gabrielli at the controls. The target was *Indomitable*. But the awkward missile had a mind of its own, and as the general cursed and pounded the remote control, it flew over the convoy, over the coast, and on for another 150 miles south over Algeria until it crashed into a mountainside. The crater smoked for days afterward. The Algerian French were not impressed.

Meanwhile, Admiral Da Zara continued to steam east from Sardinia with two light cruisers and three destroyers. Two heavy cruisers and five destroyers steamed west to meet them, having left Sicily's Messina Harbor at sunrise. They intended to rendezvous that night in the Tyrrhenian Sea north of the tiny island of Ustica, turn due south, and drop down into the Mediterranean, swing around the east side and under Pantelleria, and come out with guns blazing as the convoy cleared the west side of the island.

Da Zara knew that the aircraft carriers and battleships were planning to turn back to Gibraltar before then, as they always did. Operation Pedestal might have dodged the attacks by *motobombe* and torpedo bombers and the flying buffalo loaded with explosives, but it would not be able to fight off the Italian warships.

CHAPTER 26 • • •
ITHURIEL AND *INDOMITABLE*

T he afternoon air attack had scarcely ended when the eleven Italian
submarines lying in wait for the convoy, just north of the island of
Galita and the Algerian coast, began closing in. Admiral Burrough suggested to Admiral Syfret that each destroyer in the U-boat screen drop a
depth charge at random every ten minutes, to try to keep the subs away.
Maybe it helped and maybe it didn't. Over the next two hours the convoy
was harassed by *Emo*, which fired four bow torpedoes at a cruiser but
missed; *Avorio*, which was depth-charged and hid motionless for five
hours; and *Dandolo*, frustrated by the ships' sharp zigzagging and chased
by dogged destroyers with more depth charges.

When a depth charge is launched from a destroyer, it looks like an oil
drum that's trying to fly. It's packed with 300 pounds of TNT and thrown
off the ship for 50 yards before gravity takes over and pulls it into the sea
like the clumsy can it is. For a few seconds after it goes under, the water is
still. The drum wobbles and tumbles as it sinks at 8.5 feet per second, until
it reaches the depth where it's been set to explode. There's a muted
whump, and a single white ring speeds out from the spot on the surface
where the depth charge landed. Bursting upward from the center of the
ring comes a beautiful white geyser, shooting skyward like a spire of snow
50 feet tall, with an avalanche rolling out of the top. But it's white only if
the depth charge misses. If it finds its target, the water is an ugly, oily,
deathly brown.

The *Santa Elisa* carried three depth charges, but they were only to be
used if she got separated from the convoy and were being stalked by a
U-boat. Because the compressed air launcher was mounted on the main

deck and the main deck was third mate Larsen's territory and he was curious about anything mechanical, he had the depth-charge drill all figured out, just in case. Ensign Suppiger was technically in charge of depth charging, but Suppy was in charge of a lot of things that Larsen could handle better. A .45-caliber pistol, for example, which would soon come between them.

At 1649, the destroyer *Ithuriel* spotted the periscope of the Italian sub *Cobalto* 1,500 yards off the starboard bow. *Cobalto* had already been depth-charged by the destroyer *Tartar* and then by *Zetland* and then by *Pathfinder* and *Zetland* again. She'd been battered so hard that she was leaking all over and driven so deep that the crew's noses and ears were bleeding.

"Speed was increased to 24 knots, wheel put hard-a-starboard," reported *Ithuriel*'s captain, Lieutenant Commander D. H. Maitland-Makgill-Crichton. "U-Boat alarm given. Stopwatch started for a visual attack. Asdic [sonar] put on to the bearing. Depth charges set to 50 foot. Many others had by now sighted the periscope, and the Conning Tower actually broke surface for about 10 seconds or more."

Cobalto quickly submerged, knowing she had been busted. *Ithuriel* dropped five depth charges. "One of the charges brought up oil," said Captain Maitland-Makgill-Crichton.

Cobalto resurfaced, desperate for air.

As *Ithuriel* sped back toward *Cobalto*, sharp bullets from the five-inch gun on her bow blasted holes clean through the sub's conning tower. Armor-piercing shells had been loaded into the gun by mistake. But the only weapon that mattered now was the sharp end of the destroyer.

"Full speed ahead was ordered to Ram," reported the young captain. "Some of the U-boat's crew were seen to be abandoning ship." Wide-eyed at the destroyer bearing down on them, they were diving off the deck and frantically swimming away as fast as they could.

"Full astern was rung down so that our speed on impact was about 12 knots. We struck her at an angle of about 60 degrees, half-way between Conning Tower and Stern, the starboard side."

There was a terrific gnash of steel and shower of sparks, and *Ithuriel* pulled back. Crewmen boarded *Cobalto*, but not for long, as the submarine quickly sank. *Ithuriel* picked up forty of *Cobalto*'s crew, including the captain.

Admiral Syfret didn't think much of Maitland-Makgill-Crichton's exuberance. "Our vigilant A/S [anti-submarine] screen had the satisfaction of achieving a 'kill' of one Italian submarine," he reported. "H.M.S. *Ithuriel* delivered the coup-de-grace to this submarine by ramming it, and in doing so badly damaged herself and put her asdic gear out of action. The submarine, when it came to the surface after being depth-charged, was obviously 'all in,' and I thought the expensive method chosen by the Commanding Officer to sink it quite unnecessary. Moreover, I was disturbed at the amount of time he wasted in picking up survivors, and at his absence from the screen when an air attack was impending."

But an air attack was always impending. That was the state of Operation Pedestal.

General Fougier, chief of Regia Aeronautica, wanted to be sure his air force was cocked and ready when the convoy approached Sicily. He had rushed 101 more planes from the mainland to three Sicilian airfields: Catania on the east coast, Comiso in the southeast, and especially Trapani on the tip of the west coast, 130 miles from where the convoy would appear at dusk: dive-bomb time.

Fougier had sent every Stuka he could spare to Trapani. His scheme with the remote-controlled, megabomb-carrying flying buffalo had failed, but he was still determined to get the aircraft carrier *Indomitable,* which he and others among Comando Supremo still believed might be the *Wasp.*

"At 1830 the first enemy formation was sighted," reported Admiral Syfret. "It is believed that there were from 100 to 120 enemy aircraft in the vicinity, many of them fighters. Against them we had 22 fighters in the air, who continually harassed and broke up the enemy formations."

It's funny how the admirals saw things differently. Syfret, the warship man, saw gallant outnumbered fighter pilots breaking up enemy formations. Lyster, the aircraft man, saw the enemy formations dividing into smaller groups and spreading out, so his fighters could only scatter to chase them, losing any protection they might have been able to give one another.

The Axis aircraft had come from Sardinia and Sicily, joining forces in the sky. The Italian dive-bomber pilots had been trained by the Luftwaffe in their Stukas, and the German torpedo-bomber pilots had been trained by Regia Aeronautica in their SM.79s. And after getting thrashed in the morning, this time the Axis bombers had escorts, led by the swift Messerschmitt Bf 109s.

The *Indomitable*'s captain, Tom Troubridge, a direct descendant of Horatio Nelson's Captain Troubridge, was fat and fearless. He had commanded the battleship *Nelson* during three previous convoys to Malta. This time he watched the attack coming on the radar screen of his aircraft carrier. He thought there might have been as many as 170 enemy aircraft, lined up in layers and coming from all directions.

"In all there were at least 11 formations at heights varying from 10,000 to 25,000 feet," he reported. "The Ju87s appeared suddenly from up sun, out of the smoky blue sky which was rendered hazy by funnel gases, and delivered their attack before adequate gunfire could be brought to bear."

"We had been taken in by the oldest trick in the book," said airman Hector Mackenzie, who had been standing on *Indomitable*'s stern. "A major force draws off the defenders down sun, whilst a hitting force dives out of the sun during the diversion. There, diving at us in perfect formation of two Vees, were the Junkers 87s.

"The pilots were very brave men. They held their course straight down at us, through the flak. At around 500 feet, we could see the bombs drop away, and whilst they hit home, the Stukas pulled out of their dive at sea level and flew up the lines of the ships, in confidence that they would not be fired at for fear of hitting one's own ships."

"The *Indomitable* looked as if she had disturbed a hive of bees," said Roger Hill. "The dive bombers were zooming down on her, and our own fighters were following the enemy planes right into the carrier's gunfire. It was an amazing sight to see. This synchronized attack by over 100 planes, covered by German and Italian fighters, almost swamped our fighter defense."

Three near misses blew holes in *Indomitable*'s hull, the biggest one 40 by 20 feet, causing immediate flooding and listing to port. One direct hit bounced off a pom-pom turret and exploded on the rebound, causing damage for 52 feet inward. Two direct hits on the flight deck peeled back the thick steel, 20 by 12 feet forward and 20 by 16 feet aft. Fire leaped from the gashes and ignited tanks of aviation fuel, which poured over the flight deck and into the sea like a flaming waterfall.

In the smoke and confusion on the bridge, Captain Troubridge's microphone was bumped into the on position. His voice boomed over the ship as he spoke to Admiral Denis Boyd: "Christ, Denis, I believe they've buggered us."

Fifty men were killed, including all the off-duty pilots and observers in the port wardroom, and fifty-nine men were seriously injured. One of the pilots had been defying the odds all day in his Hurricane, and he died in a soft chair, murdered by irony. Many of the casualties were Hector Mackenzie's mates. They found his best friend's head on the other side of the wardroom.

"The stink of death was everywhere," he said. "Although not the most terrible thing we had to put up with, it is one of the most enduring memories of the awful aspects."

Captain Troubridge turned the *Indomitable* away from the wind to stop the fanning of flames, as Admiral Syfret sent the cruiser *Charybdis* and destroyer *Phoebe* to protect the disabled carrier. The destroyer *Lookout* helped fight the fires with her high-pressure hoses until they were under control. The wounded were taken to dressing stations. Spaces on the starboard side were flooded to reduce the listing to port. The engines were restarted, and *Indomitable* turned back for Gibraltar.

Captain Troubridge believed that *Indomitable*'s fighters had shot down nine more enemy planes, with two probables and one damaged during the attack, which had lasted less than twenty minutes. The *Indomitable* had lost but one Hurricane and one Martlet.

"So ended a great day," he actually wrote in his report. "In the course of the day *Indomitable*'s fighters accounted for no less than 27 enemy certain, 6 probables and 8 possible, a total of 41. The number of sorties was 74, which is thought to be a record for aircraft carriers and would have been 78 but for the bombing. All the pilots were up twice and some three times—they responded to every call. The men in the hangars and on the flight deck worked without a break for 14 hours, being then called upon to fight the fires and repair the damage from the enemy bombing attack. The teamwork between *Victorious* and *Indomitable* was one of the outstanding features of a notable day. Fighter carriers had proved their worth."

Admiral Lyster didn't think it was such a great day. "It is a great disappointment to me that the fighters did not take a greater toll of the enemy," he reported.

Lyster's Fleet Air Arm got one more kill, the next day on the way back to Gibraltar. The Air France flying boat that had discovered the convoy seventy-two hours earlier was making another run from Paris to Algiers. The first time, Captain Troubridge had decided not to shoot the bastard down. But that was before his ship had been bombed and fifty men had been killed.

Four Hurricanes from *Victorious* intercepted the airliner.

"The planes followed us for some minutes," said Commandant Marceau Meresse, the Vichy French pilot, "when suddenly they approached square on to our right side, from which I could see the leader and one of his wing. As was traditional in our service, I waggled my wings in greeting. At this precise moment I noticed the leader's plane go vertical and begin a turn towards us. Premonition? I don't know, but I pulled back on the four throttles, reducing the motors to a minimum and accentuating my descent, and turned to the left. At almost the same instant I heard clearly the dry clack of the bullets hitting our plane from the machine-gun burst from the fighters, and, curiously, I also smelled the odor of gunpowder."

Commandant Meresse managed to bring the flying boat down in the sea. Two hundred bullet holes were counted, and four passengers had been killed. "The majority of the passengers were more or less seriously wounded," added Meresse.

The French called it barbaric, but it didn't create a stir in England. It made the front page of London's *Daily Express*, but only as a six-line item, about half an inch. The war went on.

"During the forenoon of the thirteenth, we put our dead over the side," said Hector Mackenzie. "It was a moving service, with as many as could be spared from gun stations attending. The ships in company flew their battle ensigns at half-mast until the bodies had gone. I cannot remember how many there were, all laid out on the flight deck in their shrouds. I recall being vaguely surprised that we carried a large enough stock of White Ensigns to cover them. It looked an awful lot. While most were the shape you would expect of a sewn-up corpse, some were no more than two-foot-or-more cube-shaped parcels, the assembly of odd pieces which had been found. I do not know why, really, but we all felt better when that was over."

F rom the "Most Secret" notes of the War Cabinet Meeting of Saturday, August 1:

THE PRIME MINISTER outlined the main features of the Operation. A crucial stage would be reached on the night before the convoy reached the narrow passage between Cape Bon and Sicily. In making the plan, the Admiralty had had to decide whether the heavy ship escort should carry the convoy right through to Malta at the risk of our two 16-inch battleships being heavily attacked by air or whether, during the final stage of the journey, escorting forces should be confided to cruisers and destroyers. If ill befell our heavy ships in the narrow waters approaching Malta, the whole balance of naval power would be affected. On the other hand, if it was decided not to risk the heavy ships during the final stage and the convoy suffered severe losses from attack by enemy surface ships, some searching questions would be asked. In view of the grave issues involved, he asked the War Cabinet to support any decision which might be taken.

Malta was Churchill's rock, and everything else was the hard place. He said Malta had to be held at all costs, but not at the cost of the balance of naval power. The *Ohio* had been worth asking FDR for, but she wasn't worth losing two battleships and two aircraft carriers for. The decision to turn back the battleships recognized that an attack on the convoy in the Sicilian Narrows might be so advantageous to the enemy that not even the biggest guns in the Royal Navy could fight it off.

Admiral Syfret was now the "man on the spot," as the Royal Navy referred to a leader in position to call the shots. The Admiralty had determined that his Force Z—two aircraft carriers, two battleships, three cruisers, and thirteen destroyers—would turn back at the mouth of the Skerki Channel or dusk, whichever came first, and at 1817 he had signaled the convoy that Force Z would be turning back at 1915. But flaming aircraft carriers have a way of changing things.

It was now 1850, about an hour before dusk and ninety minutes to the channel. The air attack had lasted just twenty minutes, and six ships were scattered. The *Indomitable* was on fire and going off downwind, chased by her cruiser and two destroyers. The destroyer *Foresight* was disabled and rudderless, her stern blown half off by a torpedo bomber, and she was being towed by *Tartar*.

The ships of Force Z needed to stay together to protect one another, but Admiral Burrough's Force X needed them too. It was up to Burrough to deliver the merchantmen to Malta with Force X, which included the cruisers *Nigeria*, *Kenya*, *Cairo*, and *Manchester*, and eleven destroyers. He wanted air cover for at least another hour from *Victorious*, but her flight deck was a nightmare, so slimy with spilled gas and oil that men could barely stay on their feet; damaged planes were being pushed over the side to make room for those still serviceable, which needed to be refueled.

Burrough knew that fighter support for Force X wasn't going to happen, despite the fact that it was dusk and another enemy air attack was possible. He accepted that sometimes you have to go to war with the convoy you have, not the one you might wish to have.

Syfret might have wanted to escort Force X farther toward Malta, but he knew that the deeper the battleships and aircraft carriers went, the harder it would be for them to turn around, especially when there were still submarines waiting to strike as the sea narrowed. The tighter it got, the better it was for the enemy subs.

It was a weighty decision, but it didn't take him much time. At 1855 he sent his friend Burrough a message of "God speed" and turned Force Z around, twenty minutes early, instead of possibly thirty or forty minutes later than the planned time of 1915. He could have left a couple of the Force Z destroyers with Burrough, or even one of the cruisers, but he didn't. Burrough was on his own with four cruisers and ten destroyers to escort thirteen merchantmen. One freighter, *Deucalion*, was damaged and lagging behind with a destroyer escort.

"In view of the magnitude of the enemy's air attack at 1830 to 1850 it seemed improbable that a further attack on Force X on any great scale would be forthcoming before dark, and having reached the Skerki Banks, it was hoped that the submarine menace was mostly over," reported Syfret, explaining his decision to turn back early. "The dangers ahead of Force X seemed to lie principally from attacks by E-Boats during the night and by aircraft the following morning."

Admiral Syfret's confident voice leaves him on this one, and equivocation defines the decision. "Seemed" improbable. It was "hoped." Menace "mostly" over. Dangers "seemed to" lie.

But he underestimated the combined powers of the Luftwaffe, the Regia Aeronautica, and the Italian and German Navies. They had some experience with Malta convoys, too. They knew Force Z would be leaving, and they were waiting. They had all night.

"We felt very lonely when the battleships and cruisers left us," said Larsen.

The freighter *Deucalion* was feeling even more lonely. Her hull had been holed by a bomb's near miss, one of five within 20 feet, and flooding in number one hold had brought her main deck to within three feet of the waterline. Unable to keep up with the convoy, she had plowed south toward Tunisia in an attempt to sneak along in Vichy French territorial waters, escorted by the destroyer *Bramham.* When some of the crew of *Deucalion* had abandoned ship without the master's orders to do so, Captain Eddie Baines of the *Bramham* had told his men to step on the fingers of any merchant seamen who might try to climb onto the destroyer from their lifeboats. He barked at the *Deucalion* crewmen to get back onto their ship where they belonged.

Near the coast of Tunisia, *Deucalion* was discovered by an enemy reconnaissance plane. It didn't take long after that. "Just after sunset, when the light was very bad, two planes attacked simultaneously, the first from the port quarter, and the second from the starboard bow," said *Deucalion*'s master, Ramsay Brown. "Both planes dived steeply, with the engines shut off. The first plane flew along the port side without attacking, then flew off, whilst the second plane flew along the starboard side at a distance of only fifty or sixty feet and dropped a torpedo, which was slung athwartships, from a height of seventy-five feet."

It was as if the phantom dead-stick dive-bomber knew where the aviation fuel was stored, as the torpedo hit the hold with the gasoline. "Immediately the octane spirit ignited, flames rising to twice the height of the mast," said Brown. "In a few minutes the stern part of the ship was a blazing inferno and I realized the ship was doomed, so I gave the order to abandon ship."

They left the *Deucalion* burning bright in the dark, and boarded the *Bramham*, which raced to rejoin the convoy.

The Skerki Bank is a broken limestone reef that lies like a row of bad teeth across the mouth of the Strait of Sicily, blocking the entrance for ships with deep drafts such as the heavy cruiser *Nigeria*. But there's a missing molar, a deepwater gap between Cape Bon and the first big rock, and Admiral Burrough signaled the convoy to merge from cruising disposition 24 to 21, four columns into two, in order to squeeze through the gap.

He sent the three minesweeping destroyers—*Intrepid, Icarus,* and *Fury*—to the front because it was assumed that the Skerki Channel would be mined. The ships in the second and fourth columns slowed to 8 knots, while those in the first and third columns moved to starboard and slipped between them. Burrough wanted to complete the maneuver before the convoy got too close to the channel, where the sandbars bounced false echoes back to the destroyers' sonar, providing perfect cover for the subs.

So far the convoy's destroyers had dominated the subs. When Force Z was along, the convoy had depth-charged its way through Regia Marina's Zones C and B, patrolled by six Italian subs. There had been two dozen destroyers in the screen for most of that time: four destroyers per sub. Now Force X was in the heart of Zone A, with five more subs, and Burrough had but nine destroyers to protect the merchantmen from attack by the eleven submarines in the area.

Lieutenant Commander Renato Ferrini had watched the evening air attack from a distance, through the periscope of the *Axum*, although all he could see were the towers of smoke from the flaming *Indomitable*. When the bombers returned to Sicily he began chasing the convoy at full speed and a depth of 60 feet. By 1927 he had closed to 4.5 miles, and he entered in his log:

> Alter course parallel to study situation.
>
> 1933: Fresh observation. Am able to establish that the formation comprises about 15 steamers, two cruisers and numerous destroyers.

1937: Fresh estimate of distance 4,000 meters.

1942: After a quick look at periscope depth, dive to 15 meters and go half speed ahead on both engines to close.

1948: Periscope depth. Angle of sight of cruiser in the second line 28 degrees. In the nearer line, ahead and astern of the cruiser, are respectively a destroyer and a large merchant ship.

He had two out of three right. The cruiser was the *Cairo*, and leading her was not a destroyer but another cruiser, Admiral Burrough's flagship, the *Nigeria*. The large merchant ship was the *Ohio*.

"At about a quarter to eight that evening there was a welcome lull in the air combats," Anthony Kimmins told his BBC radio listeners from the bridge of the *Nigeria*. "Remember that everyone in those ships had been fighting almost continuously since daylight, and apart from the heat of battle, there had been the grueling heat of the Mediterranean sun. Now in the temporary lull, men slipped off their antiflash helmets and gloves, and seized the opportunity of cooling off."

1955: Fire bow tubes in order 1, 4, 3, 2 of which 1 and 2 straight, 3 and 4 angled respectively to 5 degrees to starboard and 5 degrees to port. Directly after firing, disengage. Distance at firing from first line 1,300 meters, from cruiser 1,800 meters. 63 seconds after firing hear first explosion.

"Some of us had gone down for a moment to the navigator's station," continued Kimmins. "Suddenly there was a flash, a terrific explosion, and complete darkness, as the lights and most other things were shattered. A U-boat had got a torpedo home on us. The ship immediately started to list, and as we groped our way to the door and forced our way out through the fumes, the ladders were already well over at an angle. By the time we reached the bridge, Admiral Burrough and the captain were leaning across the starboard side, looking rather like yachtsmen at the tiller of a boat heeling well over to a fresh breeze. Some of the ship's company were already grouping on the upper deck in the most orderly fashion, and as they did so they looked up to the bridge for orders. There was never a sign of panic, but the ship was assuming a somewhat alarming angle, and the memory of the *Eagle* was still fresh in our minds.

"But any doubts anyone may have had were immediately removed by the admiral. 'Don't worry, she'll hold!' he shouted. 'Let's have a cigarette.'

"And whatever momentary effect that great explosion may have had was removed in a flash by that casual remark. From that moment, everything in that ship was carried out like an ordinary peacetime exercise."

Except that men don't die, fifty-two at a time, during an ordinary peacetime exercise.

"On the 12th August, 1942, I was on the sloping deck of a torpedoed ship, and in what appeared to be a hopeless situation," recalled Alfred Longbottom, a twenty-one-year-old seaman at the time. "With massive damage amidships, we could hear water rushing into the HMS *Nigeria*. Down by the bow, and with the stern rising, she was in danger of going down. Everything was out of action—the guns, radar, radio, steering—all gone. Flames were leaping out of one of the funnels, with the diesel on fire. Down below, 50 officers and men had perished, and others were wounded—some mentally."

"The ship immediately assumed a list of approximately 15 degrees, and I realized that she would not be able to take further part in the operation," reported Burrough. "I immediately ordered *Ashanti* to close as I felt that it was vitally important that I should regain contact with the Convoy who were moving South-East at about 14 knots.

"At 2020 *Ashanti* came alongside *Nigeria* and, after satisfying myself that *Nigeria* was in no danger of sinking, I embarked with my Staff and proceeded to rejoin the Convoy."

Thirty seconds after *Nigeria* was hit, Captain Ferrini heard two more explosions through the hydrophones of the *Axum*.

This leads me to assume a hit on a unit in the first line and successively on one in the second line. Calculating from speed of torpedoes, distance on firing was less than estimated, being actually about 1,000 meters from the first line and 1,400 from the second.

There was a blinding flash when the second cruiser was hit, as chunks of steel and sailors from the *Cairo* flew hundreds of feet into the evening sky. Twenty-six men were lost with her stern, after she was hit by the *Axum*'s second and third torpedoes.

" 'Look out for debris!' somebody shouted, and we all dived for cover as wreckage fell all round us," said Norman Smart of the *Daily Express*, who was being sunk for the second time in the war. "The explosion had blown Y gun, aft, clean off its mountings into the sea. Royal Marines, manning the gun, had been blown overboard. I could hear them shouting for help— tiny black heads bobbing in the water."

"Almost immediately *Cairo* lost way and started to settle by the stern, taking a slight list to starboard," reported Captain C. C. Hardy. "I received a report from the Engineer Officer that the port propeller had been lost, that the starboard engine was unserviceable and that there was no prospect of getting it into action again; also that the stern had been blown off. On considering the factors, I decided to sink the ship."

Like the *Eagle*, the *Cairo* had been gallantly serving the British Empire since 1918. But she had used up the last of her luck, after surviving an un-exploded bomb in the engine room during Operation Harpoon and escaping the guns of Admiral Da Zara.

Captain Hardy transferred his men to the destroyer *Wilton*. With more than two hundred survivors aboard, *Wilton*, along with *Bicester* and *Derwent*, followed *Nigeria* back to Gibraltar.

The new destroyer *Pathfinder* was armed with eight torpedoes, so Captain Hardy asked her to finish off the *Cairo*, which was going down at the stern.

"Captain Hardy sat on the bridge, chin in hands, and watched the destroyer wheel about," wrote Norman Smart. "A torpedo hit *Cairo* amidships and she went up in a cloud of smoke. It was a heartbreaking sight after getting so far towards Malta."

After the *Pathfinder* took her shots at *Cairo*, she raced away at full speed. Her captain had just received a message: "A force of Enemy Cruisers was now being reported on a course and at a speed which would enable them to reach the convoy during the middle watch," he explained.

It was Admiral Da Zara's fleet. The Italian warships were closing in.

CHAPTER 28

CAPTAIN FERRINI'S AMAZING HAT TRICK

Although Captain Dudley Mason had only been master of the *Ohio* for twenty-eight days, he had established a reputation with the crew for carrying himself with a great deal of equilibrium, even in stormy seas. "He didn't have a great lot to say," said the ordinary seaman Allan Shaw, who was then nineteen and is now eighty-three, living in Blyth on the North Sea and nearly as nimble as he was back then.

Before the Italian submarine's strike at sunset, Captain Mason hadn't appeared to be very excited by the day's activity. In fact, he didn't have much to say about it.

WEDNESDAY, AUGUST 12TH.

The day passed fairly uneventfully. One or two isolated planes got through the outer screen and kept the gunners in action, and some bombs were dropped. Continuous salvoes of depth charges and emergency turns to port and starboard every few minutes. Several vessels reported submarines, and I believe two were accounted for this afternoon. The signal had been given that a concentration of submarines were expected inside a given area (approximately our position for dusk). We were then 75 miles north of Cape Bon, on the edge of the 100-fathom line.

But when *Nigeria* and *Cairo* were torpedoed, Captain Mason's "uneventful" day suddenly ended, and the long night in the narrows began. Lieutenant Barton, the *Ohio*'s young liaison officer, was on the bridge with Mason when the two cruisers were hit. "I saw great bits of *Cairo* flying for

400 yards," he said. "Then, while we were still looking at *Cairo*, there was a tremendous sheet of flames just about on the bridge, and we too had been hit."

Captain Ferrini of the *Axum* had scored an amazing hat trick: four torpedoes fired, three ships hit. Force X had lost two of its four cruisers—its heavily armed flagship *Nigeria* and antiaircraft specialist *Cairo*—and the crux of the convoy, its raison d'être, the SS *Ohio*, was aflame. One sweet salvo of Italian torpedoes was all it took to radically tilt the balance of Operation Pedestal.

"There was a bright flash, and a column of water was thrown up to masthead height. There were two seconds of absolute quiet, and then flames shot into the air," said Mason, who was blown to the deck by the blast. He crawled toward the chart room, where he bumped heads with the third mate, who was crawling out. "The vessel heeled over and shook violently. We were struck amidships in the pump room on the port side, halfway between the bow and stern."

The freighter *Empire Hope* was in formation behind *Ohio*, which suddenly veered; *Empire Hope* came so close to the tanker that her seamen threw fenders over the fo'c'sle to cushion the crash they thought was coming. From the bridge of the *Ohio*, behind the wall of flames and over its roar, Captain Mason heard the *Empire Hope* ring for hard astern, and a collision was avoided by mere feet.

"Some of us were standing on the poop deck when the torpedo hit," said Allan Shaw. "We all thought this was it—when a tanker goes afire, you haven't got a great lot of chance. There was the flames, and there was an awful big goosher, which seemed to put some of the flames out. A lot of water, it went up like a big geyser. Then someone shouted, 'Get the fire extinguishers.'"

Because the ships were in the middle of their formation change, the *Ohio* was close off the port bow of the *Santa Elisa* and moving nearly twice as fast. The *Santa Elisa* had slowed to 8 knots, to allow *Ohio* to move to starboard and slip in ahead of her, in the change from four columns to two. If the torpedo had missed the *Ohio*, it would have hit the *Santa Elisa*.

At their battle stations on the port bridge wings of the *Santa Elisa*, Larsen and Dales got a face full of flaming *Ohio*.

"A tremendous black cloud rose on our port beam," said Dales, watching from his gun. "The tanker *Ohio*, with its cargo so vital to Malta's existence, had just been torpedoed! We could feel the heat. I saw men dragging fire hoses across her deck. The black smoke swallowed them up."

Shaw, who's a wee five feet, six inches and the same 147 pounds he was back then, continues. "We grabbed some big fire extinguishers at the after end, and ran along the flying bridge and lowered them down to some lads who were fighting the fire. It's good the sea was washing in and out; that was helping keep the fire down."

"The *Ohio* did not list," said Mason, "but the deck on the port side was torn up and laid right back inboard, nearly to the centerline. There was a hole in the hull on the port side twenty-four feet by twenty-seven feet, reaching from the main deck to well below the waterline. The large Samson derrick post fell over to an angle of forty-five degrees, the flying bridge was damaged, and the pump room was ablaze and completely open to the sea. Four kerosene tanks were opened up to the sea on the port side; their lids were blown off, and flames were coming up through the hatches. The steering gear telemotor pipes were carried away by the explosion, also the electric cable and all steam pipes in the vicinity of the pump room.

"I had the crew mustered on the deck at boat stations provisionally, but engines had been kept running. I had previously told the chief engineer that he was not to stop the engines whatever happened, until I gave him the order to do so, but now I rang, 'Finish with engines.' I gave the order now, in order to get the men out of the engine room for the time being. I had been forced to stop, not only to fight the fire, but because our steering was out of order and we were turning in circles, making us a danger to the other ships which were lying stopped near us, including the *Nigeria* and the *Cairo*."

Mason joined the firefight, facing the searing heat, directing the hoses, and shouting for more fire extinguishers.

"It was then a case of fighting the pump room fire," he continued. "I thought it was a forlorn hope, but we set to work with foam extinguishers and managed to put out the flames much more easily than I expected. We also put out the flames in the kerosene tanks and replaced the tank lids, although these could not be screwed down as they were badly buckled."

The destroyer *Pathfinder* circled *Ohio*, dropping depth charges, as the rest of the convoy left the burning tanker behind, dead in the water at dusk.

On the *Axum*, Captain Ferrini had no time to enjoy his success.

1955: 4 min 30 sec after firing, while at 65 meters depth, the hunt begins with a pattern of depth charges; dive to 100 meters and stop all machinery. The hunt continues with deliberate attacks for two hours, patterns of depth charges being fired. It is noticed that each time the boat rises to between 80 and 90 meters the transmissions of the asdics are clearly heard, followed immediately by depth charges. Decide to remain between 100 and 120 meters.

While the *Axum* was hiding at 300 feet and the *Ohio* was smoldering on the water, the dive-bombers arrived, right on schedule.

"Whilst we were fighting the fires," said Mason, "enemy planes commenced attack at masthead height. Near misses were many and frequent, throwing deluges of water over the vessel. I sent for the chief engineer to ask him how long it would take to raise steam, as the steam had dropped back whilst we were stopped, and fortunately, owing to being fitted with a diesel generator, we were able to raise steam again within ten minutes, instead of the usual three or four hours."

From Mason's log:

Apparently Gunners (Army Ratings) E. Smith & W. Hands also Galley Boy M. Guidotti paniced [*sic*] & attempted to lower no. 5 Boat. This overturned throwing these men into the sea. They were not seen again. At approx the same time vessel was bombed & R. Morton (Asst. Steward) was found to be missing. It is assumed he was washed overboard with the deluge of water as he was assisting at Gun on the port side.

Ray Morton, alive and living in Australia, isn't sure how he ended up in the water that day, from his position at a Browning machine gun. "I remember the ship being torpedoed," he said. "Tank lids, flames, and oil shooting mast high, probably even higher. And the oil coming down on us, on the boat deck. I was soaked in it. I know that. But then there's a big gap and I just can't remember what happened at all. I've been given various stories about what happened, and all I can say is, it could be any one or all of the above. I just don't know. But I found myself in the water. Had a lifejacket on, and I was just bobbing about in the water and then I realized there were three others there with me, and we just drifted around and hoped to God somebody would see us. You could see other merchant ships steaming past, and nobody on board them even gave us a wave. We knew they weren't allowed to stop to pick up survivors, because that was putting their ship and crew at risk.

"We'd probably just about given up hope of getting picked up. Pilots came over, German pilots, and machine-gunned us while we were in the water. Fortunately they missed, and Mario, the fifteen-year-old galley boy, is yelling, 'You stupid bastards, you couldn't hit a barn door!' And I'm yelling out to him, 'For God's sake shut up, they'll hear ya and they'll come back!' We were there for about three hours when a destroyer came and circled round toward us, and we all sort of heaved a mental sigh of relief."

It will never be known why the dive-bombers didn't finish off the *Ohio*. Maybe it was fate, maybe it was an act of God, maybe it was sharpshooting by the gunners manning the Bofors on the stern. Or maybe it was just because there were more targets, farther ahead. The convoy was miles away by this time, and the enemy planes flew on, pursuing the other ships.

Captain Ferrini:

> 2250: Surface. 3,000 meters ahead is a big ship in flames. On starboard bow another burning with much smoke. 70 degrees on port bow a third ship already burnt out from which still comes, however, the characteristic dense grey-black smoke. The flames of the first ship clearly illuminate me and immediately afterwards I see two destroyers in motion and signaling; since it is essential for me to replenish air bottles and recharge batteries, I submerge to avoid being further hunted, and leave the area.

It would appear that these three burning and smoking ships were the *Nigeria, Cairo,* and *Ohio.* But no, three hours had passed. More likely, they were the next three ships in the convoy to get blown up.

PART VI

HELL IN THE NARROWS

CHAPTER 29 • • •
THIS ONE'S FOR MINDA

The commanding officer of the cruiser HMS *Kenya*, Captain A. S. Russell, according to the ship's doctor, was "the ideal type of captain—handsome, humorous, and a very brave and wonderful man." He was also the type of man to take charge when he believed it was necessary. "I immediately assumed control of the convoy," he reported after the *Nigeria* was hit and while Admiral Burrough was transferring his flag to the destroyer *Ashanti*. Russell had sent a signal to Burrough that wasn't answered, and that was enough for him.

As the convoy steamed away from the disabled *Nigeria*, *Cairo*, and *Ohio*, Captain Russell sounded *Kenya*'s siren to order the ships to make two emergency turns to starboard and signaled for an increase in speed. Then he ordered a turn back to port, another turn back to the original course, and then a reduction in speed. "By this time the formation of the convoy was chaotic," he reported, not surprisingly. Admiral Syfret later objected to Russell's use of the word "chaotic"; at least the ships that hadn't been hit were still headed more or less east, he pointed out.

Captain Russell might have been handsome, humorous, brave, and wonderful, but that didn't keep him out of the doghouse with Admiral Syfret. In fact, Syfret didn't accept that Russell had been in charge. "The Commanding Officer, HMS *Kenya*, reported by emergency signal [to all the ships] that he was in command of Force X," said Syfret. "This statement, as it proved incorrect, did not help to improve an already confused situation."

Syfret was getting the picture by radio, and he could see that it was ugly, if not chaotic. He pulled the antiaircraft cruiser *Charybdis* and the big

Tribal-class destroyers *Eskimo* and *Somali* out of Force Z and sent them racing back to help Force X.

Air support was also on its way to Force X. Four Beaufighters had left Malta before the convoy had been torpedoed, without being sure where it was. But *Nigeria* and *Cairo* had been the only ships with high-frequency radios to communicate with the fighters. The pilots managed to find *Kenya*, leading the scattered convoy just west of Skerki Bank, but she opened fire on them, not knowing they were friendly. They turned and flew back to Malta.

And there were still submarines in the water, converged near the mouth of the narrows, licking their chops for a fat target like the *Kenya* to come along.

"At 2111, Kenya was hit in the fore-peak by a torpedo," reported Russell. "Another torpedo passed under the ship, about abreast the bridge, and two more narrowly missed the stern, passing down the port side. The main machinery and all communications were found correct, but the maximum available speed was not known. I joined [the heavy cruiser] Manchester, and hoped the convoy would get reformed."

It was now about thirty minutes past sunset. As the remaining two dozen ships in the convoy ran in helter-skelter zigzags from the unseen wolf pack, thirty Ju 88s came in high, hiding themselves from the convoy's gunners in the gray area between sea and stars. While the antiaircraft guns were pointed skyward into the dull buzzing void, seven He 111 torpedo bombers zoomed in low. It was the gunners' turn to be swamped by confusion. They didn't know where to aim: up, down, left, right, hell if they did, hell if they didn't.

And then a dozen Stukas, flying like deadly dark vectors in formations of three, approached the leading ships from four directions. The *Santa Elisa* was among them, with Larsen and Dales at their battle stations.

Even the shape of a Stuka is scary. Anything so aggressively awkward must be lethal. It flaunts its ugliness with cranked wings and wheel spats sharpened at their trailing edges, making the plane look like a monster bird of prey, a nightmare from the sky, like the mythical Roc that Sinbad encountered on his Fifth Journey in the Grimm Brothers' story:

> The two Rocs approached with a frightful noise, and carried between
> their talons stones of a monstrous size. When they came directly over my

ship, they hovered, and one of them let fall a stone so exactly upon the middle of the ship that it split into a thousand pieces.

The North African Stukas were especially weird, with camouflage paint that looked like leopard skin. The Italians called their Stukas *"picchiatelli"*—"strikers"—and painted them a sinister black. The German Stukas wailed like banshees when they dived at their human targets, particularly Russians and Europeans or fleeing people pushing carts along roads, such as the Maltese. The evil machines carried wind-driven sirens called "trombones of Jericho," which were mounted on each strut, canisters with propellers looking like two baby airscrews flying along under their mother. The sirens were meant to strike fear on the ground, or on the decks of a ship at sea, and they succeeded.

Like the Roc carrying a stone under its belly between its talons, a Stuka could carry a bomb of monstrous size, 1,800 kilograms. But its normal total payload was 700 kilos: two 50-kilo bombs dangled from each wing, and under the fuselage hung one bomb of 500 kilos. The weight made the Stuka sluggish in any direction but down.

"The Ju 87D did not appear to find its natural element until it was diving steeply," said Captain Eric Brown, chief test pilot for the RAF, who got some seat time in a captured Stuka. "It seemed quite normal to stand this aircraft on its nose in a vertical dive, with the speed climbing up to 373 mph. During the dive it was necessary to watch the signal light on the contact altimeter, and when it came on, a knob on the control column was depressed to initiate the automatic pullout, with forces on the pilot reaching 6 g during completion of the manoeuvre."

Among all the dive-bombers, including Japanese and American, only the Stuka could dive vertically, taking bombing accuracy to new levels. The pilot released the bombs, and the plane began to pull out of the dive at 1,475 feet, using a system tested in 1938 by a famed female pilot, Melitta Schiller. But it didn't level off until it was sometimes as low as 100 feet. That's when it was most vulnerable to antiaircraft fire, but by then the bombs had often hit home. At sea, the line between a Stuka and a kamikaze could be fine.

Roger Hill lay on his back on the hot steel bridge of the *Ledbury*, wearing his striped rugby shirt and studying the dive-bombers in the sky. When a Stuka pitched down at his destroyer, he would shout to the helmsman,

"Hard over port!" or "Hard over starboard!" or "Full for'ard!" or "Full back!" It was a deadly game of dodgebomb, as the destroyer danced between the splashes and heaved on the swells of the explosions.

It was also a quick-draw contest, *mano a mano* between destroyer captain and dive-bomber pilot. The pilot moves first, and it's the captain's duel to lose. He needs to watch the falling black bombs long enough to judge their trajectory, but not so long his ship can't respond to avoid them. If his shouted order is quick enough and correct, and the destroyer breaks sharply enough, he can dodge the bomb with the ship's name on it. Winning is defined by survival and rewarded by the chance to dodge the next stick of bombs.

Under the falling bombs, the gunner at an Oerlikon virtually wears the cannon. He raises and lowers the long barrel with his shoulders, which are pressed into C-shaped supports, and moves it from side to side by pushing and pulling on a bar with hand grips. "The controls were like the handlebars on a motorcycle," said Lonnie Dales, "and the trigger was like the brake lever, which you squeezed with your right hand."

"The gun was mounted on a trunnion, allowing an elevation of some eighty-five degrees and only limited by the gunner's ability to crouch low enough in his buckled-in position," added Frank Pike. "If the gunner was tall enough, he could get on tiptoe to depress the barrel below horizontal, aiming at an E-boat. The gun was rotated by the gunner moving his feet sideways, and there were stops fitted to the turret to prevent the gun being aimed inboard. Sighting was through a ring sight consisting of concentric circles with the outer circles giving a guide for deflection shooting at a plane crossing in front."

Sixty rounds filled a magazine, with each cartridge greased by human hands and inserted into the cannister in alternating order: tracer, armor-piercing, incendiary, and solid. The shells were as thick as a deck ape's thumb and twice as long, and were squeezed onto a spiral track. The magazine weighed thirty pounds and was lifted onto the shoulders of one loader by the other, then clipped into the breech by both of them. Because the Oerlikon fired at a rate of 450 rounds per minute, an excited gunner could use up a magazine in eight seconds, so they were instructed to fire in bursts of no more than three seconds. Any longer than that, and the barrels got red hot anyhow. According to the manual, loaders wearing asbestos gloves were to swap hot barrels for cool ones, which were kept alongside the gun. But reality was different. "We never had time to replace the barrels," said Dales.

As the Oerlikon fired away, the brass casings streamed out of the gun and clattered onto the bridge, making a golden pile that rolled over the deck like flaming oil on water. When the spent shells got so thick the loaders couldn't walk around anymore, they were shoveled up and tossed over the side.

Stuka pilots were sometimes teenagers, like many of the Hurricane and Spitfire pilots. They were all daring, but if the British boys were dashing, the Italians were wild and the Germans steely. It took one trait or the other to fly a Stuka. They tried to get as close to their target as possible. They squirmed their Stukas through silent streams of red and gold tracer from the Oerlikons and Bofors and dodged bursts of flak from the pom-poms that rattled their planes and ripped holes in them. The steeper the dive, the lower the exposure to antiaircraft fire, because guns from the target ship couldn't point straight up. And the other ships' guns couldn't easily hit a plane falling at more than 350 miles per hour.

Thirty Ju 88s and twelve Stukas were over the ships now. "Personally, I found this the most unpleasant moment of the whole operation," admitted the BBC's Anthony Kimmins. "The combination of recent events, the fact that it was nightfall, and the determination of these dive-bombers made it all rather eerie."

"Down they came, lower and lower," wrote Dickens, on the *Dorset.* "The convoy put up an absolutely terrific barrage of fire, but still the swine came on, screeching louder and louder; when they let go their bombs, one could even see them coming straight for us. The roar and rattle of ack-ack guns, the incessant whistling of bombs and aircraft, the ghastly rending of crashes of torpedo hits made the whole thing like a bad dream."

"This was the most concentrated attack of all," said Ensign Suppiger on the *Santa Elisa.* "Three more merchant ships were hit by bombs. One ship astern of us was hit, exploded violently, and burst into flames. A Junkers 88 dropped a stick of bombs on us, again straddling the ship."

"A bomber drops a stick of 500-pounders so close to our port bow that I can almost reach out and touch them," said the engineer Ed Randall. "As he cuts away from us, a seaman picks up a monkey wrench and lets fly at him with a beautiful side-arm delivery. I feel like telling him not to be a damn fool, throwing away equipment like that, but I know how helpless he feels, and I say, 'Nice try.' He grins sheepishly."

The gunners on the bow and the bridge of the *Santa Elisa* got soaked by the splashes, cooling them off under their woolen antiflash hoods and long gloves. "Thanks!" they yelled at the Huns in the Junkers, as the hot barrels of their guns hissed clouds of steam.

Apparently, the gunners on the *Santa Elisa* had a reputation. "They enthusiastically blazed away at everything that crossed their sights," according to one report. The *Santa Elisa*'s shooters were hardly alone on that score, but because the ship was American, their eager trigger fingers seemed to be the typical Yank thing.

The other American freighter, *Almeria Lykes*, was also doing some serious shooting. Her Bofors gunner had shot down two enemy planes, and the gun's barrel had been worn smooth from all the firing. A twenty-year-old manned one of the Oerlikons on the bridge and in the middle of this dusk attack had shouted these memorable instructions to his loader: "Get a bucket of water, Bud, the barrel's melting and there's more of the bastards coming!"

Larsen was at his Oerlikon on the forward port bridge wing of the *Santa Elisa*, his two loaders hefting the magazines and snapping them into the breech. He'd been at the gun for most of the day, from the first attack at dawn until this one at dusk, despite the strain on his legs, back, shoulders, and neck, as well as the heat under his feet and assault on his eardrums. But he wasn't about to leave the gun tub. He'd been hungry for kills from the moment the ship left Brooklyn.

"Fred, one of my closest friends aboard the *Santa Elisa*, had good reason to seek revenge against the Germans, in addition to self-preservation," said Jack Follansbee. "His wife and small son had been in Norway when the Nazis invaded that country, and they were still there. He kept a picture of his beautiful wife on the desk in his cabin.

"I asked him why he spent so much time at the gun, and he said, 'Jack, I am just so mad at those damn Germans. They have my Minda.' "

A mile above the *Santa Elisa*, a German spotted her bridge through the large greenhouse canopy of his Stuka. There were ten items on his checklist, things that had to be done before he began his dive. Landing flaps, elevator trim, rudder trim, and airscrew pitch all had to be set in the cruise position. The contact altimeter had to be switched on and set to the bomb-release altitude. The supercharger had to be set to automatic. Then he had to pull the throttle back, close the cooler flaps, and open the dive brakes.

This final step nosed the Stuka over into its dive toward the *Santa Elisa.*

"In order to judge the steepness of the dive, there were lines marked on the starboard side of the canopy, which when aligned with the horizon indicated a dive angle of up to ninety degrees," said Captain Brown of the RAF. "Now, a dive angle of ninety degrees is a pretty palpitating experience, for it always feels as if the aircraft is over vertical and is bunting. But as the speed builds up, the nose of the Ju 87 is used as the aiming mark. All this while *terra firma* is rushing closer, with apparently suicidal rapidity."

If the German had any such thoughts of death, they were misplaced. His threat was not terra firma, nor the sea, nor the cold steel deck of a ship. It was an angry Norwegian gunman who was taking the war personally. If the fight between freighter and dive-bomber got down to *mano a mano*, this time the pilot didn't have a prayer.

Larsen stared the Stuka down, through the concentric circles of his scope, as the 500-kilo bomb on the plane's belly raced toward his bull's-eye. Tracer fire streamed from the other ships and slipped beyond the Stuka, disappearing in diminishing gold streaks into the darkening sky, like hundreds of shooting stars traveling in reverse. The young pilot watched them whizzing past his wings, his heart beating like the thump of a Bofors as he desperately waited for the red light on the altimeter to flash so he could whack the knob that would release his bombs and pull his plane out of the dive that seemed as though it would never end.

Larsen held his fire until he was sure he couldn't miss. He never went off half cocked about anything. The Stuka kept diving. Larsen kept waiting.

When it was time to shoot, he was calm and cold. He squeezed the trigger in his right hand.

This one's for Minda.

He watched his tracers silently speed between the circles in his sight. It was nearly night, and the small dark Stuka in the scope looked more like a bat than a bomber. As the tracers met their target at top dead center of the concentric circles, the Stuka flashed like a bulb in an old camera. Chunks of German steel scattered into the evening sky, and red flames streamed like blood over the fuselage, charring the swastika on the Stuka's tail.

"Third Mate Fred Larsen, stationed at a 20mm Oerlikon gun amidships, shot down a Stuka at about 1,000 yards range," reported Ensign Suppiger. "It crashed into the sea on our starboard beam, about a ship's length off."

The dive that the pilot thought would never end had ended, about five hundred feet short of his target.

When Fred Larsen was three years old, he lost his father, mother, a sister, grandfather, and grandmother to the global flu pandemic. He was sent to Norway to be raised by an uncle, who died when Larsen was ten. He went to sea at seventeen, and never looked back.

Lonnie Dales, an all-American boy from rural Georgia, was born brave. He boarded the SS *Santa Elisa* at eighteen, fresh out of the new U.S. Merchant Marine Cadet Corps, and was assigned to an Oerlikon rapid-fire cannon on the bridge, under the mentoring eye of Third Officer Fred Larsen.

Larsen attended mariners' college in Norway, where he married Minda, the farm girl who stole his heart. He returned to sea in the summer of 1939. On April 9, 1940, their first wedding anniversary, Germany invaded and occupied Norway. Nazis came by sea, their ships looming off Norway's rugged coast. Minda and Jan—the infant son Fred had never seen—were trapped.

GRENZZONEN-BESCHEINIGUNG Nr.: 1137
Crenzzone West
GRENSEBOERBEVIS
Grensesone Vest

Polizeidirektor/Lensmann in
Politimesteren/Lensmannen i   Farsund

Inhaber dieser Grenzzonen-Bescheinigung,
Innehaveren av dette grenseboerbevis

Minda Larsen   geb. am 5/9 1916; in Lista
                                födt den

Beruf: Fiskerdreng   Staatsangehörigkeit: Norsk
Yrke: Nasjonalitet:

hat seinen ständigen Wohnsitz in: Farsund   Langt.
har sin faste bopel i:

Polizei/Lensmanns-Bezirk: Farsund
Politi/lensmanns-distrikt:

Diese Bescheinigung berechtigt zum Verkehr in folgenden Polizei-
bezirken der Grenzzone West: Minda Larsen
Dette bevis gir innehaveren rett til å ferdes i følgende politi-   Eigenhändige Unterschrift
distrikter i Grensesone Vest: Vell. Byder politidistrikt   Egenhendig underskrift

                                                      O Irue
Ort: Farsund   Siegel   Unterschrift des Polizeidirektors bzw.
Sted: Stempel   Lensmanns
Datum: 5/4 - 1941   Politimesterens eller lensmannens
Datum: underskrift

The Gestapo issued Minda an ID. German soldiers filled the streets outside her small apartment. They staggered back to their quarters late at night, loud and drunk, just outside her bedroom window. She held her son to her breast, and whispered in his ear that his father would bring them to America.

The attack on Pearl Harbor put the U.S. at war with Germany, and U-boats soon began sinking merchant ships along the Atlantic Coast. The *Santa Elisa* was the target of *U-123*. In a mystery at sea, the *Santa Elisa*'s hull was ripped open, and her cargo of fuel ignited. Larsen and the chief mate led the firefight for nearly five hours. When lives were at stake, Larsen was the first to arrive, and the last to leave.

More bombs fell on Malta in April and May 1942 than on London during the entire Battle of Britain. Axis planes came in hordes from nearby Sicily. Limestone rubble filled the streets, and Maltese lived in caves as enemy submarines and bombers kept Allied merchant ships from bringing in supplies. With no natural sources for food or water on the arid island, some 270,000 people starved.

For the first two weeks after the siege on Malta began, the island's entire air force consisted of these three overachieving Gloster Gladiator biplanes, called Faith, Hope, and Charity.

Night bombing raids were frequent, and the Royal Malta Artillery painted the sky with streaks of white light from antiaircraft fire. The guns could be controlled by one man in a bunker, like a wizard showering the sky with shrapnel and big bangs.

The tanks of the RAF planes were filled by cans of aviation fuel carried to Malta at great risk by merchant ships. Enemy pilots often buzzed the airfields and bombed the planes as crews frantically serviced them.

Hitler planned an invasion of Malta with Admiral Raeder, commander-in-chief of the German Navy. But at the last minute, he canceled it. "I am a coward at sea," he said. "It was the greatest mistake of the Axis in the whole war in this theater," said Admiral Weichold, the German commander in the Mediterranean.

The *Ohio* steamed from Texas to Glasgow, where she was turned over to a British crew, and a new master, Dudley Mason, was assigned.

With Malta facing capitulation to the Axis, Prime Minister Churchill met with FDR and borrowed the SS *Ohio*. The Texas Company ship was the biggest and fastest tanker in the world. She was Malta's last hope, because there was no survival without the 107,000 barrels of oil carried in her thirty-three honeycombed tanks for antiaircraft generators on Malta and the Royal Navy submarines hunting Rommel's supply ships.

The Operation Pedestal convoy sometimes stretched ten miles wide at sea. The *Ohio*, the *Santa Elisa*, and twelve more freighters were defended by five aircraft carriers, two battleships, seven cruisers, and thirty-two destroyers, plus oilers, corvettes, minesweepers, motor launches, tugboats, and nine submarines patrolling nearby waters. As the ships passed from the Atlantic Ocean into the Mediterranean Sea, Admiral Neville Syfret, commander of the fleet, sent them a message: "Remember that the watchword is: THE CONVOY MUST GO THROUGH."

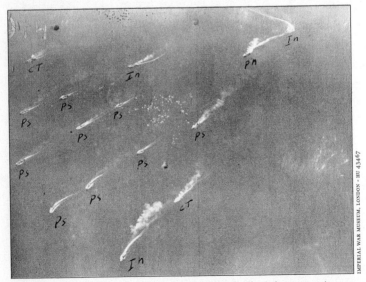

Operation Pedestal was top secret, but it was too big to hide. This Italian reconnaissance photo, taken after the convoy passed into the Mediterranean Sea, has ships marked for attack.

Warning communication is soon given, urgently flashed from ship to ship. . . .

The aircraft carrier *Eagle*, serving the British Empire since 1918, was blindsided by three torpedoes from U-73. She listed to port, dumping the planes off her flight deck, and sank in eight minutes, taking 231 men down with her. Larsen and Dales watched from their battle stations on the bridge of the *Santa Elisa*—the same point of view as this photo, taken from a destroyer. "It was a pathetic sight to see as the *Eagle* rolled over. In a matter of minutes she was gone," said Dales.

Then the air attacks began on the freighters. There were at least 540 Axis bombers and fighters on Sardinia and Sicily, all focused on sinking the fourteen merchant ships carrying vital fuel, ammunition, and food to Malta. The enemy planes attacked at all times of the day, as hundreds of guns from the convoy fought them off. "The din was unholy," said the *Santa Elisa*'s engineer.

The Junkers Ju 87—Stuka for short—was capable of diving vertically at the ships, and sometimes did so. This Stuka is dropping its total payload of 700 kilograms: two 50-kilo bombs from each wing, and one 500-kilo bomb from the fuselage.

Larsen and Dales each triggered a 20-millimeter Oerlikon rapid-fire cannon on the port bridge wing of the *Santa Elisa*. Larsen shot down a Stuka dive-bomber from 1,000 yards.

A bomb landing near a freighter could blow a hole in its steel hull. The merchant ships were often surrounded and sometimes obscured by huge explosive splashes. Here, a freighter is near-missed; later she would be sunk by a direct hit.

A twin-engine Ju 88 heavy
bomber passes over a cruiser
after having dropped its
bombs on the convoy.

Near the Sicilian Narrows, Italian submarines waited; the *Axum* fired four torpedoes and hit
two cruisers (sinking one) and the queen bee of the convoy, the tanker *Ohio.* This photo was
taken at the moment of impact. At their battle stations on the port bridge wings of the *Santa
Elisa,* Larsen and Dales got a face full of the torpedoed, flaming *Ohio.* "A tremendous black
cloud rose on our port beam," said Dales. "We could feel the heat. I saw men on deck and the
black smoke swallowed them up." This torpedo explosion blasted a 24-by-27-foot hole in the
hull. The *Ohio* fell behind the convoy, but the smoldering tanker resumed steaming toward
Malta, ever so slowly.

In this enemy photograph of the convoy under attack, the *Santa Elisa* is seen in the center, guns blazing, as an Italian SM.79 torpedo bomber keeps its distance.

Nighttime E-boat ambushes shattered sleepless sailors' nerves. Spooked gunners fired into the blackness. The loader of Lonnie Dales' Oerlikon was shot through the neck and killed by an E-boat machine gun; Dales loaded the gun himself and blew up the E-boat. But a second E-boat put a torpedo into the *Santa Elisa*.

After the *Santa Elisa* was torpedoed and dive-bombed and went down in flames, Larsen, Dales, and the rest of the crew were picked up by the destroyer *Penn*. Meanwhile, the *Ohio* was bombed and repeatedly near-missed; she lost her engines and rudder, and began slowly sinking. Two shot-down dive-bombers crashed on her decks. Captain Mason ordered her crew to the lifeboats. Too heavy to tow, she was sandwiched by the *Penn* and destroyer *Bramham*, with *Penn* on *Ohio*'s port side, which kept her afloat.

Larsen boarded the *Ohio* in the middle of the night. Joined by Dales, they repaired the 40-millimeter Bofors single-barrel antiaircraft gun on the stern. A twin-barrel Bofors is pictured here.

While the *Ohio* was being nudged along by the destroyers, four of the thirteen freighters reached Malta's port city of Valletta, greeted by bands and cheered by hungry Maltese lining the ancient battlements around the harbor. The other nine freighters were sunk. With each ship carrying about 100,000 cans of aviation fuel, many men died in flames.

The attacks at sea continued. For two days, a handful of volunteers manned the *Ohio* as she was dragged toward Malta at 4 knots.

When the swarms of enemy aircraft appeared, the destroyers released their lines and moved away from the leaking, explosive tanker. The Italian Regia Aeronautica sent its best Stuka pilots after the *Ohio*. Larsen and Dales stayed at the Bofors on the stern, and fought off the dive-bombers. "I believe it is the duty of every man to act as though the fate of the world depends on them," the U.S. admiral Rickover would say. "Surely no one man can do it all. But one man can make a difference."

OSWALD BREIT 66

"When we entered Valletta Harbor, we were saluted like a victorious Navy ship," said Larsen. "Crowds of people were singin' and shoutin' and screamin' and playin' bands, and it was quite a thrill comin' in. I was sittin' up on top of the Bofors, with Lonnie and some of the volunteers."

"They were playing *The Star Spangled Banner* for us," said Dales.

With the delivery of the *Ohio*'s oil to Malta, the 10th Submarine Flotilla had diesel fuel again, and was able to resume its attacks on Axis convoys supplying Rommel in North Africa. The Royal Malta Artillery had kerosene for the generators that powered the anti-

aircraft batteries. And four freighters with aviation fuel got the RAF bombers airborne again.

Without the Operation Pedestal convoy, Malta would have fallen into Hitler's hands and become a base for the Luftwaffe; Rommel's drive toward the oil in Iraq and Iran might have been unstoppable. That's what it was all about. Three months later, with supplies cut, Rommel was on the run, and General Eisenhower was able to lead the Allied invasion of North Africa.

FORM NO. 68.

WESTERN UNION
(THE WESTERN UNION TELEGRAPH COMPANY)
(INCORPORATED IN THE STATE OF NEW YORK, U.S.A. WITH LIMITED LIABILITY.)

ANGLO-AMERICAN TELEGRAPH CO., LD.

CABLEGRAM

CANADIAN NATIONAL TELEGRAPHS

RECEIVED AT 22 GREAT WINCHESTER STREET, LONDON, E.C.2. (TEL. LONDON WALL 1234.)

99 UK

BEO 1942 AUG 16 A 2 08

TELEGRAPH 16 AUG 42 OFFICE

WU 133 ORANGE NJ 28 15 319P

LC FREDERICK A LARSEN

THIRD APT SS SANTA ELISA GRACE LINE GPO LDN

LINDA AND SON JOHN ARE IN BROOKLYN WITH US THEY ARE WELL

SISTER CHRIS LEONARD

PASSED BY CENSOR No. 2485

1087

PASSED BY CENSOR No. 2897

Please send your Reply " Via WESTERN UNION " You may telephone us for a messenger

While Larsen was steaming in convoy he was unaware that his wife, Minda, and son, Jan, were crossing the Atlantic Ocean from Lisbon to New York on a Red Cross mercy ship. His two years of diplomatic efforts to free them from Nazi-occupied Norway had been successful. The day after the *Ohio* arrived in Malta, he was told that this cablegram (*above*) was waiting for him.

THE PRESIDENT OF THE UNITED STATES TAKES
PLEASURE IN PRESENTING THE MERCHANT MARINE
DISTINGUISHED SERVICE MEDAL TO

FREDERICK A. LARSEN, JR.
JUNIOR THIRD MATE ON SS *SANTA ELISA*
AND
FRANCIS A. DALES
DECK CADET-MIDSHIPMAN ON SS *SANTA ELISA*

For heroism above and beyond the call of duty

UNITED STATES MERCHANT MARINE ORGANIZATION

CHAPTER 30

SCREAMS ON THE WATER

Fred Larsen spent almost all of his time on the *Santa Elisa*'s flying bridge, on top of the enclosed bridge and open to the sky, a protected parapet between the Oerlikon gun tubs standing like castle towers on the port and starboard bridge wings. "There was very poor visibility from the lower deck, so we controlled the ship from the flying bridge, where we could see what was going on," he said. When he was able to leave his gun, he usually stood in the center of the flying bridge with Captain Thomson.

They were standing there as darkness crept in, when the *Clan Ferguson* was hit by a torpedo dropped by a stealthy bomber.

"A signalman on watch saw the torpedo approaching from our starboard beam," reported her second officer, Mr. Black. "He shouted, 'Hard to starboard!' but the ship did not swing quickly enough."

The *Clan Ferguson* had survived other Malta convoys, and her experienced master, Arthur Robert Cossar, wasn't afraid to fight. She was the smallest freighter in the fleet, but she carried the most armament: two Bofors instead of one, eight Oerlikons instead of six, four FAMS, four PAC rockets, two pig troughs, and extra machine guns. She also carried 2,000 tons of aviation fuel and 1,500 tons of ammunition and high explosives. She went up in a gigantic fireball and down in seven minutes.

"One minute there was this fine vessel, the next a huge atomic-like explosion, and she had gone, disappeared with just a bluish ring of flame on the water and a mushroom of smoke and flame thousands of feet into the sky," said a sailor on the cruiser *Kenya*.

As Larsen and Thomson watched the *Clan Ferguson* burn, they believed they were witnessing the incineration of fellow Americans, because they thought she was the *Almeria Lykes*.

"There were screams, quite a lot of screams, and we assumed that people were getting burned," said George Nye, one of the British soldiers on the *Santa Elisa*. He's tried to forget them for sixty-three years. We could hear screams for half an hour. You know how sound travels over the water."

"It was a ghastly funeral pyre of burning petrol on the water," said the liaison officer of the *Brisbane Star*, whose turn at the sharp end of a torpedo would soon come.

Some accounts say there were no survivors, because it was assumed that there couldn't have been. None of the nearby destroyers stopped to look for unlikely survivors because it was dark and their orders were to keep zigzagging toward Malta unless survivors were evident. Protecting the cargo was the highest priority.

However, the explosion observed by witnesses had occurred some minutes after the torpedo had hit between the engine room and number four hold, igniting the fire that spread before it burst skyward. In those minutes Captain Cossar had given the order to abandon ship and men were able to release one intact lifeboat and three rafts that they paddled with their steel helmets. More men dived over the side and swam frantically, chased over the water by silent blue flames. When the fire on the ship reached the number five hold where the 1,500 tons of ammunition were stored, she blew sky high.

"The oil on the water around the position in which my ship had sunk blazed furiously for about 48 hours," reported Mr. Black. "Cans of petrol kept floating to the surface and catching fire, and at one time there was dense black smoke rising which I think must have been caused by the fuel oil which was ignited on coming to the surface."

Mr. Black's surreal story goes on for five days. There were sixteen men on his raft. At daybreak they thought they saw a signal and paddled toward it, but it was one of their own lifeboats, burning with no one in it. They found the other rafts with 48 more survivors, accounting for 64 out of 114 men now. The sea was flat and spooky, the sky overcast with the smoke of burning ships. Two dead bodies floated by. At high noon under the blazing sun, they thought they saw a corvette on the hazy horizon so they raised red sails, but it was an Italian submarine with an image of Pinocchio painted on the conning tower. The *Bronzo* came alongside, and one of its crewmen asked them if they were in distress before it chugged off. Then a flying boat landed on the water near the raft, nearly crashing in the flotsam; a German ordered thirty-two men at gunpoint to board the plane. Mr. Black sent the most seriously injured men, in unimaginable agony as the sun seared their burns. The Germans handled them gently.

The next morning they tried to sail to Zembra Island, expecting to be interred by the Vichy French. The wind turned offshore and they paddled for fourteen hours as the rafts were separated. That evening an Italian Red Cross plane landed and took on seven more injured men. At daybreak on August 16 they were about one mile from the island. "We could see the telephone wires and I thought we could perhaps use the telephone if we were able to land," said Mr. Black.

They had come within a hundred yards of their destination when the wind blew them back. An Italian E-boat came and took three officers off the raft. Some Vichy French authorities watched from shore, furious that the Italians were trying to take British prisoners inside their territorial waters; they sent out gendarmes who wrestled the three Brits back.

The men on the raft paddled toward a small village down the beach, but the village turned into an Italian destroyer as they approached. They tried to surrender but the destroyer morphed into a ghost ship, piled up on the rocks. They beached in a cove. Italian fishermen took them to a farm, where they were given food, wine, and cigarettes. French authorities arrived and carried the injured men away on donkeys. They reached a French village where many of the two thousand locals came out to welcome them. "All the women of the village joined together to give us a good meal from their rations," said Mr. Black, the second mate.

The *Clan Ferguson* survivors were questioned by French Army and Navy officers, who hid them from the Italian authorities. The next day they were taken to a camp where they were reunited with their shipmates who had outraced the flames in the lifeboat and been picked up by the submarine *Alagi*. Captain Cossar was among them. They were all taken to another camp, where the Italian commandant was pro-British. They were there for some time, apparently escaping their loose incarceration during Operation Torch in November. Mr. Black wrote his report in December. "I do not know how many men are missing," he said.

Mr. Black didn't report how they had gotten out of Africa. It seems to be a miracle enough that they survived.

• • •

Three sticks of bombs, a total of eighteen, rained down on the *Empire Hope* from three Ju 88s. Near misses blew a fifteen-foot hole in her side and knocked out the engines, pumps, and cooling system. While she was dead in the water, a direct hit penetrated the afterdeck and exploded in the number four hold, which contained ammunition and kerosene. Another two bombs burst in a 200-ton pile of coal stacked on the decks. The ship was smothered by coal dust, as a tower of orange flames shot through the top of the black cloud. "The fire by this time was spreading rapidly and the decks were red hot, so I gave the order to abandon ship," said Captain Gwilym Williams.

The destroyer *Penn* took the survivors aboard, many of them badly burned and screaming, and sank the *Empire Hope* with a torpedo.

The *Brisbane Star* had been steaming so close to the *Empire Hope* that she had to make an emergency maneuver to stay out of the fire. She turned into the path of a torpedo dropped from an He III, which blew a hole through her bows big enough for a speedboat to race through. But she could still make 5 knots, so she steered toward the Tunisian coast and the ostensibly neutral Vichy waters, which were open to ships in distress.

"We turned south, and proceeded along close inshore," reported the *Brisbane Star*'s liaison officer. "We were passed by all the remaining ships in the convoy, including, to our surprise, the tanker *Ohio*."

Captain Mason and his engineering officer, James Wyld, had gotten the *Ohio* going again. She could make only seven unsteady knots, and she was ten miles behind the other ships, but at least she was moving toward Malta. As liaison officer Lieutenant Barton said, "The sea was washing in and out of the hole in the hull, and the decks were nearly white hot, but we were still floating."

As the destroyer *Ithuriel* was ramming the submarine *Cobalto* that afternoon, Winston Churchill was landing in his Liberator bomber at an airfield at the edge of Moscow. He'd flown there from Cairo, in order to personally inform Stalin that he and President Roosevelt had decided to invade North Africa before Europe. It was a secret mission, and FDR had authorized Churchill to speak for him in telling Stalin that there would be no second front in 1942. "It was like carrying a large lump of ice to the North Pole," said Churchill, who had never met Stalin.

He had no illusions about the spiritual depth of Stalin's commitment to freedom. "We had always hated their wicked regime," he said, "and, till the German flail beat upon them, they would have watched us being swept out of existence with indifference and gleefully divided with Hitler our Empire in the East." But now their relationship was shackled to their survival.

Churchill was driven from the airfield to Stalin's villa, which the Soviet premier had lavishly prepared for his guest. White-jacketed servants roamed the rooms, and in the dining room, a long table was "laden with every delicacy and stimulant that supreme power can command," said Churchill. But he seemed more impressed by the separate hot and cold water taps in the bathroom.

As always, the prime minister's entourage included his personal physician, Sir Charles Wilson, and his valet, Sawyers. They were in the foyer when Sir Charles heard loud shouts coming from upstairs. He ran up the steps two at a time and found Churchill in the bathtub, shivering and cursing. "The water is bloody cold and I don't know which is the hot tap!"

"Their taps do not work like our taps, and the Russian lettering did not help," explained Sir Charles. "I took a chance. There was a sudden big gush of icy water under terrific pressure. It caught the P.M. amidships. He gave a loud shriek, and when he got his breath he cursed me for my incompetence. I flew to get help."

About ninety minutes later, as the *Indomitable* was being buggered by Stukas, and fifty men were dying in the explosions and flames, Churchill was breaking the news to Stalin that there would be no forthcoming Allied invasion to draw German troops out of the Soviet Union.

The first two hours were bleak. He explained with maps and arguments why there could be no second front. "If Stalin was bitterly disappointed, he listened patiently to my explanation," said Churchill. "He never once raised his voice, never once lost his temper. When I had told him the worst, we both sat in silence for a little."

At ten in the evening, Moscow time, as fifty-two men were dying from the torpedo hit on the *Nigeria*, chunks of steel and sailors were flying hundreds of feet into the sky from the *Cairo*, and merchant seamen on the SS *Ohio* were fighting to keep the wall of burning kerosene from becoming the mother of all infernos, Churchill was still sitting across the table from Stalin. He was drawing a picture of a crocodile, which represented Nazi Europe.

Churchill loved to use crocodiles as metaphors. The British Army had a flamethrowing tank that he had nicknamed the "Crocodile." He said that Communists were like crocodiles. German historians have long wondered how Churchill managed to persuade Stalin to join the Allies. It started with this sketch of a crocodile. But he still needed Operation Pedestal and Malta to close the deal.

"I explained to Stalin with the help of this picture how it was our intention to attack the soft belly of the crocodile as we attacked his hard snout," said Churchill. The soft belly was Sicily and Italy, and the hard snout was northern France and western Europe. Stalin's interest was now piqued, and Churchill continued, describing the military advantages of freeing the Mediterranean. "In September we must win in Egypt, and in October in North Africa, all the time holding the enemy in northern France," he told Stalin.

As Churchill was dissecting his crocodile and describing the military advantages of freeing the Mediterranean to Stalin, Fred Larsen was doing his part to deliver Malta to Churchill: at that moment, he was at his Oerlikon on the bridge of the *Santa Elisa*, shooting down the Stuka from a thousand yards.

"At this point Stalin seemed suddenly to grasp the strategic advantages of Torch," continued Churchill.

> He recounted four main reasons for it: first, it would hit Rommel in the back; second, it would overawe Spain; third, it would produce fighting between Germans and Frenchmen in France; and fourth, it would expose Italy to the whole brunt of the war.
>
> I was deeply impressed with this remarkable statement. It showed the Russian Dictator's swift and complete mastery of a problem hitherto novel to him. Very few people alive could have comprehended in so few minutes the reasons which we had all so long been wrestling with for months. He saw it all in a flash.

As the *Clan Ferguson* was going up in a fireball and down in seven minutes, and eighteen bombs were raining down on the *Empire Hope* from three Ju 88s, and the *Brisbane Star* was getting a hole blown in her bows big enough to for a speedboat to race through, Churchill was back at his villa eating a huge evening meal. He put his half-finished cigar across a wineglass, rose, and stretched.

"Tired as I was," he said, "I dictated my telegram to the War Cabinet and the President after midnight, and then, with the feeling that at least the ice was broken and human contact established [with Stalin] I slept soundly and long."

As Churchill slept soundly in his spacious bedroom, the Operation Pedestal convoy steamed deep into the flaming jaws of Hell in the Sicilian Narrows.

CHAPTER 32 • • •

RETREAT OF THE COMMODORE

It might be difficult to imagine how a huge hole in the hull of a ship could be a blessing, but because the *Ohio* had been left behind by the convoy, most of the bombers hadn't discovered her, having come from the other direction. But still some planes strayed from the swarm and harassed the big tanker.

"The bombers didn't seem satisfied that we had a raging fire on board, because they came screaming across and giving us a couple dozen near misses, sending deluges of water from stem to stern," said Allan Shaw. "It was a hell of a hectic time."

Admiral Burrough ordered the destroyer *Ashanti* to pull along the starboard side of the burning tanker, and between the blast of his own starboard guns at enemy aircraft, he yelled up through his loud-hailer to Captain Mason.

"How bad is the damage? Are you going to be able to proceed?"

"Well, it's not good," Mason shouted back down. "But we seem to be gaining on this fire, and my chief engineer tells me he thinks he can have steam in the boilers and the turbines going again in about 40 minutes. We're not giving up. We'll do all we can to get to Malta."

"Good show!" said Burrough. "But if you can't get her up to speed, you might want to head for the coast and proceed independently, because I don't have enough destroyers to provide an escort for you. Good luck, God speed, and I'll see you in Malta!" And with that he raced off to the head of the convoy.

"I was most impressed by the gallant and cool manner in which Captain Mason handled the situation," Burrough reported.

Besides the hole in the pump room, the deck was buckled and ripped open between the longitudinal beams, but the tanker's back was unbroken. "That's a welded hull for you," said the chief engineer, Jimmy Wyld. "Rivets would never have stood it."

The hydraulic steering lines from the bridge to the rudder were blown apart, so they had to rig up emergency manual control of the rudder. Ordinary seaman Allan Shaw and three others who weren't manning guns were grabbed by the twenty-six-year-old chief mate, Douglas Gray, and they climbed down to the steering flat, a compartment about twenty feet below the poop deck.

"It was pretty hairy down there," said Shaw. "Our own ack-ack fire was continuous, and you could feel the thud of every bomb that landed in the water. The deck of the steering flat was jumping up and down."

They worked under generator-powered lights to rig up blocks and a one-inch chain that led to an emergency helm, about the size of an automobile steering wheel and mounted on a bulkhead on the poop deck. Chief mate Gray manned the wheel, guided by phone from Captain Mason in the wheelhouse. "Gray was on the emergency helm most of the time," said Shaw. "I think he enjoyed it, because he wouldn't let anyone else have a go at it."

They were now in the narrow Skerki Channel; to starboard lay the shallows of the African coast, and to port were Italian minefields. There wasn't much room for error, but error defined their direction. There was a big flap of metal extending from the edge of the torpedo hole, turning the ship to port, so constant starboard helm was needed in an attempt to correct the torque, which wasn't easy because the rudder indicator had been knocked silly. The gyro compass and magnetic compass were both blown out, so Mason and Lieutenant Denys Barton set a rough course for Malta by fixing on a star.

"Thank God for an American ship with telephones," said Mason. "The phone in the wheelhouse was a Godsend." He kept Gray on the line: "Give it some port helm . . . some starboard helm . . . no, that's too much, now back," that sort of thing. It's no wonder the *Ohio*'s direction was described in reports as "erratic."

Gray, a quiet Scot, remembered that he had a gallon of rum in his quarters. He sent an ordinary seaman down for it, and all hands on the poop had a big tot, toasting the star that was guiding them and wishing for a safe arrival in Malta.

• • •

Meanwhile, the destroyer *Ledbury* was running down those ships that had scattered in other directions. "The merchant ships were steaming on a northerly or northwesterly course, after the bombing and emergency turns," said Captain Hill. "I chased after them, and found the Commodore's ship turning back."

Hill went easy on Commodore A. G. Venables of the Port Chalmers in his report. The commodore, a retired Royal Navy officer, had turned and run. Apparently he hadn't gotten the message that the convoy was supposed to reach Malta at all costs. Commodore Venables's own report confirms his retreat.

"Course was altered to port and I determined to try and save the ship by leaving the convoy from the rear," he said. "*Port Chalmers* proceeded full speed to Westward. Two other rear ships were informed of my intention and turned to follow me: they were not seen again, as presumably a destroyer found them and ordered them to rejoin the convoy. This destroyer overtook me and gave instructions to proceed to Malta, which was my intention as soon as circumstances appeared favourable."

But other reports don't support Venables's claim that his flight back toward Gibraltar was only temporary. One of the two other ships he mentions was the *Dorset*, whose captain, Jack Tuckett, reported that he had asked Venables for a course and speed.

"He told me he was returning to Gibraltar. I fell in astern, but five minutes later, realising I did not wish to return, reversed course. *Melbourne Star* was in company and she also turned. We left the *Port Chalmers* steaming towards Gibraltar."

The liaison officer of the *Melbourne Star* added that he too had signaled the commodore for orders and received the reply "Turn back." But the officers on the bridge were unanimous that their destination remain Malta, so they didn't follow *Port Chalmers*.

"The state of affairs at this time was chaotic, with some ships on fire, some sinking, and destroyers going to the rescue," said *Melbourne Star*'s liaison officer. "The captain was determined that the only thing to do was make for Malta."

The *Melbourne Star* caught up to the *Santa Elisa* and signaled Captain Thomson: "Will you follow me?" Thomson signaled back: "Yes." They raced toward Malta at 16 knots, as the *Port Chalmers* steamed alone back toward Gibraltar.

• • •

Captain Hill in the destroyer *Ledbury* continued to chase after other merchant ships. "I went alongside the others to turn them, and got them round by talking to them on the loudhailer. The last ship, the American *Almeria Lykes*, wanted to go back to Gibraltar, but I pointed out he hadn't a hope in hell without an escort, and if he joined up with the others he would be in Malta the next day. I added, 'All the English ships are heading for Malta,' and round he came."

After Captain Hill turned the *Almeria Lykes* around, he looked through his binoculars into the last of the light and saw a big dark shape on the horizon. He steamed toward it and found the *Ohio* weaving like a drunken sailor in a dark alley.

"I went close alongside near the bridge and talked to Mason, her captain, and Lieutenant Denys Barton, the Naval Liaison Officer on board. I found that she had been hit in the pump room, and that her bridge steering was out of action. Her engines and propellers were all right.

"I tried to sound very cheerful and confident, and said, 'The Admiral is waiting for you with the cruisers and destroyers.' "

Captain Hill was a mere megaphone voice in the darkness to Mason, who didn't know the name of the destroyer that was alongside.

"You need to steer 120 degrees if you want to catch up with the convoy," the voice said. "Or do you want a tow?"

"No thank you, we're under our own steam, but we haven't got a compass," replied Mason from the bridge. "Can you lead us?"

"I'll switch on a stern light, and you can follow it," Hill told him. "We will go close in to the shore and join up with the others before daylight. We'll get the Malta Spitfires tomorrow and be in Malta for lunch."

"So off we went, starting very slowly, with the tanker steering all over the place, and gradually getting more steady," said Hill.

The shielded blue light on the stern of the *Ledbury* was easier to follow than a star, at least. And there were other things to guide them: the beam of the Cape Bon lighthouse and patches of burning oil on the sea, tall flaming tombstones marking the grave of the *Clan Ferguson*.

As the *Ohio* was about to steam through the fire, Mason suddenly realized that she was still leaking kerosene. He grabbed the loud-hailer and shouted to *Ledbury*: "For God's sake, steer clear of the flames!"

"We felt naked and exposed, silhouetted against the fire, and it seemed an agonizing age before we got clear of it," said Hill. "But the oiler was grand. She yawed heavily at the beginning, but was soon steadied and we had worked up to 15½ knots before reaching Cape Bon."

When the destroyer *Bramham* returned from the Tunisian coast after leaving the *Deucalion* blazing, she was lost in the dark.

"We went around Pantelleria about three times in the middle of the night," said Reg Coaker, the petty officer in charge of the armament, ninety-one years old in 2006 and exceptionally keen. "I suppose we were only doing about five knots, and we could see this silhouette of a hump, and we weren't exactly whispering but we were speaking softly, because we didn't want to wake the enemy. I can remember Captain Baines saying to our navigator, 'Where in bloody hell are we?'

" 'Well, sir, I think we're a little north of Pantelleria.'

" 'I can bloody see that! There it is over there!'

"We had a signal that the Italian fleet was coming to finish us off. And then, out of the darkness, the bows of a ship began getting closer. We all thought, 'Oh God, maybe the Italian cruisers are out.'

"The yeoman said to Baines, 'Challenge, sir?'

"And the captain sort of muttered, 'Yes, why don't you.'

"And we had no answer.

" 'Challenge again?'

" 'Yes, righto, yeoman.'

"Still no answer.

"I was in the control tower over the bridge, and I can hear the metallic click of the breech blocks of the twin four-inch guns snapping shut. I think Baines' idea was to give it one big broadsides and get the hell out of there. We were looking at her head-on, and we thought it was an Italian cruiser. She was looming large, and she was getting ever closer, there she was getting larger and larger . . . and not answering our challenge.

"And just as we closed the breech blocks and were training onto this ship, we saw the ship's signal light going, and got a belated answer back.

"It was the *Port Chalmers*."

She was headed west. Captain Baines signaled Commodore Venables to come about and to follow the *Bramham*.

But it took a second destroyer to bring the commodore back to the convoy. The *Penn* had also been out looking for wandering merchantmen.

"Returning to the southwestward of Zembra Island, I found *Bramham* escorting the *Port Chalmers*," reported Lieutenant Commander J. H. Swain, the Irish captain of the *Penn*. "*Port Chalmers* seemed to be in some doubt as to what to do, but I told him to follow me, and stationed *Bramham* astern of him."

Commodore Venables offered a slim explanation. "The evening of 12th August was a severe trial to all, as escort afloat had also vanished at a critical moment, after the disaster at entrance to Skerki Channel," he said in his report.

There might have been other gripes by merchant sailors that their escorts had deserted them, but no such complaints appeared in any master's report, other than that of the commodore of the convoy.

CHAPTER 33 • • •

IL DUCE'S PAJAMAS

All that day, Admiral Da Zara's two light cruisers and three destroyers had been steaming east from Sardinia, to rendezvous in the Tyrrhenian Sea with two heavy cruisers and six destroyers that were steaming west from Sicily. Also, the battleship *Trieste* had left Genoa in northern Italy, escorted by a destroyer and an E-boat, and was steaming south to meet with the light cruiser *Attendolo*. That was a total of seventeen Italian warships coming from four directions, intending to form a battle fleet by the next morning.

Reconnaissance planes from Malta had watched the progress of the Italian warships moving west. Air Marshal Keith Park had sent out nine sorties, seven by Baltimores and two by Marylands. Park was still fuming over the missing Liberators; if they had been delivered as promised by the RAF command in Cairo, the Italian warships would have been bombed by now.

Air Marshal Park, a New Zealander, six feet five inches tall and easily recognized around the island behind the wheel of his red MG Roadster, was serious about winning. He had led the RAF to victory during the Battle of Britain. When Churchill said, "Never in the history of human conflict was so much owed by so many to so few," he could have narrowed it down to Park. Recalled Malta Spitfire pilot Peter Rothwell, "He'd come down to the mess with his long cigarette holder and a gin in his hand, and he'd say, 'Right, what I want you to do today is kill the Hun, all right? Kill the Hun!' "

As Da Zara's warships steamed toward the reeling convoy, Comando Supremo in Rome was arguing about whether or not to provide them with air support. In two morning meetings attended by the German and Italian honchos in the Mediterranean, there wasn't much agreement.

Admiral Riccardi, chief of the Italian Navy, had requested eighty Luftwaffe fighters to defend the warships against RAF bombers that were expected to fly out from Malta. But Field Marshal Kesselring said he didn't have any fighters to spare.

General Cavallero said that air cover was absolutely necessary, because the convoy might be an invasion of Libya.

General Fougier seemed to think his Regia Aeronautica could defend the fleet without the Luftwaffe; "Fourteen Macchi 202 should clean the sky," he said, looking at his watch. His remote-controlled flying buffalo carrying two 1,000-kilogram bombs would be taking off from Sardinia soon. He smiled and told the others that he had the *Wasp* handled. He still believed that the American aircraft carrier was part of the convoy.

The really big guns of the Italian fleet, including four more battleships, could have gone after Operation Pedestal, but they remained in port with nearly empty fuel tanks. As surely as oil lies under the sea, oil governed the movement of the Italian warships.

At the beginning of the war, Italy had said it would need 200,000 tons of oil a month from Germany, but by May 1942 it was being offered just 45,000 tons—not delivered, merely offered. "From this moment on, the fuel question really became the fuel tragedy," writes Marc'Antonio Bragadin, the official Italian historian, who as a naval commander was involved in the daily watch of the oil supplies.

> The Italian Navy had to base its every movement, not on the situation at sea nor on its operational capacities as to ships and firepower, but rather on the day-to-day availability of fuel.
>
> The anxieties and the responsibilities in those days, which weighed on Supermarina every time that some movement in the enemy camp was noted, were truly terrible. Supermarina was haunted by the possibility that the British might attempt a large-scale operation and the Italian fleet would not even be able to leave port! The decisions to be made in that period weighed on the naval chiefs—in a really dramatic way and sometimes brought them to the verge of desperation.

The Italians had a powerful ally in Admiral Weichold, commander in chief of the German Navy in the Mediterranean, who steadily argued for more support of the Italian Navy. "The German High Command, as well as the German Naval General Staff, remained deaf to my every effort to have fuel oil shipments increased," he wrote from his cell after the war. "That the German General Staff observed all this with indifference proved once again its under-evaluation of naval power in the over-all conduct of warfare, and, in particular, of the meaning of the Mediterranean within the general scheme of the whole conflict."

The link from oil to air cover for the Italian warships from the Luftwaffe on August 13 was emotional but tangible. Mussolini already carried an attitude about Germany's limited support and its "niggardliness," as Bragadin called it, with its oil.

Kesselring didn't show much respect for Regia Marina in general, and in particular its efficiency; he believed the Italians were wasting hardearned German oil, infinite amounts of which were needed in Russia and vital amounts by Rommel in North Africa. He said their fleet moved around too much, with harbors all over the mainland, Sicily, and Sardinia. The ships sucked up all their fuel just assembling for battle.

"There were extraordinary technical deficiencies which deservedly earned the Italian navy the nickname 'Fine-weather Fleet,' " he wrote. "Its doubtful seaworthiness called for increased air protection, and that, with the limited strength of the Axis air forces in the Mediterranean, imposed ridiculous demands on the German Luftwaffe, whose hands were already full protecting convoys; the German airmen, who flew 75–90 percent of all sorties, had consequently to be bled white."

The meetings in Rome moved from Kesselring's headquarters to the Comando Supremo war rooms. The debate raged into the night, as ships in the convoy continued to be blown up and sunk. Reports were sent to Supermarina by the submarines *Alagi* and *Bronzo*.

Weichold sided with Riccardi (both navy men) in demanding air support for the Italian fleet, while Kesselring and Fougier (air force men) resisted.

Said Weichold, "The cruisers naturally had to be provided with a certain air cover. The naval C. in C. [Weichold] made every effort with the German and Italian Headquarters to procure air cover for the Italian cruisers, as only they could be in a position to complete the destruction of units of the convoy which had broken through. It developed into a heated difference of opinion between the Headquarters of the different Services, during which the representatives of both navies stood alone against the other leaders."

The German Naval Staff War Diary confirms Weichold's account: "The Admiral, German Naval Command, Italy, has done everything in his power to support the planned fleet action. The Admiral feels it will mean missing a big chance of annihilating the largest convoy undertaken so far in the Mediterranean after the heavy enemy forces, superior in numbers and arms, have withdrawn."

Just before midnight, while Winston Churchill was sleeping soundly in Moscow, Admiral Da Zara's warships were steaming south at 20 knots. A radar-equipped Wellington had located the ships west of the island of Ustica and was tracking them. The battleship *Trieste* had turned back, to save fuel for another day.

The six-man crew of a second Wellington was on standby at Luqa airfield on Malta. Dennis Cooke was the wireless operator.

"We had no idea there was a convoy on its way to Malta," he remembered, sixty-three years later. "We knew there was a flap on, because we were put on standby in G shelter, which was underground; but only the top brass had knowledge of Operation Pedestal. We minions on Malta knew nothing of the mayhem that was taking place.

"After a while, AOC Park told us we could leave for a couple of hours, just let him know where we were, and we went to the cinema. We're watching this film, and suddenly it stops and there's a message on the screen: 'Members of Special Duty Flight, report to Luqa.' We got up to go, and the civilians in the theater all clapped for us. There was a lorry waiting outside to take us to our plane, and soon we were off with a full load of eight 250-pound bombs.

"We were told that the other Wellington had located twelve Italian cruisers and destroyers and were given the latitude and longitude, but we had no idea of their importance. Our orders were simply to illuminate and attack."

Da Zara's warships began blipping on the radar screen of Cooke's lumbering Wellington at about 0300.

"We illuminated the target with a string of flares with about two million candlepower," he said. "The Italians put up a barrage, but we were in the dark so it missed us by quite a lot. I don't know what our altitude was because I was focused on the wireless. If we were brave we'd sometimes go in at about a thousand feet, but not often. There were a few RAF heroes who would press home the attack, but they tended to get shot out of the sky. Air crews had a different interpretation of our patriotic duty. We tended to look after our own skins more.

"We dropped our bombs, scored some near misses, and as far as we were concerned, that was the end. We done what we were sent to do.

"But at 0319 something extraordinary happened. I picked up a message in plain language that said, 'Report result your attack, latest enemy position for Liberators, most Immediate.' Plain language was never used in special ops, and I knew there were no Liberators in the area. I told the crew, 'I think this is a fake.' "

Keith Park had been seething for two days about the lack of Liberators, and in the middle of the night, when he needed them most, he created them out of thin air. He sent out the radio signal in plain language so Da Zara couldn't miss it.

The navigator of Wellington Y looked at the blipping ships on the radar screen. "Bloody 'ell, they're changing course!" he said.

When the Operation Pedestal veterans get together on Malta, they like to tell the story about how Keith Park's magic turned back the Italian fleet that night, by faking the Italians into thinking the Liberators were coming.

But there was more. Kesselring, Weichold, Cavallero, Fougier, Riccardi, and others had finally gotten tired of arguing and recognized they were at a stalemate. The only thing to do was ring Il Duce on the phone; get him out of bed to settle it. Commander in Chief Cavallero explained his version of the situation to Mussolini. Without air cover for the warships, the Malta bombers would inflict heavy damage on them. And Cavallero added something new: more British warships had been seen east of Malta.

Mussolini never confessed to being a coward at sea like Hitler, but sometimes he acted like one; two years of thrashings by Admiral Cunningham hadn't done much for his confidence. But mostly there was the ongoing issue with the allegedly niggardly Germans over oil. He told Cavallero that he wasn't willing to risk the warships of the Italian Navy if the Germans weren't willing to protect them. He believed the Italian bombers and E-boats could still destroy the convoy before it reached Malta. So he ordered Da Zara's warships back to their ports.

In the morning he congratulated the fleet for its "success in annihilating the enemy forces, which have dared to venture into the seas of Rome."

Bisogna far buon viso a cattivo gioco, the Italians liked to say. It's often necessary to disguise a bad game with a good face. Regia Marina and Regia Aeronautica competed to impress Mussolini, who only wanted intelligence that told him what he wanted to hear. When he spoke, his staff stacked the crowd with supporters, called "applaud squads."

"In this fashion," said Weichold, "a splendid opportunity for a crushing victory by the Italian ships was thrown away, even as they were already at sea and heading for the battle area. It was a strategic failure of the first order on the part of the Axis, the repercussions of which would one day be felt."

Admiral Burrough put it even more succinctly. "I was always grateful to Mussolini," he said. "There is no doubt in my mind that had the Italian cruisers arrived that morning, there would have been a massacre. We would have been wiped out."

CHAPTER 34

NIGHT OF THE E-BOATS

F red Larsen was at the helm of the *Santa Elisa* during the moonless midwatch, as Lonnie Dales remained at his battle station manning his Oerlikon.

"Night had finally fallen, but darkness did not accompany the night," said Jack Follansbee. "As far as the eye could see, the Mediterranean was filled with fire. Fire shooting from the torches of doomed ships, fire from burning heaps of wreckage, fire from burning oil on the surface of the sea."

In order to avoid the mines—"They were popping up all over the place," said Larsen—and the fire around the *Clan Ferguson*—"a square mile of flaming sea," said the engineer Ed Randall—Captain Thomson turned the *Santa Elisa* northward, but not for long.

"A destroyer then hailed us and ordered us to steer 120 degrees to rejoin the convoy," reported Lieutenant Commander Barnes, the liaison officer. "We joined up with three other stragglers, and followed the route of the convoy round to the south of Zembra and Zembretta Islands, towards Cape Bon, 200 miles from Malta. During this time, we lost contact with the other ships, station-keeping in the *Santa Elisa* being particularly difficult owing to the very heavy derrick gear forward of the bridge."

Minefields squeezed the path of the convoy to within four miles of the Tunisian coast. The *Santa Elisa* was running with no lights at 16 knots, racing toward the white-hot horizon that was lit by attacks on the ships ahead. Larsen watched the other ships' tracer fire, desperate shots in the dark at every E-boat shadow, streams of gold and green flying into the night at a half mile per second. The ships were shooting off star shells, great bursts of white light like the Milky Way come to Earth, bringing shine to the sea and hope to a gunner trying to see the enemy. It was hide-and-seek out of the pages of the Catch-22 rulebook: light up the enemy without lighting up yourself.

The neutral lighthouse at the tip of Cape Bon was working to the advantage of the Axis. Operation Pedestal was exposed by three white flashes every twelve seconds, as gunners pleaded with their captains for permission to shoot out the light. And 20 miles farther south there was another, Kelibia Light, whose beam could be seen for 23 nautical miles and was bright enough to spot the ships for Vichy guns on shore.

If that weren't enough, creepy searchlights from unknown sources scanned the black water. "Long beams of light were streaking out over the sea," said Follansbee. "The searchlights slowly swept from left to right across the water. One of the beams shone full against our stack, hovered an instant, and moved on.

"Then, from the distance, came a series of flashes, followed by the sound of distant gunfire. They were opening up with their shore batteries!"

"Resume zigzagging!" the captain shouted to Larsen.

"You could see the big bullets come at us and pass us, these big shells they were firing," said Larsen, awed by the black projectiles silhouetted against the star-shell white sky. "You could see them coming, they were so big."

The *Santa Elisa* raced northward again, out of the range of shore batteries and into the relative security of the black night. The first mate took over the helm, as Captain Thomson huddled in the chart room with Larsen, the liaison officer Barnes, and the navy armed guard Suppiger.

"The captain asked me to find our exact position off Cape Bon and lay out the course for Valletta," said Larsen. "I could still clearly see the flashes from Cape Bon lighthouse. I took the bearings from my gun position on the flying bridge and went back into the chart room and plotted them to determine our course to steer."

"They decided to head west out into the open sea toward Pantelleria, instead of south as was our designated course," said Suppiger. "This would take us out of range of coastal batteries, but would take us into what we knew to be a minefield near Pantelleria. We decided to risk the minefield."

The island of Pantelleria, code-named "Hobgoblin," was a mountain-

ous forty-two-square-mile chunk of volcanic rock. There were sixteen batteries with eighty guns squeezed into its irregular shore, an inland airfield
with a strip for Stukas, and a small hidden harbor with docks for E-boats.
Its reputation was so spooky that sailors believed the E-boats lived in caves
like vampire bats, flying against their prey at night to strike blood.

Ensign Suppiger mustered his navy crew on the stern. Guns needed
cleaning and repairing, ammo needed to be carried up from holds, and
Oerlikon magazines needed to be loaded, endlessly; 60 rounds per magazine at 450 rounds per minute didn't go far. Suppiger moved on to the forward gun position, with the Bofors and two Oerlikons; there were 400
rounds of Bofors shells left, and the springs in the barrels of all the Oerlikons had softened from the heat of repeated firing. Suppy told the crew to
find or make new ones.

"After leaving there, I went to the top bridge and supervised prepara-
tions, including loading ammunition for engagement we knew we would
receive by daybreak. I instructed my gunners to carefully inspect all the
machine guns and make sure they were in operating condition.

"I inspected all the guns and gun positions again and saw that everything was in as good operating condition as was possible. I warned everyone stationed at guns to be on the lookout for E-boats."

On the moonless night of August 12, sixteen bloodthirsty E-boats raced
south from Sicily, with at least one of them carrying a film crew to shoot
footage of the anticipated slaughter for newsreels; Il Duce was looking forward to using the film for propaganda. Two more boats came north from
the tiny island of Lampedusa, joining four from Pantelleria. Even more
German E-boats prowled the waters around the Hobgoblin, although the
Italians would dominate the action on this night.

Italy had led the development of these boats in World War I, when they
were all called motor torpedo boats, or MTBs. E-boats came in different
sizes, but large or small, they were about stealth and speed, on the way to
a big explosion. The Italian boats were usually painted black for the night,
which they owned, and their captains were the Stuka pilots of the sea.

Because they ran flat-out so much, E-boats needed huge fuel tanks,
sometimes holding more than 4,000 gallons. But weight mattered, so
armor was spared. The hulls were made from aluminum or wood, easily
penetrated by shrapnel or machine-gun bullets. But, the E-boat could run
from enemy fire, using its two or three engines making more than a thou-

sand horsepower each, and could maneuver like a Jet Ski. E-boats were armed with their own machine guns, usually 20 mm, but their real firepower was in the 600-pound torpedoes, launched at 50 miles per hour from two tubes in the bows.

Under the command of Captain Harold Drew, the HMS *Manchester* was the only cruiser as yet untouched by enemy bombs, mines, or torpedoes. But deep in the Sicilian Narrows, the big E-boats MS16 and MS22 were waiting to ambush the first cruiser that came through. They floated in flat water with dead engines, hiding behind the hulk of the *Havock*, a British destroyer that had run aground on a sandbar in April, and whose crew was still interred in Tunisia. The two E-boats waited until the convoy was nearly on top of them, then fired up their engines and sprinted out to attack.

MS16 fired a torpedo at *Manchester* from 800 yards and MS22 fired one from 600 yards, but the torpedoes missed, skimming past the bow of the *Kenya*. Each captain kept coming, holding the hammer down on nearly 4,000 horsepower and roaring out of the night at 40 knots. *Manchester*'s lookouts couldn't see them until they were 100 yards from the cruiser's 600-foot-long broadside. They fired their second torpedoes at point-blank range and retreated into darkness at full speed.

The two more torpedoes zoomed underwater for a mere six seconds before hitting home, as the E-boats cut away and threw up a curtain of spray. A starboard lookout saw them coming just before the brilliant flash and ear-splitting bang that blew a hole and started a fire in the after engine room. The second torpedo hit farther astern and knocked out the propellers. The ladder leading to the hatch at the top of the boiler room snapped, and thirteen men were trapped and steamed alive, with two more dying later.

"The screaming went on and on," said Rob Cunningham, a petty officer who had been standing near the steaming hatch. His eyes show shock that six decades haven't been able to erase.

"It was something terrible.

"Screaming.

"Only screaming.

"Terrible screaming."

"At 0112½ the E-boat was located and engaged," reported Captain Russell from the *Kenya*. He didn't know that the *Kenya* and/or *Manchester* had hit both E-boats with their 4.7-inch guns, which could be aimed low and fired rapidly. The E-boats were riddled with holes as they raced toward shore. The massive fuel cells of one or both caught fire, and thirty Italian sailors were injured and burned before their pilots were able to run the boats aground, as more men dived screaming into the water.

On the *Manchester*, two propeller shafts were snapped and the third was twisted, driving the listing cruiser around in a wide arc to starboard. The freighters *Almeria Lykes* and *Glenorchy* followed her, thinking she was taking avoiding action, until she signaled, "Steer clear of us, we are out of control."

Captain Henderson of *Almeria Lykes* shouted, "Let's get the hell out of this!" and they steered hard to port and out to sea, cutting off and nearly colliding with *Glenorchy*.

Captain Drew shut down the *Manchester*'s engines. The destroyer *Pathfinder*—always in the right place at the right time, as Admiral Burrough said—came along at 0154 and embarked 172 of the *Manchester*'s crew, then raced off to try to catch and protect the merchant ships.

"About 45 minutes after Pathfinder left, the captain said that it might be possible to get the ship underway by the morning at about 12 knots," reported Lieutenant F. H. Munro, "but that should we then be engaged, 75 percent of the ship's company would be casualties. He therefore intended to scuttle the ship. Demolition charges were placed and the ship was abandoned. The motor boats had to be rowed as there was no petrol in the ship. All hands had been told to make for Cape Bon where they would be interred."

After the explosion of three charges, the *Manchester* sank in 240 feet of water. Her stern hit bottom as her bow reached starward, a noble cruiser holding her head high before easing beneath the black sea. Captain Drew and about five hundred men rowed to Tunisia, where they were interred until freed by the Allies during Operation Torch.

A Royal Navy inquiry found Captain Drew guilty of negligence, although it hadn't charged him with it. He had abandoned and scuttled a potentially navigable warship in the face of the enemy. Later the Board of Enquiry informed Drew that the inquiry had been a court-martial. Many among his admiring crew believed the action against him had been a gross miscarriage of justice. To the end of his career and his life, Captain Drew, DSC, maintained dignified silence. Sixty years later the *Manchester* was located three miles offshore in 260 feet of water, showing damage that the Board of Enquiry had dismissed, and that same year the transcripts of the inquiry were declassified and found to be one-sided.

At the head of the convoy, Admiral Burrough's flagship, the destroyer *Ashanti*, engaged in a running battle with two E-boats on the port side and two starboard, which were tracked by *Ashanti*'s radar. "The E-Boats used smoke to avoid punishment," said Captain Onslow. "But one was seen to blow up, and it is probable that at least one more was seriously damaged."

On the *Dorset*, Captain Jack Tuckett tried to ram an E-boat but missed. "The boat just slid past, then accelerated away," he said. It lay in wait ahead, before it attacked a second time. "Black shape on the port bow, sir!" Dag Dickens shouted when he saw it speeding back at them, firing a torpedo that missed by just six feet.

"Helm was put hard aport, and the E-boat passed very close to our bow and starboard side," said Captain Tuckett. "The starboard bridge Oerlikon jammed, and the Gunner on watch was unable to get a shot at the E-boat, which was an easy target as it passed under the bridge."

"You could hear the voices of the swine on board," spat Dickens.

Commander Gibbs also tried to ram an E-boat with the new destroyer *Pathfinder*, but he couldn't get close enough. The *Pathfinder*'s 44-inch searchlight played on the E-boat and her guns opened up, but the boat threw up a smokescreen like ink from an octopus and outsped the *Pathfinder*'s 30 knots.

The *Rochester Castle* was zigzagging at 14½ knots when Captain Wren saw an E-boat at 150 yards. "It suddenly loomed up out of the darkness, and I noticed that its engines were stopped," he reported. "Gunner Turney immediately opened fire with the bridge Oerlikon, and I observed approximately 50 tracers hit the E-boat. Some five to ten seconds later, we were struck by one torpedo from this E-boat. The ship shuddered, and heeled to port. The explosion was much duller than I would have expected, and I think the flour stowed in number three hold acted as a shock absorber. The hold was flooded to water level, but there was only a very small trickle into the engine room. The engines were undamaged, so I continued at full speed."

At 0200 a searchlight played on the side of the *Glenorchy*. It seemed too high to be from an E-boat, and a Royal Navy commander on board told the helmsman to turn toward it, because it was the *Kenya*. The light snapped dark, and MS31 fired two torpedoes from 700 yards.

"It was a very loud explosion," said the second mate, Mr. Skilling. "The engine room flooded immediately, and the galley collapsed on top of the emergency dynamo, putting the emergency lighting system out of action. When the Captain gave the order to abandon ship, there was a certain amount of panic. The men had seen the burning ships during earlier attacks, and knowing the nature of our cargo were frightened lest another torpedo should hit the ship."

Four lifeboats were blown up by the explosion, but survivors filled two lifeboats, each towing a raft. Eight men were never found, including the chief mate. Captain G. Leslie refused to abandon ship. The third mate reboarded and tried to persuade him, but Leslie tricked him into getting back into the lifeboat.

Mr. Skilling returned to the ship three times, trying in vain to get the captain to board the lifeboat. He kept both boats near the *Glenorchy* that night, and at daybreak they rowed three miles, close to shore, because they didn't want to be near the *Glenorchy* when enemy planes showed up. When an Italian bomber circled the ship ten feet over the water, they rowed to the beach.

"At 0800 we could still see the ship, which was well down in the water," said Mr. Skilling. "She turned over on her side and sank, and two minutes later there was a heavy explosion which set fire to the oil in the water."

Captain Leslie was presumed to have gone down with his ship as he had wished. He might have scuttled her himself, lighting the fuse to two depth charges that were strapped to a bulkhead in the engine room, and waiting. Or he might have died screaming in the burning oil on the water.

B etween manning his Oerlikon and standing watch at the helm, Fred
Larsen had scarcely left the bridge of the *Santa Elisa* for more than
two days. But he wasn't alone; few of the ships' gunners had gotten much
sleep in the previous sixty hours. Doctors were handing out Benzedrine,
and some sailors flipped the little white bennies down their throats like
popcorn, although not Larsen. "I didn't care for those things," he said. "I
never even tried one. They made guys jumpy. They were shooting at sea-
gulls."

"The captain told me to rest for a while," he continued. "Shortly after, a
British cruiser or destroyer came alongside and with a bullhorn called us
to follow him, and he would sweep the minefields. It was dark and we did
not expect any air strikes before daybreak, so I laid down with my life pre-
server on the sofa in the deckhouse."

As the *Santa Elisa* steamed in the wake of the antiaircraft cruiser
Charybdis, the freighters *Waimarama* and *Wairangi* began tagging along.
The four ships zigzagged in the dark at nearly top speed, praying their paravanes would catch the mines—the Axis had placed more than a thousand fresh mines around Pantelleria in the previous two weeks.
"Sometimes the mines came so close you could see their horns, when
there was enough light," said Larsen. With no light at all, it was like Russian roulette with cannonballs full of TNT. Captain Thomson kept the
Santa Elisa directly behind *Charybdis*, reducing the odds that a mine would
find them.

Two E-boats watched the *Charybdis*, *Santa Elisa*, and *Waimarama* pass.
Wairangi was in the dreaded "tail-end Charlie" position, and she was

picked off by a shot from 500 yards. There was no fire, but the engine room flooded. "Fearing further attack on the now stationary ship," said Captain Richard Gordon, "I ordered the crew to lower the boats, and suggested in a message to the escort ships that the ship should be sunk by gunfire."

Captain William "Willie" Henderson, of Galveston, Texas, master of the American freighter *Almeria Lykes*, was the most experienced master in the convoy. Born in London in 1883, he'd spent most of his life at sea. He had been a Royal Navy officer before he had moved to the United States, become a citizen, and joined the merchant marine to be a skipper for the Lykes Brothers Steamship Company.

He wasn't having much luck with his crew of old Yankee salts. There were only three fellows under the age of twenty-six among the crew of fifty-one. Some wanted four eggs for breakfast and talked about demanding more pay when they got to Malta because they weren't eating well enough on the ship.

"They were a mixture just labeled American," reported the British liaison officer, Lieutenant Commander H. S. Marshall, as if that said it all. "To me they did not seem to realise properly that there was a war on—let alone that they were in it."

Captain Henderson thought it was a good idea to keep his men from mingling with the liaison officer at mealtime, so Marshall sat at a separate table with the other British officer, a midshipman. Marshall said it was just a precaution, "as the Captain was afraid some of his crew were not very pro-British."

When the cruiser *Manchester* had been torpedoed by E-boats, Captain Henderson had gotten the hell out of there, as he had said. "The Captain then wished to make a bee-line for Malta at top speed," said Marshall. "However, after a bit of discussion, he did agree to follow the course laid down for the convoy, and we then steered down the coast, but at least one mile to seaward."

Between Henderson's beeline for Malta (it was more than a wish) and the "bit of discussion," which was evidently lengthy, the *Almeria Lykes* lost ground, and the *Ohio* caught up to her as they passed Kelibia Light at 0200. The destroyer *Ledbury* was still leading the *Ohio*, and Captain Roger Hill tried to rein in *Almeria Lykes*.

"*Almeria Lykes* was told to follow," he reported, "but she went off on her own. I could not leave the tanker, so I had to let her go."

Almeria Lykes zigzagged at 13 knots. Twenty-one lookouts, brain-numbed by lack of sleep and propped up by pills, struggled to spot E-boats in the choppy black sea. The unseen, smaller MAS554 launched two torpedoes from 550 yards, with one hitting the freighter's forepeak.

"Time was about 0420," reported Marshall. "The Captain ordered 'Abandon ship.' This was, in my opinion, entirely justified as (a) the bows were going down rapidly and (b) the crew would most certainly have gone anyway."

The destroyer *Pathfinder* arrived, but her captain, Commander Gibbs, refused to pick up the *Almeria Lykes*' crew.

"The ship appeared to be perfectly all right," he reported. "I persuaded her ship's company to return to her and endeavor to steam her to Malta." It was a gentle way of saying that he told them to get the hell back on their ship where they belonged.

"The ship itself, though well down by the bows, did not seem to be going further," said Marshall. "With some trouble, the Captain got his reluctant crew to put him on board. Three of his younger officers went with him."

Henderson and the three men examined the ship and returned to the lifeboats.

"The ship's engines were undamaged," reported Marshall, "but owing to the damage forward, it would not have been possible to go at any speed, and the Bofors gun, our main A.A. weapon, which was right forward, had been put out of action. The Captain said that the crew would not go back to the ship. It would not have been possible to work the ship with a volunteer crew, because although she is driven by steam turbines, in every other way she is all electric and so needs a specialised staff.

"Considering the state of affairs, I decided to scuttle the ship. We were under observation by the enemy and possibly also the French, so I decided to sink her before I was prevented.

"I went to the ship with the Captain and his volunteer crew. The feelings of the ship's crew seemed to be that while the boats were very likely to be machine-gunned anyhow, they were certain to be if they went near the ship. The only engineer officer from the ship who would come with me was the most junior one."

Henderson, Marshall, and the first assistant engineer, Henry Brown, rowed back to the ship, and Henderson set the depth charges in the engine room. The charges went off, but the ship didn't sink.

At 0900 the destroyer *Somali* came by, picked up the *Almeria Lykes'* crew, and steamed east to Gibraltar.

In the five pages of Admiral Syfret's orders to the convoy, stamped MOST SECRET, only one sentence is underlined: *No ship is to be scuttled if she is capable of steaming and there is no immediate risk of capture.*

"The *Almeria Lykes* was hit before the bulkhead of No. 1 hold and could well have continued steaming to Malta," Syfret said. "The tale, as recorded in the report by her Naval Liaison Officer, of the abandonment of this ship is one of shame."

The merchant mariners of the *Almeria Lykes* steamed back to New York on a cargo ship. They had survived their night of hell in the narrows. But one man failed to survive the hell of the aftermath. On September 5, the ship's first assistant engineer, Henry Brown, the most junior one, jumped out of the window of a New York hotel and killed himself.

F rancis Alonzo Dales was the youngest man on the *Santa Elisa*. When he joined the merchant marine after high school he was made for heroism, if not hell-bent on it. Lonnie had always done the right thing, because that's how he was raised. Like Fred Larsen, he didn't need rum for the jitters or little white pills to stay wired for battle. The other kids hadn't called him "Admiral" for nothing.

The third mate Larsen was twenty-seven years old and the cadet-midshipman Dales was eighteen, a Norwegian American who had seen the world and a kid from the Deep South who hadn't. Fate had brought them together to form a perfect union in time of war.

At the gunnery school in Cardiff, where they had shot virtual Stukas diving from the ceiling of a dome, Dales had emerged as a sharpshooter. At the artillery range on the coast, manning a Twin Marlin that fired blanks at a plane zooming 50 feet overhead, he'd proved himself cool, outscoring all of Ensign Suppiger's navy gunners.

Larsen had told Captain Thomson that he wanted Dales at the Oerlikon near his own on the bridge. "Mr. Larsen and I had been placed in charge of the 20 mm anti-aircraft guns on the port side of the vessel, Mr. Larsen being in charge of the forward gun, and I the after one," Dales wrote in his report to the supervisor of the U.S. Merchant Marine Cadet Corps.

Jack Follansbee manned the port Oerlikon on the main deck below the bridge. He dozed off at his gun, with a blanket over his shoulders.

Six bells (3 a.m.) was striking when I felt someone's hand upon my shoulder. I opened my eyes and stretched my cramped legs.

"Sorry to wake you again sir, but some bloke says 'e 'ears what sounds like 'undreds of aircraft."

"He must be nuts," I replied. "Who thinks he hears them?"

"One of your Navy gunners on the four-inch on the stern. I can't 'ear a bloody thing, can you, sir?"

I listened. Only the whine of the turbine and splash of our bow wave met my ears.

"Wait a minute, sir!" the Britisher said excitedly. "I 'ear what he means now. Don't you 'ear it?"

A new sound had joined the noises of the night. It was a low roaring sound, and it did remind you of aircraft engines. It seemed to be coming from the port side.

"Everybody's 'eard it now," the Britisher said. "They think it must be motor boats. Maybe motor torpedo boats!"

I strapped myself into the gun. I shivered.

Lonnie Dales had first heard the E-boat engines at midnight, when he had begun the midwatch at his Oerlikon on the port bridge wing. Their powerful low rumbling carried for miles over the sea, crossing the water in threatening murmurs. He'd been anticipating an attack for more than four hours, as the *Santa Elisa* steamed along its shortcut to Malta. In just thirty more minutes it would be daybreak, and the E-boats would return to the caves where, it was whispered, they lived.

"We were alone again, as the escorting vessels were trying to get the other ships back in formation," reported Dales. "The night was very dark with visibility poor. The enemy planes and torpedo boats were trying to locate us by the use of flares."

There are at least five versions of what happened next, each one clouded by the fog of war and colored by time. About all that can be said for certain is that the man standing next to Lonnie Dales went down with a bullet through the neck, dying in a pool of blood at Dales's feet, and the *Santa Elisa* was hit by a torpedo in the number one hold, the hold that scared them, because it carried the aviation fuel.

Captain Giovanni Battista Cafiero, piloting the small and fast MAS557, had played a hunch and disobeyed orders, leaving the other E-boats from his Trapani, Sicily, squadron and moving to a point about forty miles southwest of Pantelleria. He shut off his engines and waited for a merchant ship that he hoped would be steaming alone. He heard the *Santa Elisa* but she was out of range, so he refired his engines and began chasing her.

Lieutenant Commander Barnes, the *Santa Elisa*'s liaison officer, spotted the MAS557 first. "It had barely started to get light," he reported. "Through binoculars, I sighted an E-Boat coming up astern about a cable [600 feet] away, and crossing from starboard to port. The alarm was passed to the guns, but they did not sight the boat until she was about level with the stern and about ½ cable distant."

"We had an Oerlikon on the bridge, but it couldn't be depressed sufficiently to hit anything at close range," said Captain Thomson, who thought the E-boat had come around the bow. He saw the phosphorescent wake of a torpedo racing over the water toward the *Santa Elisa* at 50 mph, and ordered the big freighter hard to starboard. "Fortunately, that torpedo missed its mark, passing astern of us."

If Lonnie Dales saw the torpedo, he never mentioned it in his report. But he believed there were as many as four E-boats. "They attacked, each from a different angle," he said. "Since we were unable to see them for the darkness, one was almost alongside when the Captain from the bridge wing spotted it. He personally ordered me to open fire."

Thomson's personal order went like this: "See that sonofabitch! Get him!"

"I began firing," said Dales.

The MAS557 fired back. The rattle of the E-boat's machine-gun bullets against the steel bulkheads of *Santa Elisa* woke Fred Larsen, dozing on the couch in the deckhouse behind the enclosed bridge. He snapped up, looked out the porthole, and saw flaming onions—that's what they called the enemy's green tracers—whizzing over the water at 2,000 mph. The first thing that entered his foggy mind was that the *Santa Elisa*'s tracers were red and gold. "Oh, brother," he said, and ran up the ladder on the starboard side to his Oerlikon.

Bullets from the guns of MAS557—"I believe they were .50 caliber," said Dales—bashed against the small steel shield that stood between death and Dales's square jaw. His Oerlikon loader dropped with a bullet in the throat, his blood streaming onto the deck.

It all happened so fast. Two more British soldiers were killed on the bridge, and another was gunned down at the Bofors on the main deck.

"The bullets made a steady clattering sound a few inches in front of my eyes," said Captain Thomson, who dived face-first onto the hard steel of the flying bridge along with the liaison officer, Barnes.

"All my gun crew were dead," said Dales. "I didn't notice until I ran out of ammunition. No one would pass me the drum. When I ran out and hollered for ammunition there wasn't any, just bodies and blood everywhere."

He loaded the gun himself and kept shooting. "A seventeen-year-old [sic] American cadet took charge of the gun and despite his exposed position kept it firing," said Thomson.

"Mr. Larsen's gun, my gun, and the other guns on the port side of the vessel all fired at the enemy torpedo boat," added Dales. "It burst into flames."

The flames were seen by two other distant ships, but the fog of war apparently obscured them from the eyes of the liaison officer. "Fire from the port Oerlikon and Bofors appeared to be accurate," reported Barnes, "but it was too dark to observe what effect was caused, if any."

Nor did Barnes see the second E-boat, if there was one. However, said Captain Thomson, "At almost the same moment, a torpedo, fired from the second E-boat, which had approached from the opposite side of the ship, struck the starboard bow. Water gushed up over the bridge."

Said the engineer Randall, "What's happened is this: That first E-boat turns out to be a damned decoy. While we're blasting her, another slips up on the other side and sends a torpedo into us."

The torpedo might have been a second shot by the MAS557; the account in the book *La battaglia aeronavale di mezzo agosto* makes this claim, although it's a work riddled with contradictions and omissions of Italian losses. But if MAS557 did survive the *Santa Elisa*'s fire, she might have sheered off to port and circled behind the *Santa Elisa*, whose starboard side would have been exposed after Thomson had turned hard-a-starboard to dodge the first torpedo. That's what Barnes believed happened.

The book *Pedestal* states that after the attack by MAS557, the *Santa Elisa* was hit by a torpedo fired at point-blank range from the Pantelleria-based MAS564, a version which appears to have been taken from more confused Italian reports.

Wherever it came from, "The torpedo struck the starboard side of our number-one hold, igniting the high-test gasoline and setting our entire ship afire," said Dales. Blue and yellow flames rose for 600 feet. The Italian report called the fire "incandescent."

"We'd better get out of here!" shouted one of the British loaders. "She'll blow sky-high any minute!"

"The guns' crews at the forward gun platform were unable to get past the burning hatches, and either jumped or were blown into the sea by the explosion," reported Barnes. "In view of the highly explosive nature of the cargo and the extremely small chance of controlling the fire, the Master decided to abandon ship."

"The ship began to settle at the head," said Captain Thomson. "In spite of my fears the aviation gas didn't explode, although it did catch fire. It ran out slowly over the surface of the water and lay there burning. I ordered the engines stopped, since the ship had settled so rapidly that our propeller was already out of the water. Then I rang to abandon ship. It was a hell of an order to have to give. It was my first ship. But I had the crew to think about."

"There was fire everywhere," said Larsen. "Two British Army radio operators were running up and down and couldn't get out, because fire was all over the deck. I grabbed an emergency light and led them up to the wheelhouse. It was a mess. Windows broken and water on the deck. I think I heard the abandon ship signal, and I grabbed my sextant and went to my boat station. I was in charge of the number two boat on the port side.

"The two Army soldiers got out on the starboard wing of the bridge deck and tried to get in the number one lifeboat, but the tackle wasn't released correctly, and she dumped over in the water. Some fool had tied the pelican hook with a knot."

Larsen saw that the captain was having trouble launching the fifty-man number four lifeboat on the deck below him, so he ran down a ladder to help.

"Someone in the confusion had cranked the davits back in, after they had been cranked out and ready for lowering," he said. "Someone else had commenced lowering the boat and it landed in the gutter. With the help of some men we managed to tighten up the tackles and get the boat clear."

Captain Thomson shouted to Larsen that he had forgotten about his dog, so Larsen ran to the skipper's cabin. "I think he was already gone," he said. "The water was a foot deep in the captain's quarters. I tried like hell to find him but it was too late. I think he had already drowned."

Larsen scrambled back up to his lifeboat, where he found that the men from the balzupped launch of the number one lifeboat had climbed up the slippery slope of the listing bridge and jumped into his number two boat.

"The whole boat was loaded with people, and nobody was doing anything about lowering it. So I unlashed the trapping gear and started to lower the boat. An ordinary seaman showed up and helped me, and we released the scramble net and climbed down it into the lifeboat.

"When I got down in there, soon as I got in the boat, the two radio operators, with their heavy army boots on, they had come from the other side because their boat got tangled up and tossed everything in the water; and they were coming down the scramble net, and they figure the boat's gonna leave without them, so they jump from the scramble net and landed right on top of me. Shoved me right down in the bottom of the boat. I was bending over to release a lever at the bottom of the boat, and these two guys drop on top of me. Luckily I had my steel helmet on, because they would have knocked me silly. So I'm laying in the bottom of the boat with guys on top of me, and I hear someone say, 'Hey, isn't the deck officer in this boat?'

" 'I'm down here! Here I am!' "

Larsen's back had been fractured by the impact of the soldiers in their heavy boots, but there was no time for pain. Nor was there time for Ensign Suppiger's problems. Suppy had dropped his .45-caliber pistol, and the second engineer had picked it up, but Larsen took it from the engineer.

Said Larsen, "I held the .45 automatic up in the air and I said, 'Calm down! Let's get this show on the road!' And we took off. So with a few orders and waving the pistol, we got the lifeboat away."

According to Suppiger, the number two lifeboat had been lowered into the water directly under the overboard discharge from the ship, and it was rapidly being flooded; he and some others tried to push it away, but it wouldn't move.

"Then some people jumped out of the boat into #4 boat, which had been successfully launched astern of us," he said. "I jumped out and attempted to reach #4 boat, but could not leap far enough and fell into the water."

Said Larsen, "My boat was so heavy loaded, I had at least twenty-eight men aboard a twenty-two-man boat, so I rowed toward the captain and asked him if he had room for some of my men. They all wanted to get in the captain's boat. I had to control them by holding the pistol at them. I said, 'Hey: you, you, you and you go into the Captain's boat. Everybody else stay here.' A couple of guys jumped anyway, but I let them go."

Larsen used Suppiger's own pistol to order him back into the lifeboat, but Suppy swam on. He furiously stroked to escape the burning gasoline as the ship's propeller, spinning slowly and skimming the water, missed his head by about two feet, he said. He drifted away and found himself 1,000 yards astern of the ship. "I shouted as loud as I could, and in about an hour's time number four lifeboat, which contained Captain Thomson, made its way toward the direction of my voice and picked me up."

"The water wasn't calm but it was no big sea," said Larsen, commanding the unflooded number two boat. "We were picking up crew members. The Navy gun crew was all covered with fuel and shit. And they had been on fire. Some of the gasoline had dropped down on top of them from the number one hatch, and they had been burned very badly, some of them. We picked those guys up out of the water. We couldn't do much for them. We had loaded hidden whiskey beside the water tanks in the lifeboats, and gave that to them."

"When we lifted one Navy gunner aboard, I saw that his face and neck were badly burned," said Follansbee. "He sat for a while without speaking, then slowly and deliberately, without seeming to address anyone in particular, said, 'We got cut off when the fire started back aft. Couldn't get up to the lifeboats. Finally decided to jump. But the gasoline on the water caught fire.' "

"As the men rowed, I heard a strange sort of whisper starting among them," said Captain Thomson. "I had never heard anything like it before. I guess it was what you'd call panic. Usually I keep my voice to myself, but this time I stood up in the bow of the boat and said, 'Listen, you men. If anybody opens his yap, I'll clout him.' I guess the men were surprised to hear that kind of talk from me. Anyhow, after that there was silence."

The number three lifeboat was the only one to get away without problems, but it too was overloaded. It carried men from the aborted number one boat, as well as Dales, Follansbee, and Randall, and had also picked up some of the burned men in the water. "Suddenly," said Randall, "we hear a shout: 'Help! Sharks are after me!' "

It was Frank Pike, the British gunner, who had been sleeping on the stern and had leaped overboard with some others because they were separated from the lifeboats by the wall of flame. "The day before we were torpedoed, we had seen several sharks on the surface, and I was reminded of these when I felt something brush against my leg," he said. "The next time I felt it, I took a swipe at it with my jack knife—and speared a submerged cardboard carton, to my great relief."

The chief mate, Englund, a Swede, was in charge of number three lifeboat. "Row like hell!" he had shouted as it was released. "She could blow up any minute!"

A sense of panic followed the chief mate's lead and swept over the boat. The British soldier George Nye remembers the panic ending when Cadet-Midshipman Dales took charge.

"It was every man for himself," said Nye, at home in Dartford in 2005. "We'd have tipped the boat over, the way we were going. I don't remember any of the crew of the *Elisa*, because I had only been on the boat for a few days, having boarded at the Clyde. The only one that stood out in my memory was this lad who stood up in the boat and brought order to chaos. And I thought, what a brilliant young lad of eighteen or nineteen, the same age as me, what a brilliant leader of men he was going to be. He calmed everybody down, including his senior people, officers senior in age and rank. I didn't know his name, but as long as I live I've got a picture of him standing up in the boat and raising his voice—not nasty or anything, but masterly, and everybody did more or less what he told them to do."

The destroyer *Penn* had been helping the destroyer *Bramham* keep Commodore Venables and the *Port Chalmers* on the path toward Malta. From a distance, the *Penn* had seen the flaming E-boat that Lonnie Dales had shot up.

"At 0430 Oerlikon fire was seen ahead, and then an explosion," reported the captain of the *Penn*, Lieutenant Commander J. H. Swain. "Shortly afterward the engine of an E-boat was heard proceeding away from the scene of the explosion. I steered for this point, and as it became light the *Santa Elisa* was seen to be stopped and on fire."

The three lifeboats from the *Santa Elisa* were rowing away from their sinking ship. "We had decided we were closer to Pantelleria than any other place, so we started rowing to Pantelleria," said Larsen.

Said Follansbee:

The sun was just climbing above the horizon as one of the men in my boat suddenly pointed astern. "Look you guys! Here comes a warship, or something!"

A vessel was rapidly bearing down on us from the north.

"Holy Christ!" another man shouted. "It's probably a Wop coming out of Sicily!"

"Looks like a destroyer," said the Navy gunner with the burns on his face.

"Maybe they'll fire on us!" someone exclaimed.

"Shut up, goddammit!"

The British Lieutenant Commander who was our Liaison Officer stood up in the lifeboat and watched the approaching vessel intently.

"It's a destroyer, all right," he announced finally. "I can almost make out her flag now . . . Yes, I believe . . . Yes, by God, she is . . . she's one of ours!"

The *Santa Elisa* survivors scrambled up the nets that were lowered over the side of the *Penn*, as an officer on the bridge shouted through a megaphone, "Make it snappy down there! We can't sit here any longer!"

As the last man boarded the destroyer, Captain Swain said to Captain Thomson, "We've got to cut your boats loose now. Is there anything else you want out of them?"

"No," said Thomson, "cut them loose."

The destroyer leaped forward, and the lifeboats twisted and turned in its wake. Follansbee suddenly remembered the rum he had hidden in the biscuit tins and kicked himself for leaving it behind.

"As the *Penn* was steaming away from the *Santa Elisa*, down in the bows and burning fiercely, the dawn bombing attack came in right on schedule," said Follansbee. "One of the *Penn*'s gunners shouted into his phones, 'Enemy aircraft coming in on the starboard quarter!'

"There's one now! Right over the *Elisa*!" shouted another crewman.

A Ju 88 dived on the abandoned *Santa Elisa*. The Italian pilot had been saving a 500-kilogram bomb for her. "We could see the ship with its propeller partially out of the water," said Larsen. "The airplane came in and dropped a bomb on the foredeck and she blew up. She was fully loaded with explosives. We were about a half a mile away. Pieces from the ship's explosion rained all around us."

"The ship was seen to blow up in a cloud of smoke and sink almost immediately," reported Barnes. "The officers and men behaved excellently under a very trying ordeal and did everything possible to get the ship to her destination."

"The smoke cleared away," said Follansbee. "The *Santa Elisa* had disappeared completely."

"There wasn't a smear left of her," said Larsen.

n the four hours after midnight, E-boats had sunk one cruiser (*Manchester*) and four freighters (*Glenorchy, Wairangi, Almeria Lykes,* and *Santa Elisa*), while damaging another cruiser (*Kenya*) and a fifth freighter (*Rochester Castle*). The previous evening, bombers had sunk three freighters (*Deucalion, Clan Ferguson,* and *Empire Hope*) and damaged the *Brisbane Star,* while the submarine *Axum* had sunk one cruiser (*Cairo*), blasted another back to Gibraltar (*Nigeria*), and crippled the *Ohio.* The aircraft carrier *Eagle* had been sunk by U-73 the previous day, and the carrier *Indomitable* was mortally wounded and staggering home.

From the bridge of the destroyer *Ashanti* at daybreak, Admiral Burrough could see just three merchantmen. *Rochester Castle* was in front despite flooding in the number three hold, with *Waimarama* and *Melbourne Star* right behind.

Ohio was five miles back, still following the destroyer *Ledbury* at 12 knots—"I consider the greatest credit is due to her Master for this magnificent effort," said Burrough. *Port Chalmers* was another five miles back, with Commodore Venables finally lifting his eyes from the rearview mirror, while *Dorset* was on her own course farther north. *Brisbane Star* was hugging the coast, south of Point "R," where the rest of the convoy had turned southeast, making slow progress with the hole through her bows.

The RAF flew off Beaufighters from Malta at dawn. On the *Ashanti,* radio operators had worked all night to patch a system to reach the pilots, and a lieutenant nicknamed "Flags" repeatedly called out in code for nearly an hour, listening intently all the while. Flags was excited by a cryptic answer, until he realized he was talking to the cruiser *Charybdis,* steaming alongside. A torrent of blue words spouted from his mouth as he slammed down the receiver. Meanwhile, Admiral Da Zara's warships—three heavy cruisers, one light cruiser, and eight destroyers—were on their way back to Italy. But the submarine HMS *Unbroken*, under Lieutenant Commander Alastair Mars, had anticipated their course and was waiting for them near the island of Stromboli. Mars was a submarine ace. He launched four torpedoes, badly damaging the heavy cruiser *Bolzano*—she was towed aground and burned until the next day—and blowing the bows off the light cruiser *Attendolo*, knocking them both out of the war. The destroyers dropped 105 depth charges and kept *Unbroken* submerged for ten hours, but Mars surfaced that evening and returned a hero to the "Fighting Tenth" at Malta.

At 12,843 tons, *Waimarama* was the biggest of the thirteen freighters—half again the size of the *Santa Elisa*, at 8,379 tons. She was also carrying the most aviation fuel. Flimsies were stacked on the afterdeck by the tens of thousands, on top of number six hold, where there were another two or three thousand tons of high-octane gas in more flimsies.

The cardboard containing the flimsies on deck had been ripped off by the saltwater splashes of near misses. The silver cans sparkled in the morning sun, calling to the bombers, which had arrived right on time. There were twenty-four Ju 88s flying at 5,000 feet, and three of them answered the call of the flashing flimsies.

First one Junkers dropped into a dive, then another, and then the third, with about 500 feet between them. They zoomed at the pile of flimsies at 300 mph from 60 degrees. The Bofors boomed without result, and the Oerlikons' tracers snaked past the planes as if their target were the sun. The pilots' focus on the bridge of the *Waimarama* was absolute. The first Junkers dived to 1,000 feet and missed with three bombs.

The second Junkers dived lower, and let go five 500-pounders. Two bombs landed abaft the bridge, and a third fell on the hatch of hold number four, which contained torpedoes and mines. The fourth bomb landed on the stack of flimsies.

The German in the third Junkers was still diving, and his plane was blown away by the blast.

John Jackson was a radio operator on the forward bridge of the *Waimarama*. "The ship was immediately enveloped in flames and on looking to the starboard I could see nothing but a solid mass of flames," he said. "I looked across to the port side and could not even see the gun mounting which was about two yards away, owing to the solid wall of flames."

Jackson ran through the bridge deckhouse, down a ladder and over debris and dead bodies and pieces of bodies, through the flames and past the burning and screaming men, and jumped into the only patch of sea that wasn't on fire. He wore a life vest but couldn't swim. There were about twenty men in the water. They were the only survivors. More than a hundred men were dead or soon would be.

The bridge crumbled as if imploded. The tips of the funnels could be seen in the smoke as they collapsed and fell into the fire. Flaming flimsies shot into the air like skyrockets. Thick black smoke rose into the blue morning sky and took the shape of some giant grim-reaping spider, as if rising over the Mediterranean from the world of Earthsea.

Freddie Treves was scarcely seventeen years old, a cadet like Lonnie Dales. He had entered the Pangbourne Nautical College at thirteen, graduated in June, and reported to the *Waimarama* on July 27. His total time at sea was sixteen days. Operation Pedestal was his baptism by fire.

The ship's master, Captain R. S. Pearce, had teamed his youngest sailor with the oldest salt, Bowdory. "Bowdory was a pantryman," said Treves, "he worked in the kitchen. He was sixty-three, a lovely old man, he looked after me. His two sons were fighting in the war, and he had rejoined the merchant navy against his wife's wishes. He said, 'If my sons are going to this war, I'm going too.'

"He and I were put in the only part of the ship which had no explosives in it, in the fo'c'sle. It was the safest part of the ship, for the oldest man and the youngest man. It was full of bags of lime. When the bombs came down, Bowdory fell on me to protect me. We were both blown through a hatch onto the bags of lime. I don't know what happened next, except I forgot the rule about jumping over the side that's listing and closest to the water, so I jumped off the wrong side. Bowdory must have jumped too. It was a long jump. About sixty feet, maybe forty feet, I don't know. I looked up at the ship. The flames were rising into the sky. I have a photograph that shows the smoke going up about six thousand feet. It was a pretty big explosion."

Treves was wearing a special lining inside his coveralls called kapok, supposedly the latest thing in flotation. His mother had bought it in London and made him promise he would wear it at all times. Which he did, despite the heat and the merciless teasing of his shipmates because he looked like a little boy in a stiff snowsuit.

As Treves swam away from the burning *Waimarama,* he saw John Jackson.

"He was struggling, he couldn't swim. He had come down from the bridge in some way, I never found out how, and he couldn't swim, so I got him over to a bit of wood. I had a whistle, because I was in charge, as the officer, part of the fo'c'sle group, and I tried to calm people down, and gave him a bit of wood to hold onto. He said he was okay then, and I said just kick your feet, hold onto the log."

"I am quite sure that I definitely owe my life to this cadet," Jackson reported.

Treves looked up and saw Bowdory on a Carley raft.

"I went towards Bowdory. His arms were outstretched, like this. And he was being pulled into the flames, by the ship going down, the water, sucking towards the ship. And he was yelling and screaming, and . . ."—he fumbles over words—" . . . the flame."

Treves is asked how far away Bowdory was. It's not a simple question. It's been haunting him for sixty-three years. Too far for me to save? Or not? Could I have swum into the sucking water of the 13,000-ton sinking freighter, wearing my waterlogged kapok, into the flames that were closing around Bowdory's raft, and tied a line from the raft around my chest and swum with all my might, towing the raft and Bowdory to safety, against the powerful pull of the sinking ship, before the flames closed on us? Could I have talked the nonswimming and panicked Bowdory into diving into the water so I could drag him kicking and screaming away from the closing flames to safety?

It's the question that haunted him through his breakdown afterward, still seventeen years old, and through his service on a destroyer, after he joined the Royal Navy the next year, until the war ended. Never mind the clear impossibility of reaching Bowdory. The question still haunts him, as he sees Bowdory on the raft through his glistening eyes, from the couch of his home in Wimbledon.

"Quite a way," he answers, his voice drifting quite a way back, ". . . but not too far. I think I could have made it, I got medals for swimming at school. But I . . . turned back. Just . . . swam away."

He swallows. "They decorated me, which is nice." The king gave him the British Empire Medal at Buckingham Palace, for saving Jackson. "At least I got Jackson."

Only Treves considers that swimming into the fire in an attempt to save Bowdory might have been the better thing to do. Only he would.

> All the world is old, my friend
> Yet all the world is new.
> And all the dead are dead, my friend
> Saving me and you.
> And all the dead are me, and you
> And all the future too.

The *Waimarama* blast was so intense that the crew of the *Melbourne Star,* four hundred yards behind, thought it was their own ship that had been hit. Thirty-three jumpy men leaped over the side, mostly army gunners at the six-inch and Bofors aft. "Mad bastards, they were," said a sailor who watched them go. "The gunners around me just disappeared overboard. It was 50 bleedin' feet down to the water."

They were mad, yes. All night at the guns they had watched the funeral pyres and listened to the screams of burning sailors carrying over water. "No one could say he was not frightened by now," said Dickens. "We had seen too much."

"It was impossible to avoid going through *Waimarama's* flames, although the Captain, who was conning ship from Monkey Island above the bridge, ordered helm hard to port," reported the liaison officer. "The Second Officer, who was in the Wheelhouse with the helmsman at the time of the explosion, rang on full speed, and this undoubtedly in my mind saved the ship.

"Remainder of men onboard tried to find the best means if any of escape, but ship came through the burning oil of *Waimarama* which was spreading rapidly, and men returned to the forecastle and so back to their action stations, the whole episode taking about three minutes.

"On coming out of the flames, a destroyer was seen to be attempting to rescue the men who went overboard, and at the time I thought it was a hopeless task. Subsequently it was found that this destroyer was H.M.S. *Ledbury*."

Roger Hill had just rescued the *Ohio* by leading her through the narrows and back to the convoy with his destroyer *Ledbury*, but his next job was what he was there for.

Admiral Burrough had known Hill for a long time and was well aware of how he felt about having been ordered to abandon the merchantmen during PQ17. Burrough knew that the *Ledbury* was near *Waimarama* and that Hill would rescue any survivors whether or not he was told to, so he sent the signal with some resignation. "*Ledbury* was ordered to pick up any survivors from the *Clan Ferguson* [*sic*], although it seemed unlikely that there could be any," he reported.

"The Admiral made [signaled] to me, 'Survivors, but don't go into the flames,' " said Hill. "It was the biggest explosion I have ever seen. It was terrible. The flames were hundreds of feet high, and a great expanse of sea was covered in rolling smoke and flames. I took the ship to the edge of the flames but did not think anyone could have survived. As we approached, there were heads bobbing about in the water, waving arms, and faces blackened with oil."

Hill could hear the cries of the ghosts of the PQ17 sailors whom the *Ledbury* had left to die in the Arctic Sea. His soul had gone down with theirs, as he felt the doom and despair of their voices over the radio. Now he could hear the screams of the men in the fire around the *Waimarama*, and he could see their mucky heads, as if these were the PQ17 sailors risen from the bottom of the sea for a second chance to be saved. But it was more the chance for Hill to save himself.

He whipped his destroyer around as if it were a Jet Ski plucking fallen surfers away from big waves. "I can not speak too highly of the sheer guts of these men," he said. "They were singing and encouraging each other, and as I went through them explaining by loudhailer that I must get the ones nearest the flames first, I received cheerful answers of 'That's all right, sir. Go and get the other chaps.' "

Mines were falling from the sky under parachutes, and a few Junkers continued to attack. Said Freddie Treves, "I remember Bunny Hill shouting through his loudhailer, 'Be back in a minute, I've just got to shoot this bloody German down!' "

Because Hill had leaped off the bridge of the *Ledbury* on the way to Gibraltar in his failed attempt to rescue the crew of the *Sunderland* downed by friendly fire, the *Ledbury* men now felt free to copy their captain's style. "All sorts of people were jumping over the side with lines and bringing survivors, some seriously burned, to the landing nets," said Hill. "The flames were spreading outward all the time—even to windward—and at one time spread the whole length of the ship, picking up two men close to the after nets. I had to take the ship after, and these men were supported by my rescuers who themselves were clinging onto the nets."

He nosed the *Ledbury* into the flames as hoses tried to push back the fire. "On the bridge, the flames and smoke towered over us," said Robin Owen, a young officer. "The first lieutenant had hoses rigged, and they played on the upper decks, as the captain maneuvered the ship with the engines and rudder to get as close as possible to the survivors while a boat was lowered."

They picked up survivors for two hours. There was one more man in the water. Hill couldn't leave him.

The coxswain reported up the voice-pipe, "There's a man on a raft in the flames." I hesitated, wishing to ignore what he reported. Then I wondered if the ship would blow up if we went right into the heat. The density of the smoke changed, and I saw a man sitting on some debris surrounded by leaping flames, and he raised his arm to us. I took the ship in and shouted to Number One, "For Christ's sake, be quick!"

The flames were higher than the mast, and the roaring noise and choking fumes were all around us.

"Jesus," said Yeoman (who had been forbidden to go over the side), "it's just like a film."

The cook came out of his galley aft, saw the man, took off his apron, kicked off his boots and over he went.

Charles Henry Walker is ninety-one years old now, built like a bull and living life to the full in Reading with ten grandchildren and ten great-grandchildren. He shows off the pictures on the wall of his room. "There's me and the queen, there's me and Margaret Thatcher, there's me and Prince Philip. Who haven't I met?" he says with a spark in his eye and a poke in his guest's arm. "The queen called me Charles Henry, so you commoners can call me Charles Henry too. I met her after I gave a fella a little help in the water."

Petty Officer Walker, the ship's cook, was the strongest swimmer on the *Ledbury*, captain of her water polo team. For two hours he rowed the whaler with chief gunner Musham and three more men, working in the channels and pools between the flames, picking up survivors. Some couldn't swim, and all of them were burned. When the rowers could go no closer, Walker went over the side of the whaler and swam the backstroke, splashing away the fire, to reach the last couple of men. Reginald Sida, a steward, also swam for survivors, connected to the *Ledbury* by a line.

"One chap I picked up, oh he was really bad, he was burned to hell he was," said Walker. "He was really cooked in diesel oil. His nose was like a little pear drop, and he was cooked in diesel, and he was going, 'Water, water . . .'

"When you see bodies floating around the ocean like that, and you can't do a thing about it . . .

"I saw a body in the water, we rowed out to get his dog tags off him. His jacket was full of air, keeping him up. I touched him and he rolled over in the water, went blub blub blub. Things like that stick in your mind." They stick in his throat, and his eyes begin to take on water, as if to splash away the memory.

"Somebody's son, somebody's dad. Somebody's sweetheart. That's the nastiest thing about war, isn't it.

"Musham said, 'All right, let's get going,' Flames were getting on the boat, he was pretty worried. I was too. I see a hand on the gunwale, I see this bloke, and I say, 'Give me your hand, I'll pull you in,' and I turn away for a second to put the oar down, and the hand is gone. I could see the hand on there, even now when I go to bed, late at night, I see the hand, I see his eyes. Christ yes, ooh wee. We survived, we survived. When you come to think of it, why? Why was it us who survived?"

Walker earned the George Cross Medal, the highest civilian honor the monarch can bestow, for what he did next. "Ah, you'd like to hear that story, would you?" he says with the spark in his eye returning.

He hasn't told the story many times. Few of the veterans have told their stories many times. When they got back from the war they didn't want to, and nobody wanted to hear them. They didn't even tell their children. Decades have passed, and now they're beginning to tell them, these eightysomethings who don't want to carry the reality of war to their graves. If anyone asks. The children are fifty and sixty years old, and they're astounded. They never knew their fathers were heroes.

"We picked these boys up out of the water, we didn't think anything," continues Walker. "I was on the upper deck and my mate was rubbing diesel off me because I was covered in diesel. The skipper give the order 'No more men over the side, we're getting under way.' I didn't hear the order, because I was over the side when he gave it.

"The flames were coming over the ship. There was Alan Burnet, he was only a young lad, someone saw him having difficulty on a raft in the flames, and I went over the side again and got him. He starts yelling, 'There's something around my legs!' I said there's no bloody sharks on you, he bloody finds his trousers had got around his ankles. So I pulled the buggers off and they sank to the bottom, and I push him alongside the ship to the scrambling net, and he's got a big bare ass, isn't he? You should have heard them on the boat. He's only sixteen years old. Lovely white bum, I can see it now. He was quite knackered, had been in the water a long time, and I had to push him up: like this."

"I felt like I could not wait any longer," said Captain Hill, "and called through the loudhailer, 'Hold on like hell, I'm going astern!' We came out fast astern, and I was sure the cook and the man would have been washed away, but he had one arm round the man's neck and the other through the net and had held on."

"I was still in the water," says Walker. "The skipper said, 'We're getting under way.' I'm in the water. 'Throw the line for Christ's sake!' I nearly go mad.

"The yeoman, oh a nice chap, really nice chap, he said to Hill, 'Excuse me sir, petty officer Walker is still in the water.' Bloody hell! Put the *Ledbury* astern! Picked us up, and that was it."

"We had been two hours picking up forty-five survivors, one of whom was dead," said Hill. "I told the admiral I was thirty miles astern and set off to rejoin the convoy."

CHAPTER 38

SWERVING TOWARD MALTA

Captain Mason conned the SS *Ohio* hard aport, around the flaming gold sea over the sinking *Waimarama*. "Weather was fine with good visibility, smooth sea, and light airs, and we were steaming at thirteen knots, steering approximately East, in position a hundred miles west from Malta," he reported. The tanker continued swerving toward Malta, shadowed by two dozen Ju 88s.

"At 0800 the heavy bombing attacks started again," said Mason. "*Ohio* seemed the main objective, as always. The planes never flew over in any particular formation, and appeared to adopt the same technique each time. Ten or twelve planes would appear over the horizon to the southward, and all guns would open fire, then the real attack would develop from the opposite direction, i.e., northward. We had got used to this method of attack by now and were ready for the enemy. Our gunners brought down a Stuka with one of the Oerlikons.

"At about 0900 we shot down a Ju 88 that crashed into the sea close to our bow and bounced onto our foredeck, making a terrific crash, and masses of debris were thrown high into the air."

"We saw it come down in the sea and fly off a swell onto the main deck," said Allan Shaw. "Luckily nobody was on the main deck at the time. A lot of the aircraft just fell back into the sea, but what stayed on deck was afire. Hot machine-gun bullets from the plane were all over the place. We put out the fire and threw it over the side."

Continued Mason, "A little later the chief officer telephoned from aft in great excitement to say that a Stuka had landed on the poop. Apparently this plane also fell into the sea and bounced onto our ship. I was rather tired, having been on the bridge all night, and I'm afraid I answered rather curtly, saying, 'Oh, that's nothing, we've had a Ju 88 on the foredeck for nearly half an hour.'

"The bombing attacks seemed to go on for ages, and we were constantly receiving orders by wireless to make forty-five-degree emergency alterations. It was quite impossible to execute these in the time given. These orders were also transmitted over the radio telephone, and the wireless orders were always several seconds behind, thus causing misunderstanding and confusion.

"The enemy planes were dropping parachutes with an object suspended which looked like a seven-pound tin of marmalade, and these fell at a considerable speed into the middle of the convoy as we were executing the emergency turns. It appeared to be impossible to avoid them, but I never saw any actually hit a ship."

With the *Ohio* finally back in the convoy, Admiral Burrough was keeping an eye on her. "The air attacks that were carried out by Stuka dive-bombers were of a most determined nature, being chiefly directed against *Ohio*, who suffered several near misses," he said.

"A large plane flew right over us at a height of about two thousand feet, banked slightly, and dropped a salvo of six bombs, three falling close to the port side and three close to the starboard side," said Mason. "The vessel seemed to be lifted right out of the water and shook violently from stem to stern. One near miss right under the forefoot opened up the port and starboard bow and buckled the plating, filling the forepeak tank and shaking the vessel violently forward to aft, amidst a deluge of water."

"We were standing around the end of the poop deck and the whole deck just heaved up in the air," said Allan Shaw. "Your feet left the deck and you were like shuddering, back down again. If it wasn't happening on one end of the ship, it was happening on the other. There was so many near misses we couldn't count them all."

The steam turbine engine room of the *Ohio* was the most beautiful place its chief engineer, James Wyld, had ever seen. After decades at sea in tubs, he had finally been rewarded with a masterpiece like the *Ohio*. He had restarted the engines just thirty minutes after the first torpedo hit, twelve long hours ago, and was dealing heroically with the 600-square-foot hole in the pump room. But the near misses kept knocking the engines out. Captain Mason counted six separate whacks.

Wyld's report:

Approx. 9.15 a.m. Violent explosion at stern of vessel, causing severe concussion.

Approx. 9.20 a.m. Engines stopped. Investigation showed that trip gear on Fuel Pump had disengaged owing to concussion.

Approx. 9.30 a.m. Full ahead.

Approx. 10.30 a.m. Violent explosion at stern of vessel, causing severe concussion.

Approx. 10.35 a.m. Engines stopped. Investigation showed that Circuit Breakers on both Fuel Pumps disabled.

Approx. 10.50 a.m. Engines started. Unable to maintain vacuum. Investigation showed no apparent cause, but most likely caused through fracture in Condensing system. Utmost available 3 inches of vacuum, and engine speed of 20 R.P.M. [4 knots].

The lighting system in the engineroom and stokehold were put out of commission by the severe concussions, so that all illumination in the engineroom, stokehold and auxiliary engineroom was hand lamps and emergency lighting, though some of the emergency lamps were also out of commission, so that work in the engine room was carried out under extreme difficulty and very trying circumstances.

Approx. 11.30 a.m. Port boiler gave out. Severe explosion inside furnace, and escape of steam, putting out fires.

Approx. 11.50 a.m. Starboard boiler gives out. Severe explosion inside furnace and escape of steam putting out fires.

Approx. 11.52 a.m. Informed Captain Mason no steam on boilers and no likelihood of getting under way again. All burner valves shut tight and manoeuvring valves shut.

Approx. noon. Engineroom staff left engineroom.

The *Ledbury* had come back to the side of *Ohio*—her massive, heaving, kerosene-leaking, ripped-up hull—about an hour before noon, while the tanker was struggling at 4 knots in fits and starts. Her funnels blew out alternating clouds of black and white smoke, from oil in water and water in fuel. Hill had offered to tow the tanker—some 30,000 tons of deadweight, half of it seawater—in the same spirit that had invited his fantasy of the little *Ledbury* ramming a battleship. He reckoned that together they could make 12 knots.

They were getting ready to toss a towline, when Hill suddenly told Mason he had to run.

Some baffling balzupped messages had been flying between the ships. Signals were relayed by sleepless men under fire, so words got lost and twisted in translation. Hill had earlier gotten a far-out signal that ordered the long-gone *Nigeria* to the Orkney Islands, or so he said; but it was from Burrough, ordering the *Ledbury* back to Gibraltar, and Hill had ignored it.

Burrough was largely out of touch on the *Ashanti* and was still unaware that the *Manchester* had been scuttled some eight hours earlier. As the convoy neared Malta, Vice-Admiral Sir Ralph Leatham played a bigger part in its direction, working with others from the damp control room in a well-lit limestone cave with a loft and vaulted ceilings.

Leatham sent Burrough a message suggesting that *Ledbury* stop to look for survivors from *Manchester*, on her way back to Gibraltar. Burrough never got the message but Hill did, and he seized the opportunity to save more men. He steamed at 24 knots to look for *Manchester* in the Gulf of Hammamet.

"We relaxed into two watches, to give the hands a chance to bath, eat and sleep," he said. "I went down to the engine room and boiler room, which I hated doing, and visited the wounded survivors in the sick-bay. Some of the poor chaps were terribly badly burned, just a mass of bandages from head to foot."

Hill was napping below when two torpedo bombers appeared in the glare of the afternoon sun; he awoke to the alarm and ran to the bridge to direct the guns through the loud hailer. He ordered the bigger guns to hold fire so the planes would come closer, and together the pom-pom and Oerlikons shot them down. They lay wrecked and sinking on the calm sea, a column of brown smoke rising from each.

"I was calling through the loudhailer, 'Bloody good shooting!' and the whole ship was cheering, slapping each other on the backs," said Hill. "Then there was a cry, 'Torpedo!' and there it was, coming straight for the after part of the ship. The second plane had dropped it while we were shooting down the first. Hard a-port was all I could do, and we waited, our hearts in our mouths, for the explosion."

The torpedo passed a few inches astern. The exhilaration was too great, the victory too sweet to go unrewarded.

"Coxswain, what are the regulations about splicing the mainbrace?" asked Hill, using an expression that dates to the days of Nelson, for tapping the rum.

"Don't know, sir. I think it's when the King visits the fleet or some special occasion."

"I think this is a special occasion, Coxswain. Pipe round the ship, 'Splice the Mainbrace, including all survivors. Stand fast the Hun.'

"The whole ship was cheering hard, and after this everything went with a swing," said Hill.

Forty-five minutes later, with the crew in what Hill called a "happy and piratical mood," the *Ledbury* sighted land. Hill thought that some of the *Manchester*'s crew might be ashore, captured by Arabs or Frenchmen.

With rum fueling their creative inspiration and courage, the *Ledbury*'s men came up with a plan: like a scene out of *Heart of Darkness*, they would charge the coast of Africa, shooting at the sky. The destroyer raced toward shore, with shells from the four-inch guns—Hill called them "Pip," "Squeak," and "Wilfred"—flying into the blue sky and exploding in the jungle.

"We arranged to send a landing party with rifles, revolvers and hand-grenades in the motorboat towing the whaler to form a rearguard or bridgehead, or some such military term. Anyhow, they were to knock off any Frenchmen or Arabs who tried to interfere, and to get the survivors off to the ship."

The men had scarcely slept or eaten, and some had washed down uppers with the rum. Hill was wearing a pair of trousers rolled up to the knees (his father had worn them fighting in India) with a faded, ragged blue shirt; "and the sailors were dressed as they pleased," he said, as they went off on their expedition to liberate the *Manchester*'s men from their bonds in Africa. All they needed were daggers between their teeth.

Hill harked back to his chicken-thieving night in port with the doctor—who didn't think much of this mission. He had watched it organize on deck before returning below to his injured survivors, "shaking his head and muttering about 'a lot of bomb-happy bloody lunatics,' " said Hill.

After a couple of hours trolling the coast and shouting into the bushes, they returned to the ship without having found anyone to rescue. The destroyers *Eskimo* and *Somali* had been there before *Ledbury* and picked up survivors in the water. Hundreds more had made it ashore and had already been marched off to be interred.

As the *Ledbury* steamed off, there was trouble: the shore station at Hammamet signaled, "Hoist your signal letters."

They still had the three-letter signal flying for "Splice the Mainbrace," so the yeoman lowered it and put an I flag on top of it. The I flag was the first letter in all Italian warship identifications.

The joke—"I splice the mainbrace"—was lost on the Frenchmen at Hammamet, who challenged the bomb-happy bloody lunatic pirates of *Ledbury* no more.

CHAPTER 39

Winston Churchill slept late that morning, in his luxurious suite in Stalin's villa. The weather was lovely, so he took a walk around the gardens. He fed some goldfish out of his hand and toured a bomb shelter ninety feet underground—"the latest and most luxurious type," he said, although he added that he had been more attracted by the goldfish.

As the morning sun was making the goldfish glisten at Churchill's fingertips in Moscow, it was rising over the Mediterranean, where the freighter *Dorset* found itself a stunning thirty miles ahead of the convoy. Her Captain Tuckett had cut a sharper corner than the others and steamed without zigzagging all night. When he looked around and realized that his ship was all alone in broad daylight, he got spooked. *Dorset* was now within range of the Spitfires from Malta, so he requested air cover; but Admiral Leatham thought the signal could only have come from the *Brisbane Star*, because no other ship was supposed to be on such an independent course.

"At 0730 as no fighter escort arrived, I decided to turn back and rejoin the convoy," reported Tuckett. He was a mere fifty miles from Malta.

"It was quiet, and there wasn't another ship in sight," said Ron Linton, a *Dorset* gunner. "Somebody said, 'Look, that's Malta!' I reckon we were about thirty miles away. It was so clear; if you know the Mediterranean air, you have unlimited visibility."

But Malta was just a mirage.

"Suddenly, the *Dorset* turned around, 180 degrees," said Linton, recalling the unfortunate U-turn from the couch of his home in Brixham on the Devon coast. "We said, 'What the hell's going on?' We figured somebody had ordered us back to join the remains of the convoy. Why that order wasn't disobeyed, I shall never, ever know.

"We steamed back and made it in two hours. We got in the tail-end Charlie position. That was where the dive-bombers came from, the stern, so they didn't have to face all the antiaircraft fire."

The Malta Spitfires had arrived to provide air cover and were chasing away Stukas. The *Dorset* promptly shot down a Spitfire.

"We opened fire with our Oerlikons," reported Captain Tuckett. "These guns were placed round the ship and were not fitted with any means of communication, hence it was impossible to establish any sort of control. The Officer on the bridge saw Spitfires overhead but was unable to communicate with the gun's crew, and within a few minutes one of our Spitfires was shot down."

"When friendly aircraft is mistaken for hostile, and fire is opened, I think it would reassure the gunners if the aircraft turned away from the ship," reported the *Dorset*'s liaison officer. "On one occasion, after a very heavy attack, 3 Spitfires flew over the ship and some of the gunners opened fire. The Spitfires continued over the ship in a steep bank and, although several officers, including myself, ordered 'Cease Fire,' we had the great misfortune to shoot one down."

If the Australian pilot had lived to tell the story from his side of the bullets, he might have said he simply couldn't bloody believe they wouldn't recognize a Spitfire on the tail of a Stuka.

"We were told if you see a plane, it's the enemy, so shoot it," said Linton. "Friendly planes would not fly over the convoy. We believed we had no air cover, so any planes that came over had to be enemy. So we just blazed away as soon as a plane appeared, and that was that."

The *Dorset* paid for her lack of discretion. Fourteen Stukas attacked her, and eleven near misses did her in. "I think probably one of the bombs had penetrated into number four hold," reported Captain Tuckett. "As the fire was un-get-at-able owing to other cargo being in the way, and was in close proximity to the high-octane petrol, also as the engines and pumps were out of commission, I decided to abandon ship immediately. This was done and the whole ship's company was taken on board H.M.S. *Bramham*."

"We'd seen what happened to the others, so the order didn't take long to abandon ship," said Linton. "It seemed like it happened about five minutes after we had made it back to the convoy. I was in the lifeboat with the second mate and the bosun. One of them said, 'If I could find the bastard that gave the order to come back, I'd shoot him.' "

"The *Dorset*'s crew abandoned ship at once and had no desire to go back to her," reported Captain Baines of the *Bramham*. He tried to tow the *Dorset* with his destroyer but stopped when a Ju 88 attacked. Later four more Junkers attacked, and a direct hit put *Dorset* afire. Along came the U-boat of none other than Kapitan Rosenbaum, who had been tailing the convoy for fifty-four hours after sinking the *Eagle*. Rosenbaum's log claims the *Dorset* for U-73, with a torpedo at 1848.

"Gradually a majestic looking ship went lower and lower, and by 1955 *Dorset* was no more," said Dickens. "What a pathetic sight that was. She went down with colors flying, the red duster had done its best. There now remained *Ohio*. By hook or by crook she must be brought in."

Spitfires and Beaufighters from Malta, four or five at a time, had taken over the defense of the convoy; they were flying on fuel that had come from Alexandria in minesweeping submarines. The merchant gunners now knew that friendly fighters were in the sky, but they were hopelessly jumpy and beyond exhausted, and had seen too much to take chances. And because the ships still had no VHF radio contact with the fighters, the pilots kept their distance; they were able to engage enemy bombers only before the bombers moved in on the ships to attack.

The morning sky was full of dogfights. Admiral Burrough said the Malta fighters "performed a magnificent job of work throughout the day," and Admiral Leatham called it "a very remarkable achievement." Stukas, Ju 88s, and Messerschmitts, as well as Thunderbolts and Flying Buffalos, fell flaming and smoking from the sky, nose-diving, spiraling, and floating gently into the water.

All the stars came out from Malta, both RAF and Fleet Air Arm pilots. The veteran Dickie Cork, a Hurricane ace who had flown off the *Indomitable*, shot down six enemy planes, either alone or with other fighters, and earned a Distinguished Service Order Medal to go with his Distinguished Flying Cross. Adrian Warburton, DSO, DFC (U.K.), DFC (U.S.), the baddest of the bad boys and rock-star reconnaissance pilot, a hero of Taranto, searched for enemy planes between Sardinia and Cape Bon, his fifth recon flight in two days—Alec Guinness would play a character like him in the movie *The Malta Story*, but it could have been James Dean.

There was also Group Captain Walter Churchill, DSO, DFC, who would be shot down and killed over Sicily two weeks later. And the inimitable Canadian George "Buzz" Beurling, DSO, DFC, DFM, Malta's top ace by a mile, with 26½ kills during his ten months there in 1942.

"We tussled it out with the Jerries and the Eyeties," said Beurling, who shot down a Ju 88 with two others, at 18,000 feet. "That's where we found our lonely Ju, cruising around all by himself."

"I yelled into the mike: 'Look out! Here I come!' and whizzed down, putting a two-second burst into the starboard engine as I went past. The engine fell off. The bomber burst into flames and down it went. Not one of its four-man crew got a chance to bale. We sure had let daylight into the Ju!"

A Beaufighter with an American pilot and Scottish observer was hit, and the men bailed out. The American was lost—the only pilot killed on the day, by the enemy—but the Scot floated in his Mae West until dark, when he was picked up by two Italians who had bailed out of their Stuka and inflated their backpack dinghy. The trio drifted together for sixty hours, sharing food, water, and pantomimed stories. A German flying boat picked them up, and the Scot, Jock McFarlane, was taken captive. Forty-five years after the war, he and Nicola Patela, the Italian gunner from the Stuka, met again in England.

As the *Ohio* was being bombed that morning, the destroyer *Penn* was skipping along in the sunny sea at 30 knots with the *Santa Elisa* survivors on board. They had to compete for deck space with the survivors from the *Empire Hope*. The injured were treated for burns with an ointment containing gentian violet, slathered on by the sick bay doctors, who sent their patients back out in the sun because there was nowhere else to put them. The decks were clogged with moaning masses of purple ooze.

"The ointment was pretty unsightly," said the *Ledbury*'s Dr. Nixon. "It made them blue. They looked like Indians that had been painted in their warpaint. Poor devils.

"There's a limit to how much your body can be burned and survive, and it was too much for some of them. But it's amazing, really, how much men can stand. Some of them must have been in terrible pain. All one could do was keep them full of morphine."

"The crew of the *Penn* did everything they could to try to make us comfortable," said Lonnie Dales, whose broken forearm was a slight injury compared to others'. "But when you have a couple hundred survivors on board a destroyer, there isn't much room to turn around. I don't think anybody who was picked up by the *Penn* got any rest, because there wasn't any place to rest, except to sit on the steel deck."

Like hurricane victims in a bread line, the survivors stood in a long, winding queue for a plate of porridge, a biscuit, and a cup of tea to wash it down. "All the whiskey, and the food and everything was left behind in the lifeboats," said Larsen. "We didn't get much to eat on the destroyer."

Follansbee suddenly remembered that he had also left behind his brief-case containing $2,000 of the ship's cash, which they would need for food if they ever got to Malta. Larsen changed the subject to the speed of the *Penn* before the others stuffed Follansbee into a depth-charge launcher and fired it.

"Thirty knots is really moving," he said. "It would take a pretty lucky shot to hit this baby."

"You spoke too soon," said Captain Thomson. "We're slowing down."

The *Penn* approached the *Ohio,* which was dead in the water.

"What in the hell?" said Larsen. "How did she get this far? I thought she was hit."

The tanker's paint was scorched and blistered, her superstructure scarred by shrapnel, her funnels riddled with bullet holes. There was a cavern in her foredeck, and daylight glared through the hole in her hull. "A dive-bomber had crashed on her foredeck, and we could make out the wreckage of the plane even from our distance," said Follansbee.

The *Penn* circled *Ohio* for two hours. "Suddenly the loudspeaker system blared forth a startling announcement," said Follansbee. " 'Survivors will stand by aft to assist with towlines.'

" 'Holy Christ!' I exclaimed. 'That doesn't mean . . .'

" 'Yes, it does,' replied Larsen. 'We're going to tow that tanker into Malta.' "

"We gave the *Penn* a 10-inch manila tow rope from forward," said Captain Mason, "but the attempt to tow from ahead was hopeless, as the ship just turned in circles, finally parting the tow rope. I signaled the *Penn* that the only hope of towing the *Ohio* was from alongside, or with one ahead and one astern to steady the ship."

"It seemed impossible under the present conditions that any progress could be made unless some other ships could assist in the tow," said Lieutenant Barton, the liaison officer. "It seemed that the ship was nothing more than a sitting target."

"We were still being bombed whilst stopped," reported Mason. "As it was useless the crew staying on board and risking life, I called up the destroyer to ask if he would take off my crew until more assistance was available, to which he agreed, and at 1400 HMS *Penn* came alongside and took off the whole crew."

The *Ohio* was abandoned.

CHAPTER 40

LAME DUCK OFF LINOSA

If Captain Mason hadn't met Captain Thomson at the skipper's meeting on the day Operation Pedestal left the Clyde, he met him now, in the wardroom of the *Penn*. Lord knows what they might have said to each other. They'd scarcely slept for three days. They were stubbled, scorched, smoky, and oily. Mason's hands were freshly bandaged—his first stop on the *Penn* had been sick bay, to have his own burns treated. Their ships had been bombed and torpedoed, and flames had swallowed large parts of them. The *Santa Elisa* had been obliterated, and the *Ohio* was slowly sinking. They'd heard the harrowing screams of men dying in the burning water. They'd been deafened by days and nights on the bridge with guns going off in their ears, and half choked from inhaling smoke and fumes from burning oil, kerosene, and aviation fuel. Eleven days earlier they'd been bragging about the power and grandeur of their new ships, and now they had abandoned them.

One of the *Penn*'s junior officers came into the wardroom. "Captain Swain would like to see you sir, if you don't mind," he said to Mason.

Swain had sent a message to Burrough at 1350 that said, "Can not tow by myself. She will not steer." He received a reply from Admiral Leatham at 1552 that said, "You must make every endeavor to tow."

But the *Penn* was only a 1,500-ton destroyer, and the *Ohio* was drawing thirty-seven feet and adding another foot every two hours. "The *Ohio* was damaged so badly where the torpedo hit," said Larsen. "She was still taking on water, and she had a big steel plate sticking out the port side, so you couldn't steer."

Mason and Swain agreed that struggling along at 3 knots while being dive-bombed and stalked by submarines, with the destroyer lashed to the target by the towline, wasn't a great call.

Swain told Mason that the towline hadn't exactly parted; at the arrival of a dive-bomber, the *Penn* had parted it. There was no sense in having his destroyer blown up too. If the tanker were hit in the wrong place, she would go up big. Her oil and kerosene were less explosive than aviation fuel, but there was six times as much of it.

And destroyers were meant to attack and shoot. The *Penn* couldn't do much shooting without movement. She could hardly protect the *Ohio* from ahead.

The ocean minesweeper *Rye* and two motor launches were on their way from Malta, and they could help tow. The *Penn* could screen the *Ohio* until those three ships got there. Mason hoped his men could get some rest on the *Penn* and reboard after dark, when the bombers would be done for the day.

The steel decks of the *Penn* were scorching under the afternoon sun, and nearly two hundred survivors from the *Santa Elisa* and *Empire Hope* were already sprawled or curled up in every corner and cranny, desperately seeking shade. There wasn't much water or space to sit down. Many of the men were barefoot, in ragged, oil-soaked clothes. Some were in pain. The air attacks continued. Each buzz from the sky stirred terror.

"The after gun's crew of HMS *Penn* behaved wonderfully," said Captain Williams of the *Empire Hope*, who would earn the DSC for his actions. "They were stripped to the waist and were fighting at their guns throughout the attacks. In between the attacks they had a quick cigarette and were laughing and joking among themselves, but immediately the alert was sounded, they were back at their gun, firing with grim determination."

There were three merchant masters on the *Penn*: Captain Williams, Captain Thomson, and Captain Mason. Allan Shaw was standing next to one of them—he won't say which one—and heard him say, "Why doesn't the old scow sink, so we can all get ashore." A crewman from the *Ohio* had to be restrained to keep from throwing this captain over the side.

Ensign Suppiger had a similar story. "One of the captains of one of the ships tried to go to the bridge of the *Penn* and tried to get Captain Swain to take them ashore," he said. "They all wanted to get off the ship. And Swain said, 'Get the hell off this bridge! My mission is to bring this tanker in, and that's what I'm going to do!' "

"The commanding officer of the destroyer had been ordered to bring the *Ohio* in at all costs, and he therefore intended to tow her in," explained Lonnie Dales.

"Captain Swain was a much respected man," said Able Seaman Andrew Forrest, the Leading Torpedo Operator on the *Penn*. "Hard but fair, with a good sense of humor."

It was a short sleep for the *Ohio*'s men. The minesweeper *Rye* and two motor launches arrived early, at 1740, and Captain Swain sent the *Ohio* crew back to their ship to be towed.

Mason:

6 P.M. APPROXIMATELY:

I called for a small number of volunteers to return to the Ohio to make the tow ropes fast, but the whole crew voluntarily returned. The towropes were made fast to HMS Penn and Rye, both towing ahead. Steering arms were disconnected and chain blocks connected to port and starboard sides of quadrant to assist steering.

Between 4 and 7 P.M., twenty-six Ju 88s and seven He III torpedo bombers had been sent out after the *Ohio*, as well as five Italian Stukas escorted by twenty-four MC.202 fighters. At least six of the lot were shot down, but some of them got through the fighters. Eight Junkers came at the *Ohio* from astern. A near miss caused more damage to the rudder, and a 500-pound bomb landed near the funnel.

6.30 P.M. APPROXIMATELY:

Enemy plane dropped bomb at the fore end of the boat deck, probably delayed action, which exploded on the boiler tops, blowing all the crew out on deck blinded and choked with asbestos lagging and powder. The engineroom boilers and after accommodation were wrecked. The engineroom ventilator and fallen debris fell on Bofors gunner P. Brown, causing numerous internal and external injuries.

Fearing such an event, Mason had ordered Wyld and the other engineers abovedecks. If they had been below, they would have been killed.

"I did not see any use in remaining on board the *Ohio* with the consequent risk to life when stopped, from continuous air attack," said Mason.

"As the attempt at towing was proving hopeless with the assistance available, I ordered the crew to the boats, from which they were divided between the motor launches and destroyers, and I lost touch with them."

When he lost touch with his crew, he lost command of his ship.

Captain Mason is careful not to use the word "abandon" in any of his reports. He only "ordered the crew to the boats." And in the ship's log, written after the fact, he distances himself more, saying only, "All crew took to the boats." If there was a distinction between taking to the boats and abandoning ship, the crew missed it.

"The Chief Engineer and Master both considered that the ship was now sinking and she was therefore abandoned, the crew getting away in the lifeboats," reported the liaison officer, Lieutenant Barton.

"About 6.45 the Captain gave orders to abandon ship," reported Chief Officer Gray to Eagle Oil and Shipping.

"Approx. 8.00 p.m. Order given to abandon ship," reported Chief Engineer Wyld. The clocks in the engine room were all smashed.

Reported Captain Swain, "There was an attack by about 8 Ju 88 at 1915, and the tanker was hit; her crew abandoned her."

"We slid down the lifelines into the lifeboats," said Allan Shaw. "I think there were only two of them. Under normal circumstances of abandoning ship, people would go to their assigned lifeboat stations, but in this case it wasn't as if the ship was sinking or on fire or anything, so we just assembled at the nearest boat. We were all sixes and sevens—all mixed up, haphazard. But there was no panic, just a leisurely walk to the lifeboats. The first boat went over to one of the motor launches, but the other motor launch came alongside the lifeboat I was in, so we really only used the lifeboat like a step between the two ships, and climbed up the ladder to the motor launch.

"Captain Mason was in my lifeboat. He was the last to leave. He did think about staying aboard, I think, but the skipper of the *Penn* shouted, 'You might as well come aboard, we've got hot cups of tea!' and things like that."

The motor launch ML 121 took the men over to the *Penn*. It's unlikely that Swain made Mason cocaptain in the towing operation. There was nothing more Mason could do. He was spent. He crashed in the wardroom, while the determined attempt to save the *Ohio* continued without him.

Larsen helped some men from the *Ohio* carry aboard the tanker's Bofors captain, British Army bombardier Peter Brown, who had been crushed by the blown-off engine room ventilator, which was about six feet square and located in the tight space between the funnel and the Bofors.

The Bofors was out of commission, but Larsen knew he could fix it. He could fix anything. And he could shoot it; he and his cadet Dales had been to the school. And now the Bofors needed a gun crew.

"On the destroyer they told me they got orders to bring the *Ohio* in at all costs," said Larsen. "Never mind what it costs, never mind anything, bring the *Ohio* in."

He figured he was the man to do it.

As the bomb was landing near the Bofors on the *Ohio*, blinding and choking a dozen or more men with asbestos, thousands of Maltese cheered from the battlements around Grand Harbour. The *Rochester Castle, Melbourne Star,* and *Port Chalmers* steamed into Valletta, escorted by minesweepers under a rainbow of Spitfires flying figure eights. They carried more than 30,000 tons of food, ammunition, and aviation fuel.

The *Rochester Castle* had been hit again, with three near misses sending hot bomb splinters through the hull and starting two fires in the fo'c'sle; men climbed into burning ammunition magazines and extinguished the fires while the master sped on. "The whole of my crew behaved magnificently throughout the many sustained and violent attacks," reported Captain Richard Wren, who was awarded the DSO.

The *Melbourne Star* was missing thirty-three men who had leaped overboard into the *Waimarama* fire, ten of them run down and killed by the flames they thought they were avoiding. "The fighting spirit of the ship was magnificent," reported the liaison officer. "Every single man on board made all effort throughout to fight off the enemy; the hotter the battle became, the stouter, if possible, were their efforts. I cannot say too much for the officers and crew."

The *Port Chalmers*, carrying Commodore Venables, had had a number of close calls, including a torpedo that passed under her hull and a parachute mine that tangled in her paravanes—"What shall we do with this?" Venables had signaled Admiral Burrough, who told him and guided *Port Chalmers* through the extraction. She was the only ship to arrive unscathed.

As the trio of merchantmen arrived in Grand Harbour, most of the warships of Force X steamed at full speed back to Gibraltar, led by the *Ashanti* with Burrough aboard. They steered clear of *Ohio*.

"Course was shaped to pass 12 miles South of Linosa Island in order that enemy aircraft shadowing *Ohio* might be avoided," reported Captain Onslow of *Ashanti*, as the 500-pound bomb was landing on top of the tanker's boilers.

"The lame duck off Linosa" is what Admiral Leatham called the *Ohio* in his report.

"Proud to have met you," Admiral Burrough signaled to the *Ohio* as he steamed off into the sunset.

As Captain Mason slept, his sinking ship inched toward Malta without him, dragged by the *Penn*. The minesweeper *Rye* was trying to steady *Penn*'s bows, connected by two minesweeping wires. The destroyer *Bramham* had returned from the coast, weaving back at 23 knots through splashing bombs, and now steamed in slow circles around the *Ohio*, screening against submarines and bombers.

"At 2024, twelve bombs fell within 20 yards of *Rye*, covering her with spray and splinters, but doing no effective damage," reported her Captain Pearson. "At 2042 H.M.S. *Penn* cast off *Rye*'s and her own tow, due to heavy bombing."

The survivors on the decks of the *Penn* had nowhere to hide from the dive-bombers. "There was no shelter," said Allan Shaw. "There was nowhere to sit down. All you could do was stand there."

When the dive-bombers came from the port side, the survivors ran around to the starboard side of the superstructure; and when the dive-bombers came from starboard, the survivors ran to port. The wardroom had been turned into a sick bay, but there wasn't enough room for the injured. Men with bandaged eyes were led by others, and men who couldn't walk were dragged. Larsen and Dales carried a survivor from the *Empire Hope* whose legs had been broken by shrapnel.

Between the attacks, Dales sat with the engineering officer of the *Penn*, on top of the engine room hatch. Born leader or not, Dales was eighteen and scared.

"The chief engineer smoked his pipe and talked to me," said Dales. "I think he sensed that I was uneasy, and he tried to make me feel better by telling me that the plating was so thin on the decks of a destroyer that a bomb would probably pass right through. He told me if you could hear the bombs, don't worry about them, because they're going to miss you. This is a matter of physics, sound going out in concentric circles. He said you'll never hear the bomb that kills you."

They were all scared. Men cowered in bunches and curled up in the fetal position in dark corners, covering their ears, closing their eyes, and waiting to die. Guns crashed over their heads, and near misses pounded the hull—they could feel the steel concussion in their bones. After a near miss comes a direct hit. Everyone knew that.

"During these attacks, the second mate Logan and I found a hiding place in the torpedo repair room just forward of the *Penn*'s torpedo tubes," said Follansbee. "The thin shell of the overhead gave us a feeling of security, even though we both knew that a bomb could crash through it like paper. Our nerves were almost completely shot now. Nothing to do but lie in the corner of a torpedo room and hold your ears to try to eliminate the whistle of the bombs and the deafening detonations of the guns."

I looked at Logan. The blood had run out of his face and his hands shook as if he had the palsy. I buried my face in my hands and started to pray, repeating a prayer I had learned in my youth at Sunday School.

I looked at my watch. Fourteen past eight. The general alarm bell rang.

I shivered and broke out in a cold sweat.

A gunner at a 20 millimeter Oerlikon pointed astern. "'Ere comes Jerry now! Two points on the starboard quarter!"

The towline was cut.

With all of her guns blazing, the Penn leapt forward again.

An inferno of flame and shattering noise. The whistle of bombs and the thud of near misses.

The Penn circled the tanker and threw everything she could throw up at the planes. Then at last the enemy had exhausted its ammunition and its supply of bombs and disappeared over the horizon in the direction of Sicily.

The towline was made fast again and we continued towards Malta at four knots.

Malta suddenly seemed very far away.

By 2052, the last bombing attack of the evening was beaten off. Rye took over the tow, with *Penn* serving as stern tug. By 2330 the ships were making about 4 knots, but at 0107 the *Ohio* suddenly sheered, and the hawsers to the *Rye* and the *Penn* were parted.

"*Bramham* then suggested that the destroyers should secure either side of the tanker," reported the *Penn*'s Captain Swain. "We did so."

Captain Eddie Baines of the *Bramham* was a young lieutenant who played by the book—he called Roger Hill a "ragamuffin," for the way he dressed at sea. But Baines wasn't afraid to step outside the box, and he was willing to do whatever needed to be done. "He was a very good seaman, mind you," said Reg Coaker, who worked alongside Baines on the bridge. "A bit of a ruffer, quite outspoken to those above him, but he knew what he was doing."

Captain Swain of the *Penn* saw the brilliance of Baines's plan, to lash the two destroyers to the sides of the tanker; that would not only keep her under control but help keep her afloat, because the three ships would be like a trimaran. "Towing the *Ohio* like that was our Captain Baines' idea, but Swain was senior to him, and he took over the idea," said Coaker.

"We went alongside of the tanker's starboard side with the *Penn*," said Fred Larsen, "while another destroyer [*Bramham*] managed to come alongside on the port side."

This was Larsen's chance to get back into action. He'd been in a passive position on the *Penn*—useless—and it didn't much suit him.

"After we tied up, some men from the *Penn* went aboard the *Ohio*," he said. "As soon as they went aboard, I went aboard, to see where the guns were. Because I figured if I can get some of these guns working, I can protect the *Ohio*."

He never said anything to anyone. He just climbed aboard. As if he owned the ship.

"I went aboard the *Ohio* because I was basically a tanker man. I had been bosun on the sister ship, the *Louisiana*. It was very familiar to me."

While men from the *Penn* were aboard the *Ohio* inspecting her damage and Larsen was seeing if he could fix her guns, Captain Swain grew uncomfortable with the fit of the tanker sandwich.

"In the darkness it was not possible to secure and fender the ship properly, and we could not see what under-water and above-water projections there might be," he said. "I was afraid of doing serious damage to the destroyers' hulls, so we cast off."

It was about 3 A.M. Larsen remained on the *Ohio*, watching the *Penn* steam off. The tanker was adrift and dead in the water, but it was where he wanted to be. There were maybe twenty men on the *Ohio*, including Allan Shaw. Lonnie Dales remained on the *Penn*—for now.

"Some of the crew of the *Ohio* was there," said Larsen, "and they were securing an air compressor. All the lifeboats were gone, all the floats, the flotation equipment was all gone out of the racks. Most of the guns were inoperative, the engine was disabled, the steering gear had been torpedoed, and the rudder couldn't operate any more. We tried to get it to work by hooking up emergency steering gear. I was down there in the steering gear room with flashlights, and we tried to hook up the emergency steering gear. I think it was already rigged. But it was not enough to be able to steer her without the propulsion of the ship's propeller.

"I examined the armament and found some of the Oerlikons in operating order. The five-inch gun on the stern was not repairable, as a Stuka had crashed on it and totally destroyed it. There was debris from the bomb that landed near the funnel all over the place, asbestos powder and junk. But the only thing wrong with the Bofors cannon was a shell jammed in the breech."

"The merchant navy's not like the Royal Navy, where you have to be told what to do," said Allan Shaw. "Everybody just knew what they had to do on the *Ohio*. It's a case of just getting on with the job. There wasn't anybody really in charge, it was just a crowd of men doing the job.

"I volunteered because it was my ship, and it was something to do. You couldn't sleep on the *Penn* anyhow, because there wasn't any room. You could doze off, but whenever someone walked past, they kicked your feet."

It's true there was no one in charge, but some men carry themselves with more authority than others. Larsen didn't need any props, but the .45-caliber pistol stuffed in his belt didn't hurt. This was the gun that had gotten away from Ensign Suppiger when he had dived out of his lifeboat in an attempt to get into another; the gun that Larsen had already used to restore order in the boat. The ensign had demanded its return when they were on the *Penn*, because it belonged to the U.S. Navy. But Suppy had lost it while abandoning ship in a hurry, if not a panic. Larsen told him he could have the gun back when he learned how to use it.

Back on the *Penn*, the men from the *Santa Elisa* noticed that Larsen was gone. There was only one place he could be.

"Several said that Larsen is so brave, having volunteered to man the tanker, etcetera," said Suppiger. "The truth of it is that he has a fanatical hatred for the Germans. His wife, who hasn't been seen for nearly three years, and his child whom he has never seen, are being held in German occupied Norway."

"The wording was to bring the *Ohio* in at all costs," said Larsen, making his motives sound simple. "The leader of Britain, Winston Churchill, sent a message to the Mediterranean Command that said to bring her in at all costs."

"The oiler remained stationary until 0420," reported Captain Pearson, "when *Rye* again took the whole in tow using a 10-inch manila found on board *Ohio*, which she secured to her sweep winch and led one part to a wire from *Ohio*'s forecastle and the other to *Penn*'s cable, *Penn* being still alongside *Rye*."

Larsen and Shaw worked elbow to elbow securing the towlines, but to each other they were just foreign accents in the darkness. "You hear voices, you think, 'He's a Yank, he's an Aussie,' you know," said Shaw. "We spent all night putting wires out and lashing them together, and when she broke them you just dumped 'em and put some more wires out."

The *Penn* came alongside *Ohio*. "I could hear the captain of the *Penn* on the loudspeaker saying he needed more volunteers," said Larsen. "So I called over to the destroyer for the officer in charge of the stern, and told him I wanted some volunteers to help me man the guns. I was in charge of the guns on the *Ohio*. In no time at all, there came my cadet from the *Santa Elisa*, his name was Francis Dales. He was one of the first volunteers that came with me. He stayed with me back aft."

It's almost eerie how similar the lives of Larsen and Dales were. Their pasts met on the crossroads between coincidence and fate. They were Gary Cooper and John Wayne, with moments when it was the other way around. They were two of a kind, separated only by experience and accents. It was as if God had created them as one, complementing halves to a diverse whole, making the warrior He needed to stop Hitler.

Dales and more volunteers were shuttled over to the tanker by ML 121, one of the two motor launches that had come from Malta.

"My biggest reason, I think, for volunteering with Mr. Larsen to go aboard the *Ohio*, was I felt much more comfortable having something to do than just sitting on the deck of the *Penn* and watching the bombs fall," said Dales, forgetting his broken arm. "At no time did I feel that I was being brave. I really didn't think about it that much.

"I had great respect and admiration for Mr. Larsen's ability and leadership. He realized that the *Ohio* had some fine antiaircraft guns, which we needed badly, so he asked for volunteers to man them.

"There was an ordinary seaman from the *Santa Elisa*, I don't recall his name, who went with us, and two of the Royal Marines, making a total of five to man the 40-millimeter Bofors on the *Ohio*."

"The British Army sergeant in charge of the gun crew and several of his men also came," added Larsen, referring to the men with Dales. "Also, several of the U.S. Navy gun crew came, barefooted and bandaged up and covered with purple burn ointment, so they looked kind of strange. They were burnt from the fire on the *Santa Elisa*. I sent them forward to the bridge to cover the Oerlikons on the bridge. All those guns needed was to have the barrels removed, because the barrels had been fired so much they were useless. So they take the old barrels out and put the new barrels in, so two of the guns that were up there could start firing.

"The other Oerlikons, one on each side of the poop deck, was also manned by volunteers. We changed the barrels on those guns too. They were a mix of people who had left the *Ohio* and other ships that had been torpedoed in the convoy, and they had been picked up by the destroyers."

Peter Forcanser, the junior engineer on the *Santa Elisa*, manned one of the forward Oerlikons. But Ensign Suppiger was not among the volunteers. "All through the night we attempted to tow the *Ohio* through submarine and E-boat infested waters," he said as he continued to find flaws. "That night I learned from one of the *Penn*'s officers that her submarine sound detection device was not operating."

"After we cleared the ventilator and all kinds of rubbish from the Bofors gun placement," said Larsen, "the British sergeant handed me a steel shield used for releasing the spring tension of the gun. I straddled the gun and pressed down with the shield and managed to get the bent and jammed shell free, and tossed it over the side. Then we changed the barrel. With the four Oerlikons we got working, we now had five guns going."

The minesweeper *Rye* managed to tow the *Ohio* for about forty-five minutes. But at 0503, the ten-inch manila hawser parted. All the volunteers were transferred back onto the *Penn,* which steamed off to a distance. Larsen, Dales, and Allan Shaw tried finally to get some sleep, in steel corners of the *Penn.* As dawn approached, the *Ohio* was abandoned and adrift once again.

TWO MEN, ONE WARRIOR

A s Larsen was climbing over the rails of the *Penn* onto the *Ohio*, Churchill was climbing the steps of the Kremlin to see Stalin. "The meeting was a flop," said Sir Charles Wilson. "It was as if yesterday's meeting, with its good humour and apparent agreement, had never taken place."

"We argued for about two hours, during which Stalin said a great many disagreeable things, especially about our being too much afraid of fighting the Germans," said Churchill. "I repulsed all his contentions squarely, but without taunts of any kind."

Tobruk had fallen while Churchill was with FDR at a critical and delicate time, trying to secure support for his cause; there was little that could have been worse than that. But now Operation Pedestal—*Malta*—was going down while he was with Stalin, needing to show strength to argue his case. He needed all he could find. Before he had left, he had cabled FDR, "I should greatly like to have your aid and countenance in my talks with Joe. . . . I have a somewhat raw job."

Churchill had requested daily reports on the progress of the convoy—he had insisted on them, to include just one subject: Pedestal. He sent the First Sea Lord, Dudley Pound, a "most secret" cipher telegram: "Shall be glad of early information about PEDESTAL if it can safely be sent to Moscow, but do not send to Teheran."

He wanted something positive to show Stalin as evidence of his commitment to his own crocodile theory. The *Ohio* should have been in Malta by now. Churchill desperately wanted to be able to lay the tanker on the table like an ace-high straight. But when he looked at his hand he saw more humiliation, this time with the Soviet premier, after the American president. He looked deeper, and saw an empty chair at his desk at 10 Downing Street. Tobruk, PQ17, Harpoon, Pedestal/Malta: consecutive disastrous defeats, in just sixty days. His leadership wouldn't be able to withstand it. "I was politically at my weakest, and without a gleam of military success," Churchill said about this period.

Although Stalin was fighting Hitler, Russia was not yet an ally of Britain and the United States. This conference needed to change that, and the pressure was on Churchill to make it happen. Stalin was not impressed by defensive efforts. He understood two things: strength and sacrifice. "His experience showed that troops must be blooded in battle," said Churchill. "If you did not blood your troops you had no idea what their value was."

Churchill had received his first report from Admiral Pound that morning, and it painted an ugly picture.

MOST IMMEDIATE

Personal for Prime Minister from First Sea Lord

A. 3 Ships have arrived and between them carry 6000 tons of flour, 2000 tons aviation spirit and a considerable amount of ammunition besides other stores.
B. There is a possibility that the oiler and one other ship may get in but chances are not good.

C, D, E, and F report the destruction to *Nigeria, Kenya, Indomitable,* and *Rodney.*

G. All forces appear to have played their part well, but the odds which were concentrated against them were too heavy.
H. TORCH appears all the more necessary.

Churchill's troops were bloodied, but he needed to show Stalin some power in the Mediterranean in order to seal the deal on Operation Torch. He still couldn't point to a Malta capable of attacking the belly of the crocodile. Stalin's open mind about Torch had snapped shut like a bear trap, and with no success from Operation Pedestal, Churchill couldn't pry it back open.

"I am downhearted and dispirited," said Churchill when he returned to his villa that night. "I have come a long way and made a great effort. Stalin lay back puffing at his pipe, with his eyes half closed, emitting streams of insults. He said the Russians were losing 10,000 men a day. He said that if the British Army had been fighting the Germans as much as the Red Army had, it would not be so frightened of them. He was most uncomplimentary to our Army. He said we had broken our word about a second Front."

The prime minister squeezed his lips together. "I can harden too," he said. "I'm not sure it wouldn't be better to leave Stalin to fight his own battles.

"Losing all these British ships," he muttered. "Only three of fourteen got through in the convoy."

Churchill was sorely tempted to walk out and go home. He stopped just short of doing so. "No, that is going too far, I think," he said.

Roger Hill raced all night in the *Ledbury* from the Gulf of Hammamet back to the *Ohio*. He found her adrift in the ghostly daybreak. There was no sign of the *Penn* or the *Bramham*. The tanker appeared to be totally and finally abandoned.

"I asked for volunteers from the survivors we had picked up from the fire, and all the men who were not injured or badly shocked said they would go onto the *Ohio*," he said. "I thought this was just about the bravest act I had ever known. If *Ohio* was hit she would go up even higher than the merchant ships they had been on, and they would not have a chance.

"I appointed the *Ledbury*'s gunner, Mr. Musham, Acting Master of the *Ohio*, and transferred him, along with the Merchant Navy volunteers, together with everyone we could spare from the action stations, to the tanker."

"Another entirely unofficial boarding party also went aboard," said the *Ledbury*'s first officer, Lieutenant Tony Hollings. "There were no members of the tanker's crew on board at the time. She was deserted. We can not have been alongside more than five minutes, but in that time we acquired one very large typewriter, a number of sound-powered telephones of which we were much in need, two Oerlikons and 12 magazines, besides a variety of smaller stuff, including a very fine megaphone with SS *Ohio* stamped on it."

"Some of the merchant sailors raided the *Ohio*'s larder to get food, because it was in short supply," said Dr. Nixon. "So they went onto *Ohio* and took as much food as they could."

"I've never told anyone this," said Charles Henry Walker, glancing over his shoulder at the queen on the wall in his room, "but when I first boarded the *Ohio*, I went looking for a bottle of whiskey. Me and George Preston—he was decorated too—we boarded the ship and went below, looking for whiskey. I was young and stupid."

Mr. Musham also went below and came up wearing Captain Mason's hat, to crown his appointment as acting master. It didn't help his shooting, said Walker. "We used to call him the Galway Bomber. If he'd see a seagull, he'd close up. He was like that."

Miles away on the *Penn*, Captain Mason awoke. He ate a quick breakfast and conducted a misty burial at sea for the Bofors gunner Peter Brown, who had died in the night.

"I was there," said Allan Shaw. "The destroyer's engines were stopped for a brief service. The body was sewn up in a canvas bag covered with the red ensign and weighted down with a shell from the five-inch gun. The *Ohio*'s bosun tipped the stretcher, and 'Gun' Brown slid off into the sea."

After the service, Larsen went to the bridge and asked Captain Swain to be returned to the *Ohio* with his gun crew. Swain agreed, and again the ML 121 carried the men over, where they found some of the *Ledbury* crew aboard the *Ohio*. Larsen and Dales went straight to the Bofors platform, where they were met with a rude shock.

"Musham had promptly dismantled their Oerlikons guns," said Don Allen, who was a radar operator working on the bridge of the *Ledbury*, recalling the day from his home near Dover in 2005. "We'd been firing our own Oerlikons so much that the barrels were worn out. So Musham said, 'We'll take the *Ohio*'s Oerlikons and put them on our ship.' So we changed the barrels over, and we gave them our worn-out guns."

He laughs fairly heartily.

"A lot of looting was going on. She *was* slowly sinking."

"There were some crew members from other ships going through the *Ohio*'s quarters," said Larsen. "One man showed up with the chief engineer's uniform jacket on. I questioned who he was, and someone said he was a messman. Another fellow brought some eggs. They were terribly spoiled, but I ate them just the same, not having had anything to eat for some time. I also found an undershirt on the *Ohio* that had belonged to one of the British soldiers, he didn't need it any more. I didn't have no shirt on when I went on the *Ohio*, so I was very happy to find that heavy undershirt."

Ledbury joined the minesweeper *Rye* in tow of the *Ohio* again. A six-inch manila rope was passed from the tanker's stern to the destroyer's midship oiling bollard, but, said Hill, "I put on too much weight and *Rye*'s tow parted."

Next they tried the *Rye* in tow of the *Ledbury*, with the *Ledbury* in tow of the *Ohio* off the tanker's port bow. The *Penn* lashed herself to the *Ohio*'s starboard side and acted as a drag to keep her straight. "This was fine and we were off," said Hill.

That morning, Regia Aeronautica sent its best Stuka pilots after the *Ohio*. All the two-man Ju 87 crews in Gruppo 102 were dive-bombing aces.

"At about 0800 the enemy air activity commenced and continued," said Mason. "I was now in one of the motor launches, about three cables astern of the *Ohio*."

"Suddenly they were over us, and peeled off one after the other to come screaming down," said Hill. "There were nine of them, and it was horrible to be secured each end, to the *Rye* and *Ohio*, moving at two knots and quite unable to dodge.

"About the fourth plane released his bomb a fraction late, and this seemed to be coming exactly at us on the bridge. 'Lie down!' I shouted, and the 500-pound bomb whistled over the top of the bridge and landed with a great splash alongside the focsle. I waited for the explosion and then the ship to go up, but nothing happened. The water came all over the ship, and then we saw a large widening circle of oil.

"We were saved by Axis thoroughness. They were dropping oil bombs, in order to set the tanker on fire."

The United States had invented napalm earlier that year but hadn't used it yet. The oil bombs near-missing the *Ohio* were a primitive Italian version of napalm.

The *Ohio*'s Bofors was mounted on a platform over the poop deck, behind the funnel. The dive-bombers always came from the rear, where a near miss would knock out the ship's screws. Larsen and Dales were dead center in the sights of the Stukas, which were diving from 10,000 feet.

"My back was badly damaged from these guys falling off the *Santa Elisa* on top of me, in the lifeboat," said Larsen. "And we were sitting in steel seats at the big Bofors, a Swedish rapid-fire cannon. It took one pointer and one trainer, and a man to spot for us. The gunnery sergeant was the one that spotted for Dales and me, and gave the orders when to shoot.

Dales' arm was broken and it was bandaged up in a splint, but he never complained about it. We also had two guys from the British gun crew there, who helped us loading this gun. We showed them how to handle the ammo, and it was a very simple operation."

The Swedish-made Bofors was the Volvo of antiaircraft guns. It was reliable under abuse and could whump out 120 rounds per minute. Churchill liked the Bofors and bought as many as Britain could afford. Arming the merchantmen had been his very first act when he was appointed First Lord of the Admiralty on the day war broke out in 1939. Britain awoke to its need for him, finally seeing the truth in his relentless warnings that Hitler must be stopped at all costs.

The Bofors weighed more than two tons, nearly as much as a Spitfire. The 900-pound barrel was 10 feet long, elevated and rotated by two men belted into seats on either side of its base. Larsen, the pointer, elevated and fired the gun, while Dales, the trainer, traversed it, using a rotating crank identical to the pointer's. Each looked through an open sight, like a spiderweb the size of a dinner plate, three feet in front of his eyes.

The shells were the size of Dales's splinted forearm, with pointed steel tips for penetration, fused to explode upon impact. There were four shells in a clip with a total weight of 20 pounds, and the breech held two clips; the first loader slammed in the clips that were handed to him by the second loader. The Bofors was an ammunition hog, but good loaders could keep up with the gun, even as it fired continuously.

Larsen's second loader scrambled down a ladder from the poop deck to the main deck and dipped buckets over the side to get water to cool the gun. He didn't have far to reach, as water was lapping at the *Ohio*'s gunwales.

"The Stukas came in droves," said Allan Shaw, "and with our guns back in action, we were busy running boxes of ammunition up to the Bofors. It seemed like they never stopped firing. There were a lot of very near misses, lifting the ship nearly out of the water sometimes. Larsen was up there at the Bofors over the poop deck."

"I remembered what one of the instructors said at the antiaircraft school in Newport," said Larsen. "He said when the planes were coming in, don't open fire until the bullets are splattering behind you. He also explained the new gunsights installed in our guns, with the system of aiming off-angle for high-speed targets."

"Some people seemed to have nerves of steel," said Follansbee. "While the rest of us were petrified with fear, Larsen was blazing away at the bombers with a 40mm Bofors. He had a personal grudge against the Germans. I remembered the pictures of his wife and son in his wallet."

"I fired at anything that came at us," said Larsen. "One time some planes came directly out of the sun, which they were not supposed to do. I fired at them, and shortly after, someone called out that they were friendly. I hope I did not hit them."

Musham was firing from an Oerlikon amidships, and he claimed a kill, but the bomber was more likely downed by Larsen from the Bofors—Musham didn't use up much ammunition, because his Oerlikon was not in a good position; and, said Captain Hill, "He complained that he was forced to use hosepipe firing instead of eyeshooting, as the sights had already been stolen by another gunner of HMS *Ledbury*."

"When the attack was over, we had four ships in a row," said Hill. "The *Ohio* with *Penn* alongside, heading more or less for Malta, then the *Ledbury* alongside *Penn*, heading the opposite direction, and *Rye* alongside *Ledbury*, also heading the wrong way. The chaos of wires, ropes and cables hanging down into the sea had to be seen to be believed.

"And of course, as we lay four ships stopped in a row, down came the next Stuka attack."

F red Larsen wasn't the type of man to say much about his own hero-
ics. He never mentioned the first Stuka he had shot down, and he
didn't claim a second one, either. Likewise, Lonnie Dales didn't initially report the E-boat he had blown up. But he had to, after he received a letter
from the commander of the merchant marine:

> Your valorous actions as well as those of Mr. Larsen's have come to the
> attention of the [Merchant Marine] Committee, and they are desirous of securing
> further information. It is noted in your report of the sinking of the Santa Elisa
> that you have refrained from mentioning any personal achievement. Your
> modesty is commendable, but in order that your deeds may be recognized and
> rewarded, it is desired that a complete factual account of all your actions and
> those of Mr. Larsen be submitted promptly.

Larsen and Dales were still on the *Ohio* when the *Rye* broke the tow yet
again. The *Bramham* came along the port side of the *Ohio,* with the *Penn* to
starboard, and the pontoonlike destroyers dragged the unwieldy tanker
along at 2 knots. When she swung off course, the *Ledbury* put her bows
against her and pushed her back in line.

"A great deal of time we were under attack," said Larsen. "We were
being attacked a lot. And every time we were attacked, the captain of the
Penn, he'd come on the loudspeaker and say, 'Volunteers on the *Ohio,* stand
by! We'll come back after the attack!' They'd back off a little bit, slacken
the line, then take off, and bust all the lines. They'd circle us and gave us
protection, and we fired the best we could to try to keep the Germans and
Italian bombers away from us."

When the bombers came in and the *Penn* raced away, she played "Chattanooga Choo-Choo" over her loudspeakers. It was the only American recording on the ship, a current hit, and they played it again and again during the dive-bomb attacks, so loudly you couldn't hear the whistle of the bombs, said Follansbee.

Another crash from above. Then the sound of music. Music? I must be going crazy. Crazy as a bed bug. I listened. It was music, all right.

"The only other people on board *Ohio* were the crew members of the *Ledbury* or the *Penn*, who were constantly trying to adjust the cables holding the ships together, and help fight fires when they broke out," said Dales. "But they immediately returned to their ships under an attack, and we were cut loose, so it left just the five of us at the Bofors on board."

"By now there was mostly dive-bombers comin' in," said Larsen, "and they were comin' in very fast, especially in the morning and late in afternoon. As the sun was setting or rising you could almost count on them comin' in. You could hear them quite a distance away, so we knew they were comin'."

The Axis was throwing everything it had at the tanker. The near misses from oil bombs showered her decks with splashes like fat flaming raindrops, and now the Stukas carried blockbusters. There were only five Stukas this time, but Regia Aeronautica was determined to get through the screen of Spitfires, so twenty-three of the fastest fighters, Macchi 202s with the hot Daimler-Benz engines, escorted the bombers.

Each Stuka carried one 500-kilogram bomb under its belly, like the bomb that had devastated *Illustrious*, even with its armored deck. Below the *Ohio*'s thin decks there were thirty-three honeycombed tanks containing 12,900 tons of fuel oil, kerosene, and diesel, minus the kerosene that had already burned or been lost.

Spitfires shot down a Macchi fighter, as well as one of the Stukas.

"As we arrived I saw one Ju 87 diving and went for it, overtook it rapidly, opened fire at 300 yards and broke away at 30 yards," said Squadron Leader Tony Lovell. "I saw strikes all over the engine and fuselage. White smoke poured from both sides. He lost height, smoke stopped, and he did a steep turn to port and flew west losing height. I turned back towards the convoy and saw the Ju 87 crash into the sea."

The destroyers saw the dive-bombers approaching and cut the tanker loose. Two Stukas broke through the Spitfires, and one of them dived at the *Ohio*. From his seat at the Bofors, Dales cranked like crazy, oblivious to the pain in his forearm from the cracked bone, and the big barrel moved sideways. Larsen cranked from the pointer's seat, blind to the pain in his fractured back. The gun climbed toward the Stuka in a diagonal sweep as the two men meshed the gears of their souls for the shot that could win or lose it all. Larsen was trying to save his family; Dales was just doing what he'd been raised to do. The Stuka screamed down at the Bofors as the loader pumped in 20-pound clips and Larsen fired bursts from the cannon at two rounds per second.

Some people seemed to have nerves of steel, Follansbee had said. *While the rest of us were petrified with fear, Larsen was blazing away at the bombers with a 40mm Bofors. He had a personal grudge against the Germans.*

Larsen missed.

The 500-kilogram bomb landed hard in the flat wake of the *Ohio,* dead astern, tossing her forward on the wave of the huge concussion. Her twenty-foot bronze screw was twisted by the underwater blast, and her jammed rudder was blown all the way off. The sea rushed in through a new gaping hole in her stern.

But Larsen's barrage from the Bofors had caused the pilot to release the bomb just early enough to prevent what otherwise would have been a direct hit on the poop deck, or on the main deck over the pump room, where her back was ready to snap. Had the big bomb landed on the *Ohio,* she would have sunk on the spot.

As the 500-kilo bomb landed in the wake of the *Ohio,* Captain Mason watched from the motor launch, about 600 yards astern.

"The *Ohio* began to settle by the stern, as the engine-room flooded," he said. "I watched the ship settling aft, and sent a message to the *Penn* for the chief engineer and chief officer to assist as much as possible with the air compressor gear, assuming these officers, and most of the crew of the *Ohio,* were now on board. The reply from the *Penn* was 'Come aboard.' "

Aboard the *Penn,* Mason discovered that all his officers and engineers were in Malta: more than thirty men, including seven navy and twelve army gunners. When the *Ohio* had first been abandoned, they had all boarded the second motor launch, ML 168. Its engines had been damaged by a near miss during the dusk attacks, so in the middle of the night Captain Swain had sent ML 168 sputtering into Malta—"much to the surprise and regret of these men," said Mason, "leaving only two firemen, two greasers and two other seamen belonging to the *Ohio*.

"I therefore boarded the *Ohio* and made a complete examination of the vessel with the assistance of these men."

By now anyone could climb over the railings from the *Penn* or *Bramham*; their decks were nearly even, with the *Ohio* having less than three feet of freeboard. As Captain Mason was belowdecks, inspecting his ship with the chief engineer of the *Penn* and trying to figure out how to keep her afloat, the unofficial acting master of the *Ohio*, gunner Musham, appeared on the bridge wearing Mason's cap and uniform jacket.

"In these desperate circumstances this was an amazing touch of humor to which all responded with a great cheer," said Robin Owen, a midshipman on the *Ledbury*. "Later he continued his temporary authority by opening the *Ohio*'s duty free locker and sending around refreshments."

Some sailors found paper party hats waiting for an occasion, and this seemed like it: Friday Happy Hour, after a long, hard week. Captain Swain cranked up "Chattanooga Choo-Choo" again and flipped the 45 over to the other side, "Elmer's Tune."

"My mate Paddy, an Irish AB [able-bodied seaman], a real character, enjoyed a tipple from a rum bottle, sitting on the boat deck," said Allan Shaw. "He said, 'Allan, I'm too drunk to stand. Do me a favor. Throw me over the side.' I told him I was too tired. He offered me a tot, to carry me over. But the bottle had only a thimbleful left."

Larsen and Dales stayed at the Bofors at the stern of the long ship, as far from the party as they could be, watching and waiting for enemy aircraft.

Over on the *Bramham*, more volunteers for the *Ohio*'s guns were being re-cruited. "The coxswain lined us up," said Ron Linton. "He asked, 'Any of you guys MSGs [merchant seaman gunners]?' Some hands went up. He said, 'Right. Over there on that tanker, you've just volunteered to go.'

"First they gave us a feed, and half of the 'volunteers' disappeared by the time he came back. I would have too, but I said, 'What the hell, I've got nothing to lose.' With the *Ohio*, at least we knew we were going to Malta. Stay on the destroyer, and we could end up in Greece or somewhere. You never know with a destroyer."

Linton manned the Oerlikon on the port bridge. "But we were up there only if needed," he said. "Captain Mason came along and said, 'Come, I'll show you where to get something to eat,' and took us to his private pantry.

Captain Mason seemed to be the only one there. He came down to us, to show us the way back up. He said, 'You better stick close by, with me.'

"We stayed on the bridge for the clean air. Another thing was, she smelled. Boy, she stunk when we first got on, but the further we went, it lessened. Because she really stunk. The smell of that stuff. There's nothing worse than the smell of burned oil.

"The one thing I can remember is I had a bloody good sleep. We found some very comfortable bunks. I think we slept solid for about six hours. We weren't just sleeping, we were dead."

Mason continued his inspection with the half-dozen greasers, firemen, and seamen, and with the *Penn*'s engineering officer, Lieutenant Commander John Sweall, who had begun reducing the flooding with pumps from the *Penn* before Mason got there.

"We sounded all the empty spaces and tested the air compressor gear," said Mason. "The empty tanks, numbers ten and eleven, were still intact and dry, but the kerosene was overflowing from the port tanks and the water was flowing in through the hole in the ship's side, forcing the kerosene up with it, as all the lids were buckled. And nothing could be done with the compressed air, because all the lines were broken. HMS *Penn* was endeavoring to keep the engine room pumped dry, but the water was gaining six inches per hour.

"From this examination I came to the conclusion that the ship could still be saved, and would last at least another twelve hours, providing she did not break in half at the main deck where she was buckling, in which case the stern half would probably have fallen off, leaving the forward section still afloat and salvable. I passed this advice to the senior naval officer and also told him that if the after end did part, towing operations would be easier and we should still get 75 percent of the cargo to its destination. This conclusion I continued to impress on all those interested, insisting that it could and must be done."

"The afternoon dragged slowly on, matched only by the progress of the tanker, as *Penn* and *Bramham*, constantly changing their engine revolutions, carried her along," said Roger Hill. "We longed and longed for darkness when the enemy air attacks must cease.

"By evening we were tense and ready for the expected synchronized attack, and I felt if we had any more bombs around, I would lie down on the deck and burst into tears."

CHAPTER 45

THE TEETERING TIRADE

A s sailors wearing party hats were having rum and biscuits on the shattered and scorched decks of the *Ohio*, the Maltese were dancing on the edge of the cliffs over Grand Harbour. The *Brisbane Star* brought another 10,000 tons of supplies into Valletta under a halo of six Beaufighters and four Spitfires, with a jagged expanse of sunlight flashing through the huge holes in her bows.

After hugging the coast of Tunisia, Captain Riley had brought her in on his wits. An exchange of signals with the Vichy station at Hammamet had gone like this:

HAMMAMET: You should hoist your signal letters.

BRISBANE STAR: Please excuse me.

HAMMAMET: You should anchor.

BRISBANE STAR: My anchors are fouled, I cannot anchor.

HAMMAMET: You appear to be dragging your bow and stern anchors!

BRISBANE STAR: I have no stern anchor.

HAMMAMET: You should anchor IMMEDIATELY.

BRISBANE STAR: I cannot anchor, my anchors are fouled.

HAMMAMET: Do you require salvage or rescue?

BRISBANE STAR: No.

HAMMAMET: It is not safe to go too fast.

He had turned his wounded ship east at dusk, to "strike across to Malta during the night, and hope that the enemy would be too busy with the convoy to take much notice of us," said the liaison officer.

A French patrol boat sped after the *Brisbane Star* and fired a warning shot that landed thirty feet from the broken and flooded bow. Two French officers came aboard, and Captain Riley invited them below to his cabin, where he stashed his Irish whiskey. Well into the balmy black night, the Frenchmen emerged smiling and wobbling. They shook the captain's hand, wished him "Bon voyage," boarded their boat, and steamed off.

There were no more dive-bombers that day, after Larsen and Dales fought off the final Stuka. Patrols of sixteen Spitfires were maintained continuously over the *Ohio* until dusk, and that pretty much ended it. That, and the Axis' belief that victory was theirs.

"The fact that an extraordinary success has been achieved is beyond doubt," said Radio Berlin.

"Britain has been forced to recognize our magnificent victory," said Mussolini. "Their ships now lie at the bottom of the sea."

"Mussolini is moderately satisfied with the results, because the guns of the Navy were not engaged in the battle," said Ciano.

But the *Ohio* was still floating. Her honeycombed holds limited the flooding from the 500-kilo bomb that had hammered a hole in her stern, and the loss of her jammed rudder actually improved her handling. The southeastern cliffs of Malta came into hazy view, their bleached limestone burned gold by the setting sun, and a cheer went up from the crowded decks of the *Penn.*

"Later in the night," said Roger Hill, "we were entertained by a circus act."

The ancient paddle-tugboat *Robust* arrived from Malta and began towing the *Ohio* by herself; her skipper, J. P. Pilditch, was the acting king's harbormaster, a position that put him in command. When he tried to increase the speed of the tow, the *Ohio* sheered to port and her nose turned starboard, whipping the tugboat into the blackness and smashing her into the *Penn,* which was standing by.

At that moment there was a dinner party in the wardroom of the *Penn* for some of the surviving officers. Captain Thomson and Captain Mason were there, along with Jack Follansbee and Ensign Suppiger. They were eating well.

> Supper consisted of vegetable soup and roast beef and baked potatoes and canned peas. I asked Logan to pass the bread to me. Taking a piece, I broke it in two and began to spread it with plum jam.

My knife froze. A loud crash came from the starboard side of the lounge. The steel plates buckled inward. The couch toppled over, spilling the lifejackets out on the deck. Two armchairs fell over on their sides. The sound of running feet and shouts came from above.

At the supper table, the men stared dazedly across the table at each other, their forks poised in mid-air. Then with calm deliberation we placed our utensils on the table and laid our napkins beside our plates. One by one we rose, as if in a dreamworld, and filed out the door leading up to the main deck.

The stern quadrant of the *Robust* had burst into the wardroom, punching a huge gash in the *Penn*'s hull above the waterline. Suppiger said it was twenty-five feet long. Captain Swain had been sitting at the head of the table and the full ferocity of his Irish temper flared into the black hole in the bulkhead, over to the churning paddle of the *Robust*. The sorry tugboat ran back to Malta with its jammed rudder like a tail between its legs. Her master, Pilditch, had previously been commodore of Operation Harpoon, a larger disaster.

Mr. Musham and most of the other volunteers had returned to the destroyers to sleep. There were only a few men left on the *Ohio* as it was dragged toward Malta in the moonless night.

Soft singing from the Bofors platform drifted over the ship's quiet wake. Larsen was trying to keep himself from falling asleep. First he sang, then he hummed, then he whistled a song popular in Europe: "Can You Whistle, Johanna?"

"Of course, we were very tired," said Larsen. "To cheer them up and to cheer myself up, I hummed a tune, I sang this little song that I knew, and they didn't know what I was singing. They laughed at me. I'd fall asleep singing, and I'd wake up and suddenly I'd say, 'Are they coming?' and they'd say, 'No, there's no bombers here,' and I'd doze off again. I was sitting in this gun seat on the Bofors, and they had a big kick out of me, the way I was falling asleep and waking up and talking and singing. That's the way it went on for the night."

"He was probably singing it in Norwegian," said Minda.

Fred liked to sing to Minda, who rode on the crossbar of his bicycle, before she could afford her own. They used to ride together into the country around Farsund for picnics.

"I remember when we were dating, he was singing to me, 'You Are My Sunshine.' That's the first song I learned in English. He had another one he would sing to me, 'I will work and slave all day through, so I can come back to you,' or something like that."

As Larsen was singing to stay awake, Captain Mason was roaming around his former ship in the dark. He ran into Ramsay Brown, master of the sunken *Deucalion*.

"I was having a look round the *Ohio* during the night when I met a man on the after deck who asked me who I was," reported Brown. "I told him, and then asked who he was. He replied, 'I am the Captain of the ship,' so I returned to the *Bramham*, leaving the *Ohio* in the hands of her own captain."

Reg Coaker was standing midwatch on the bridge of the *Bramham*. "I can only tell you what I saw," he said. "In the early hours, could be about three in the morning, of the Saturday morning, in the dark, I was on our Oerlikons deck, which was a little bit below the bridge of the *Ohio*, because we were on the port side of the *Ohio*, covering the hole in her side. I'm on the starboard side of the Oerlikons deck, and this figure appeared at the end of the bridge.

" 'Hey: over there: you!'

"It was Mason. He was shouting to our Captain Baines, who was wrapped around a binnacle and just about flaked out. Mason shouted, 'You've taken my ship from me! I want my command, and I want my ship back!' This sort of thing. And to me, he appeared as if he'd hit the bottle, and quite frankly you can't blame him, can you? I mean, what would you have done? Because here's his ship dead in the water, he can't do anything else whatever. His command is gone. Absolute dead in the water.

"His behavior led me to believe he was absolutely fed up. Mason's function was done. He'd done a good job getting the tanker to where it was—it's a credit to the way that ship was built, it took an awful lot of punishment. He got his ship that far. But there it was, it was taken from him. There was just his shouting in the night.

"Captain Baines could not suffer fools at all; four-letter words streaming down from our bridge were quite common from him. But there was no answer from our bridge. Absolute silence. Nobody answered Captain Mason.

"Having carried out his little tirade against our bridge, he just teetered away into the darkness and was gone."

CHAPTER 46

NINE DOWN, FOUR HOME, ONE TO GO

Ａs Fred Larsen's song to Minda was drifting over the wake of the *Ohio* and Dudley Mason was teetering away into the darkness, Winston Churchill was being tucked into bed in Stalin's villa. It had been another bad day.

Another "MOST IMMEDIATE" cable from First Sea Lord Pound had arrived, confirming that nine freighters had been sunk, after just three had made it to Malta.

1. The other ship, by determination and cunning, has arrived, making the total 4.
2. Determined efforts under heavy attack are being made to tow oiler [*Ohio*] in. She should be approximately 40 miles from MALTA at 1600 today.

The pins and needles were relentless. Nothing could be resolved: not Malta's survival, not control of the Mediterranean, not beating back Rommel, not Russia's support, not Churchill's own future. It was all slowly sinking, like the *Ohio*. Everything rode on the tanker.

Churchill replied to Pound, "Many thanks for your Tulip 132 [the message]. Prolongation of life of Malta was worth the heavy cost." His words were unconvincing.

"I am sure that all played their part to the utmost," he continued. "I assume you will let me have as soon as possible a fuller account of the operation and of the losses suffered by both sides, also the exact supply situation in Malta, assuming the ships which got in are successfully unloaded."

That night there was a banquet at the Kremlin, with about forty people eating and drinking, as the officers on the *Penn* were eating and drinking until the tugboat crashed their party. General Brooke called the evening at the Kremlin a complete orgy. "From the beginning, vodka flowed freely and one's glass kept being filled up," he said. "The end came at last and I rose from the table thanking Heaven that I still had full control of my legs and my thoughts!"

"Silly tales have been told of how these Soviet dinners became drinking-bouts," scoffed Churchill. "There is no truth whatever in this."

Vodka or not, Churchill was still smoldering like the *Ohio*.

"Stalin didn't want to talk to me," he told Sir Charles Wilson. "I closed the proceeding down. I had had enough. The food was filthy. I ought not to have come."

"The P.M. got up, pacing the room in nothing but his silk undervest, mumbling to himself," said Sir Charles.

"He said he wouldn't go near Stalin again. He had deliberately said 'Goodbye' and not 'Good night.' If there was any fresh move, Stalin must make it. He wouldn't. He got into bed, put on his black eye-shade and settled his head in the pillow. I turned out the light. When I left the room I looked at my watch. It was a quarter to four."

Churchill fell asleep, not knowing whether the *Ohio* was in Grand Harbour or at the bottom of the Mediterranean. The future was as dark as his vision under the eyeshade.

CHAPTER 47

GRAND HARBOUR

T here was a strange quiet in the ships, except for the gentle lapping of the sea and the singing of the straining hawsers," said Reg Coaker. "The crew and survivors were now huddling in groups, their heads down on their chests. I was at a port Oerlikons and fell asleep on an ammo locker, taking turns to catnap with another. Suddenly we were awoken by the searchlights from the cliffs of Malta."

Radar on Malta had detected what appeared to be a sub on the surface, tailing the tanker, and the searchlights were trying to find it. Supermarina had sent out a message to all the subs in the area: "Surface and proceed at once, concentrating greatest maximum strength to search for damaged enemy units." The submarine *Asteria* was specifically signaled: "At 35 miles, 205 degrees from Gozo lighthouse, proceeding toward Malta, a tanker under tow. Search and attack with utmost resolution."

But it wasn't *Asteria* or any other sub; it was just another ghost on the radar screens.

"The reaction of Captain Baines was instant, loud, and clear," said Coaker. "He could be heard in the still night air cursing the stupidity of the searchlight operators. We knew the enemy was lurking somewhere. The last thing we wanted was to be lit up as a sitting target."

Then the minesweeper *Hebe* got jumpy and fired at "movement" toward shore. The shell landed near Fort Benghisa, where soldiers thought it had come from an attacking submarine. They were poised to reply with their nine-inch guns but were stopped by frantic signals.

The shore guns opened up just before dawn, shooting at more shadows. They feared an attack on the tanker by E-boats and thought the blips they saw on their screens might be that attack. Shells passed over the *Ohio* with a *wheee*, said Roger Hill. "The shots seemed to be falling astern, but what was said on our bridge turned the air blue."

But there were no E-boats in the area, either. Two biplanes with depth charges—one Albacore and one Swordfish—had been patrolling throughout the night, along with four reconnaissance bombers: three Baltimores and a Wellington. With the Beaufighters and Spitfires that were ready to resume flying over the *Ohio* at daybreak, the RAF had her covered.

Having dodged the searchlights and friendly fire, the *Ohio* now began its most difficult navigational challenge, through the maze of minefields that protected the harbor. Her gunwales were only eighteen inches from the sea, and swells sloshed onto her main deck amidships as the jagged gash in the steel screeched and moaned. Only the grace of God and the fat welds joining the *Ohio*'s bulkheads kept her from snapping in two. She was a behemoth bloated with seawater and nearly impossible to turn. But she had to be twisted around Zonkor Point, the eastern tip of Malta, and guided northwest into the channel.

It was a final job for the *Ledbury*. "Took oiler in tow in order to get her straight for the channel," reported Captain Hill. "With the help of a Motor Launch pushing my bows, I managed to turn her 140 degrees in three hauls, turning her about 45 degrees each time."

The channel had been swept clear of mines for the convoy's arrival, but the path between the starboard mines and coastal rocks was narrow, and an offshore wind had picked up. It blew against the port beam of the tanker and swung her stern into the fringe of the minefield. Larsen and Dales sat there and watched, poised to run if they saw the black horns of a mine poking out of the water in the gloom of first light. Although Larsen probably would have tried to shoot it with his .45.

"The *Ohio* made several determined attempts to blow herself up on our minefields," said Hill. "She would start turning, and the destroyers alongside would pull her up; we would push her round, and off we went again.

"At daylight I walked round the upper deck. The sleeping bodies of the sailors lay sprawled and hunched in their duffel coats. Their friends' legs or backs made pillows. Through the growth of beard and sunburn, their faces looked so young and peaceful. I felt a great surge of affection and pride for what they had achieved, and deep gratitude that we had come through it all without a casualty."

The tugboat *Robust* came out from Malta again, bringing more tugs to help lug the *Ohio* into Grand Harbour. Spitfires began flying figure eights over the tanker, in case the Luftwaffe was thinking of bombing her at the mouth of the harbor.

"Considering position and extreme value of cargo, weakness of enemy's air attacks and a complete absence of surface or submarine attack is remarkable," reported the Admiralty. "Seems probable Axis air forces had suffered such heavy casualties unable to stage or unprepared to risk full-scale attack."

"I think myself that we had enough, so obviously the Jerries had enough too," said Ron Linton.

"If only I were a writer instead of a naval officer writing up a journal 20 years later for his family, how I would like to be able to describe the scene and my feelings," wrote Hill. "The great ramparts and battlements of Malta, built against the siege by the Turks, were lined and black with people. Thousands and thousands of cheering people—on the ramparts, on the foreshore, on the rooftops, the roads, paths, and at every window. Everywhere bands were playing; bands of all the services and Maltese bands. The uneven thumps of the drums and crash of cymbals echoed back from the great walls.

"It was Saturday morning. Years and years ago we had left Gibraltar, and that was last Sunday morning. It did not make sense, but all this had taken only a week."

"When we came in the entrance of Valletta Harbor, we were saluted like a returning victorious navy ship," said Larsen. "Crowds of people were shouting from the breakwater. The people turned to, they were down on the points with bands and ovations and all kinds of singin' and shoutin' and screamin' and playin' bands, and it was quite a thrill comin' in. I was sittin' up on top of that gun, with some of the volunteers on the gun. There was no more attacks because by now the Spitfires were up there, and they were shootin' down anything that was comin' around. Then the tugboats from Malta came out and they took over the tow of the *Ohio* and they drove her to the dock. Her decks were practically awash by now. We were greeted and saluted as a full navy ship. It was a proud moment."

"Thousands of people were standing on the batteries cheering and singing," said Dales. "There were military bands playing, and they were playing 'The Star-Spangled Banner' for us."

"The hurrahs went up again and again from the cliffs," said Follansbee. "Children on small boats shouted, 'Convoy! Convoy!' "

"When we came around that corner, we were assailed with a wave of sound that I've not heard since Stanley Mathews won the footballer cup in Wembley Stadium," said Ron Linton. "I've not heard anything since, to equal the cheer that the whole of the people of Malta put up. I think everybody that was able to walk and some that couldn't walk was there, on the cliffs."

In his home on the Devon coast, Linton pulls a photograph from a folder, a shot taken from the battlements down at the *Ohio*. He puts his finger on the bridge.

"That white cap there is Captain Mason," he says. "And that one is me. I was talking to him, all the way to Valletta. Up and down from the wheelhouse. He was just there, he was a gentleman he was, kept saying, 'I appreciate you guys coming on.'

"He just stood there. He was totally imperturbable. He was a man you're only honored to meet every so often. There aren't a lot of his type about. He just stood there, and that was it. I know he heaved a few great sighs of relief, but if he ever went wild I certainly never noticed it.

"He was still there when we got off, saying, 'Thanks very much for coming on.' "

"I'll never ever forget the proud feeling entering Valletta and seeing the crowds of people," said Allan Shaw. "A very humbling experience. Lump in your throat. I think everybody felt the same, nobody was talking. Complete silence. We were pleased to be in, but you couldn't understand all the crowds up there."

The Maltese understood. It was August 15, the Feast of Santa Marija.

"Today is the Feast of St Mary, the celebration of the Assumption of Our Lady into heaven," said *The Times* of Malta that morning. "It will be celebrated without any of the traditional manifestations of rejoicing, which accompanied 'Santa Marija,' Patroness of Malta, in the pre-war days. 'Santa Marija' is a day of thanksgiving to God through Our Lady for the mercies received, and of prayer for added strength to resist the material powers of evil, and also a day of rededication to the cause which we are convinced is sacred and just."

But the newspaper didn't know the *Ohio* was coming. When the tanker arrived, the paper rewrote the part about not celebrating. It was really the faith and fortitude of Malta's 270,000 people that had saved the island.

That and the gallant Dudley Mason, according to the king.

"The violence of the enemy could not deter the Master of SS *Ohio* from his purpose," said King George VI. "Throughout he showed skill and courage of the highest order, and it was due to his determination that, in spite of the most persistent enemy opposition, the vessel, with her valuable cargo, eventually reached Malta and was safely berthed."

"Even though *Ledbury* was leading her, the passage of *Ohio* through Tunisian waters at high speed without a compass, with extensive damage to the ship and in hand steering, was a remarkable feat of seamanship and tenacity on the part of Captain Mason and his officers and crew," added Admiral Leatham. "The towage of this unwieldy ship for a distance of nearly 100 miles from a position in sight of an Italian Island and within easy range of his aerodromes was a feat of seamanship, courage and endurance of the highest order."

The Admiralty extended its "admiration of the gallantry and determination" of all the men in the convoy.

"Thank you very much, though we should feel better if our losses had been lighter and we had got more ships through to Malta," replied Admiral Syfret.

Governor Lord Gort took the destroyer captains to lunch the next day—a modest vegetarian omelet—and told them that if the *Ohio* hadn't gotten through, Malta would have been forced to surrender in sixteen days.

Prime Minister Churchill cabled the First Sea Lord from Moscow:

Please convey my compliments to Admirals Syfret, Burrough, and Lyster and all officers and men engaged in the magnificent crash through of supplies to Malta, which cannot fail to have an important influence on the immediate future of the war in the Mediterranean.

CHAPTER 48 • • •

MOSCOW SATURDAY NIGHT

As the Maltese were celebrating the Feast of Santa Marija that evening, Churchill was asking Stalin if the Red Army would be able to hold the Caucasus mountain passes and keep the Germans from sweeping down to take the oil fields in Turkey, Iraq, and Persia.

"He spread out the map," said Churchill, "and then said with quiet confidence, 'We shall stop them. They will not cross the mountains.' "

They talked for quite a while. The only time Churchill got upset was when Stalin brought up the PQ17 convoy again and asked him, "Has the British Navy no sense of glory?"

Churchill was ready for him this time.

Admiral Leatham had cabled Pound:

Arrived H.M. Ships PENN BRAMHAM LEDBURY and OHIO.

As if the *Ohio* were one of His Majesty's own ships.

Air Marshal Park had cabled the RAF chief, Tedder, who was with Churchill in Moscow:

Able and eager to resume strikes against enemy shipping.

Finally, Churchill received the Most Secret and Most Immediate Cypher Telegram on which his political life depended, along with thousands, maybe hundreds of thousands of other people's lives. The cable contained the words that the prime minister had been agonizing to hear:

Oiler OHIO has arrived Malta.

Everything changed, after that, starting with the relationship between Stalin and Churchill and then that among the Soviet Union, Britain, and the United States.

No sense of glory?! I'll tell you about glory, Churchill might have finally replied to Stalin. Glory is fifty Royal Navy warships and fourteen British and American merchant ships fighting a flaming hell of Axis firepower to end the siege of Malta at all costs. Glory is using our submarines and aircraft and army to drive Rommel running backward all the way across North Africa, which we will do, to lay bare the soft belly of the Nazi crocodile. Glory is doing our share to keep the Germans away from the Mideast oil.

"One hour's conversation drew to its close," said Churchill, "and I got up to say good-bye. Stalin seemed suddenly embarrassed, and said in a more cordial tone than he had yet used with me, 'You are leaving at daybreak. Why should we not go to my house and have some drinks?' I said that I was in principle always in favor of such a policy."

Sir Charles Wilson was waiting for Churchill back at the villa. "When 8:30 came and there was no sign of the P.M., I found myself pacing up and down the passage by the front door," he said. "Then nine o'clock, then ten o'clock, 11, 12, and still no sign. Was it a good or bad omen, this prolonged interview? What did it mean?

"At half-past three in the morning the P.M. burst in. A glance at his face told me things had gone well."

Churchill and Stalin had drunk and talked for four more hours. Food was served at 1 A.M., when Stalin usually ate his evening meal.

"Dinner began simply with a few radishes, and grew into a banquet— a sucking pig, two chickens, beef, mutton, every kind of fish," said Churchill. "There was enough to feed 30 people. After four hours of sitting at the head of a pig, and when I refused, Stalin himself tackled it with relish. With a knife he cleaned out the head, putting it into his mouth with his knife. He then cut pieces of flesh from the cheeks of the pig and ate them with his fingers."

History doesn't record the things that leaders say to each other during such moments, when they sit down and drink together for four hours and eat pigs and chickens with their fingers and wash them down with wine and vodka—maybe it should happen more often, to give history a chance.

"I was taken into the family," Churchill added. "We ended friends. It was true that an argument broke out later, but it was a very friendly argument."

At 4:30, as dawn was breaking, Churchill left for the airfield, where his Liberator bomber was waiting to fly him to Cairo. "The safe arrival of the convoy enabled me to invite Malta's governor, Lord Gort, to Cairo," he said. "I greatly desired to hear all about Malta from him."

On the plane he dictated a long cable to FDR, which ended, "Everything for us now turns on hastening 'Torch' and defeating Rommel."

CHAPTER 49

THE CABLEGRAM

The minute the *Ohio* berthed, crews from Malta raced to unload her cargo of oil before the Axis bombers struck. Larsen gave them a hand. He was a tanker man. He knew about pumping oil.

"They hooked up the hoses and I went down to the main deck, and I was more or less helping them a little bit, you know. I was not very tired. I'd been sleepin' for a couple of hours, so I was down there helpin' them with that. The rest of the crowd of my volunteers got off, while I was down on deck there, foolin' around with those guys hookin' up the hoses. I saw some first-aid men treating a man and putting him on a stretcher. It looked like he was dead.

"Then all of a sudden the siren went off in town, the attack alarm for an air attack, which meant get back to the caves, the whole island of Malta is honeycombed with caves; some of them are quite large. They spewed out this heavy smoke screen all over the town, a camouflage fog, it was spread over the harbor blotting out all visibility.

"The guys pumpin' out the oil finally said, 'We can't do anything more,' so I said, 'Well, how do I get to my gang?' They says there's a boat now going, to take you over to the caves. A little harbor ferry boat came alongside and I went on there, and they took me over to town and they put me in a truck and they took me to one of the big military caves, where we could take showers and we got the first meal that I'd had for about four or five days, that was fried eggs and bacon and bread and coffee, or maybe it was tea.

"They also gave us . . . ah, their underwear, new underwear that was British, and I don't know if you've ever seen that British underwear but it's horrible stuff, it's more like three-quarter-length tights. And also I had this Norwegian sweater I had got for Christmas, I was wearing it when the *Santa Elisa* was hit, and still had that with me."

"We were led through a series of underground chambers to a very large room filled with hundreds of cots, and were told to make ourselves comfortable," said Follansbee. "We hadn't been stretched out on the cots for more than 15 minutes when the loudspeaker system announced, 'All survivors can line up for grog.'

"A shout went up from the men, as more than 300 of us lined up for a stiff shot of rum from a single cup passed from one to another and dipped into a washtub filled with rum."

"After a rest, I probably slept some, we were loaded on a British lorry," continued Larsen. "The Maltese on the streets screamed at us and threw rocks at us. We thought, 'What's going on?!' They thought we were German prisoners, because of our American helmets. The British had to stop them."

"As the lorries wound their way through the streets of Valletta," said Follansbee, "we could see what 3000 bombing attacks had done to Malta. The harbor below us was dotted with funnels and masts of sunken ships. High and dry on the far shore was a beached freighter. The docks were honeycombed with bomb craters, and the buildings surrounding them were broken skeletons staring at the sky. Roofless churches with their stained-glass windows gaping vacantly, and statues of saints were sprawled across the rubble on the floor. Houses without windows. Houses without roofs. Foundations without houses. The devastation was complete.

"We reached our hotel, and the truck came to a stop with a jolt. It was set high on a hill overlooking the yellow stucco houses below, and the blue Mediterranean beyond."

"We were boarded in a missionary hotel," said Larsen. "The manager was an Australian missionary and he was very sick. The hotel was in bad shape, it had been hit by bombing. There was only one flush toilet that worked. This was very busy as many of us had upset stomachs.

"I got very sick shortly after I got ashore with some kind of a Maltese fever. I don't know, it was from some kind of a rotten food I got, or something, or maybe it was sand fly fever, which was really bad in the caves. I also had a badly damaged back from those fellows falling on me in the lifeboat."

"During the night a severe air raid took place, and the building next door to the hotel was totally demolished," said Lonnie Dales. "And I didn't wake up. I was very amazed to find out the next morning that I was the only one left in the room. Everyone else had evacuated."

Ensign Suppiger spent the night in a cave, safe from bombs although unhappy that he wasn't in a hotel. At least he got some relief from the stress of his expectations of others.

"The deck cadet, Dales, as usual has been sticking his nose into other people's business and spreading malicious gossip," he said. "This outfit is a lousy bunch, drunk, greedy, jealous, hypocritical, and untrustworthy— I sure will be glad to get away from them!"

It was a beautiful Sunday morning in Malta. Church bells called the faithful to joyous masses. God and the Virgin Mary were tearfully thanked for answering their prayers. A man came to the door of the hotel and asked for Fred Larsen. There was a cablegram for him at the office a few blocks away.

By now the islanders knew the strangers were heroes, not Germans. As Larsen walked down the street, he was surrounded and followed by people who wanted to shake his hand and say, "God bless you." Others from across the street pointed and shouted, "Thanks, Yank!"

"So I went over to the cable office and I saw this message, a radio message had come from Grace Line. It said, 'Please release money for wife and child now here.'

"And I said, 'Well, it has nothing to do with my wife, she couldn't be in the States, that cannot be, that I can't believe, it must be something about the money that I sent to her before I left for Malta from Glasgow, and it has nothing to do with my wife and child. But we can send a message.' "

Larsen cabled to Grace Line, in New York:

Position unclear am I to understand wife and son actually in Newyork?

His sister, Christina, replied:

Minda and son Jan are in Brooklyn with us they are well.

he fact that the Battle of Mid-August constituted a splendid victory won by the Italian underwater and small surface units, emerges clearly from the account," according to *The Italian Navy in World War II*.

"Italian submarines and large and small torpedo boats—not even a score in all—sank two British cruisers and seven supply ships, torpedoed two more cruisers and two other supply ships, and literally put the British formation to rout, all in the course of nine hours of fighting. These exceptional results demonstrate the valor and ability of the Italian crews. A just share of the credit must also be given to the very effective attack plan conceived by Supermarina."

"To the continental observer, the British losses seemed to represent a big victory for the Axis," wrote Admiral Weichold, "and they were accordingly exploited for propaganda purposes. But in reality the facts were quite different, since, in spite of all these successes, the Air Force had not been able to prevent a British force, among which were probably five merchant vessels, reaching Valletta. Thereby the enemy had gained the strategic end of his operation, in spite of what it may have cost him. Thanks to these new supplies, Malta was rendered capable of fighting for several weeks, or, at a pinch, for several months.

"The main issue, the danger of air attack on the supply route to North Africa which was later to be smashed from Malta, remained. To achieve this objective no price was too high. The British operation, in spite of all the losses, was not the defeat it was made out to be by German public opinion, but a strategic failure of the first order on the part of the Axis, the repercussions of which would one day be felt."

Churchill called it like Weichold, again. "Thus in the end five gallant merchant ships out of fourteen got through with their precious cargoes," he said. "The loss of three hundred and fifty officers and men and of so many of the finest ships in the Merchant Navy and in the escorting fleet of the Royal Navy was grievous. The reward justified the price exacted. Revictualled and replenished with ammunition and vital stores, the strength of Malta revived. British submarines returned to the island, and, with the striking forces of the Royal Air Force, regained their dominating position in the Central Mediterranean.

"It should have been within the enemy's power, as it was clearly his interest, to destroy this convoy utterly."

Wrote Churchill's secretary, Elizabeth Layton Nel, "To me this episode, which was code-named PEDESTAL, always seemed the turning point of the war, the time when the news, after being bad, always bad for so long, despite adverse circumstances turned to encouraging."

It's true that after the *Ohio* came in, all went downhill for the Axis. The tanker carried enough fuel oil to bring the 10th Submarine Flotilla back to Malta, and the subs resumed sinking more thousands of tons of Rommel's supplies. Operation Pedestal's four freighters delivered the high-octane gas and aircraft parts that the RAF fighters and bombers needed for renewed attacks on Axis convoys from Italy to North Africa; by the end of September there were a hundred more serviceable fighters on Malta, repaired from the parts and powered by the fuel delivered by Pedestal.

The Maltese were able to put some meat back on their bones. That fall, two more convoys met little resistance, delivering nine of nine ships, carrying mostly foodstuffs.

"Malta is the war's key fortress," said *The New York Times*. "In convoying supplies to Malta, the risk was deliberately taken—a proof not only of audacity, but of the desperate importance of holding this speck of an island. That Malta still stands, isolated and interminably bombarded as it is, is one of the miracles of the war."

Operation Pedestal had lifted the siege on Malta. In July there had been 180 air raids on the island, and in September there were just 60. In July 10,000 tons of Axis shipping had been sunk, and in September that amount was tripled. The Allies zeroed in on tankers.

"Rommel is halted in Egypt on account of lack of fuel," Ciano said on September 2. "Three of our oil tankers have been sunk in two days."

"These circumstances force the panzer army to suspend the offensive," Rommel wrote in his diary. "The Army will therefore fall back slowly under enemy pressure to the starting line, unless the supply and air situations are fundamentally changed."

There was nothing to change them, in the face of Malta's renewed strength.

"This convoy sealed the fate of the Axis armies in Africa," said Admiral G.W.G. "Shrimp" Simpson, commander of the 10th Submarine Flotilla. "It was confidently felt in the 10th Submarine Flotilla that after the limited, but substantial, success of Pedestal, we had reached the top of the hill, were on level terms, and had an exhilarating downhill run before us."

The stage was set for General Eisenhower, Churchill's "prairie prince," to join with Admiral Cunningham and lead Operation Torch, the invasion of North Africa, which brought in the American forces three months later.

"While we were in Moscow, the siege of Malta was raised," said Sir Charles Wilson. "This made it possible for the Governor, Lord Gort, to fly to Cairo to report to the Prime Minister. The P.M.'s relief is a joyful sight. The plight of the island has been distracting him. We found Gort at the Embassy on our return from the desert. He is hardly recognizable—stones lighter. The fat boy, as he was called, has disappeared, and in his place is a man years older, with sunken cheeks and tired eyes. The island has been on short commons, and the Governor has been setting an example in rationing. He has character enough for anything."

"We had long talks," said Churchill, "and when we parted I had the Malta picture clearly in my mind."

"The P.M. dabbed his eyes with a handkerchief as he listened to Malta's story," said Sir Charles.

Gort returned to Malta for the presentation of the George Cross to its people. "How you have withstood for many months the most concentrated bombing attacks in the history of the world has the admiration of all civilized peoples," he told them. He unrolled the scroll written in the king's hand:

To honour her brave people I award the George Cross to the Island Fortress of Malta to bear witness to a heroism and devotion that will long be famous in history.

From the time of the Phoenicians, Malta's destiny had been survival. The arrival of the *Ohio*, with Larsen and Dales at the Bofors, was just one of the miracles of the war.

On May 22, 1943, at the direction of President Roosevelt, Frederick August Larsen, Jr., and Francis Alonzo Dales were awarded the Merchant Marine Distinguished Service Medal, the highest honor that branch can bestow, "for heroism above and beyond the call of duty."

In the dedication at the Merchant Marine Academy at Kings Point, Long Island, attended by more than 2,300 cadets, the citation was read aloud. It ended, "The magnificent courage of this young third officer and cadet-midshipman constitutes a degree of heroism which will be an enduring inspiration to seamen of the United States Merchant Marine everywhere," and the cheers and applause from the men burst into the sky.

After the ceremony Larsen was interviewed by a Norwegian radio reporter, and he was asked to say something directly to the Norwegian people. "There is no reason for me to tell about my experience at sea," he replied. "Thousands of Norwegian seamen have gone through the same thing, and maybe worse. What is interesting for you to hear is about all the provisions they got to Malta. I will also mention the happiness of the Maltese people when we got the tanker to port. It is going to be the same when the Allies land on your land."

He was promoted to master in 1944 and participated in sixty-five convoys by the end of the war in the North Atlantic, Mediterranean, and Pacific. He was the commodore of the first convoy to arrive in Amsterdam after V-E day in May 1945. The city was starving, so he encouraged the sailors in his fleet to give up their meals to the dockworkers.

He was a sea captain for nearly forty years. He died of natural causes on May 23, 1995, one day after the fifty-second anniversary of the receipt of his Distinguished Service Medal, the greatest among many he earned. He was inducted into the National Maritime Hall of Fame in 2000.

In the final year of his life, he was asked to address his local chapter of merchant marine veterans. It was the only time he ever spoke publicly about Operation Pedestal. He chose courage as the subject of his comments. "When I think of courageous people, foremost in my mind is my bride of more than fifty-five years," he said. "Her name is Minda, and I admire her for many reasons."

Along with Larsen, Lonnie Dales also received the Grace Lines Gold Medal for bravery. After Operation Pedestal, he went right back to the Mediterranean on the *Santa Maria,* a *Santa Elisa* sister. He took part in Operation Torch with the invasion of Casablanca, his fleet under the command of Admiral Syfret. He did his Christmas shopping in Casablanca with his brother Bert, who was by now an army captain on General Patton's staff.

In 1943 he finished his studies at the Merchant Marine Academy and graduated with a 95.4 percent average in the twenty-four final exams. He moved quickly up the mariner's ladder, becoming a third officer that year, second officer in 1944, and chief mate on a Victory ship by 1945—the ship was in Saipan, loaded with ammunition for the invasion of Japan, when the war ended. He earned his master's license in 1946 and by 1948 was the captain of an oil tanker steaming from New York to Texas—one of the youngest masters on the sea.

In 1949 he married Marjorie Odom and later began a career in construction. He and his wife had three children: Donna, Dottie, and Cliff. He died in 2003, taking himself off dialysis after a long illness. "He was the bravest person I have ever known," says Marjorie, who still lives in Waynesboro. "He was brave his entire life, to his final days. And until those final days, he longed to return to the sea."

In October 1942 Admiral Cunningham, Britain's greatest admiral since Nelson, returned to London as naval commander in chief of Operation Torch, the successful invasion of North Africa by the Allies, which he planned and led with General Eisenhower. One year later Cunningham was named first sea lord, replacing the dying Dudley Pound.

Three weeks after Operation Pedestal, Admiral Syfret was knighted for "bravery and dauntless resolution." He commanded the primary Royal Navy invasion force during Operation Torch. Admiral Burrough commanded a separate large fleet.

Lieutenant Commander Roger Hill was awarded the Distinguished Service Order Medal for his actions at the helm of the destroyer *Ledbury* during Operation Pedestal. He pressed the British government for salvage money for himself and his crew for their part in towing the *Ohio*, which was a thorny issue because a ship can't be salvaged unless it's recognized as abandoned. But the salvage was finally acknowledged, with Admiral Leatham's approval on the request. Hill's emotional stability soon began to waver and he removed himself from the *Ledbury*. He recovered to command another destroyer during the Normandy invasion but continued to struggle with his mental health and left the Royal Navy after the war. In 1965 he moved his family to New Zealand, where he worked as a laborer on the docks and wrote his memoir, *Destroyer Captain*. He died in 2001 at ninety years of age.

Field Marshal Erwin Rommel returned to Germany in late September 1942, exhausted and sick; his Afrika Korps was soon crushed by General Montgomery at the Second Battle of El Alamein. Hitler's insane orders at Normandy in 1944 caused Rommel's defeat there. After he was accused without evidence of supporting a failed assassination attempt of Hitler, the Gestapo gave him the option of a trial and almost certain execution or suicide by ingesting cyanide. His death was called a brain seizure resulting from war wounds, and he received military honors at his funeral. "The name of Field Marshal Rommel will be forever linked with the heroic battles in North Africa," Hitler wrote to Rommel's widow, a truth decried for its "despicable hypocrisy" by Rommel's son.

President Roosevelt visited Malta on December 7, 1943, the second anniversary of Pearl Harbor. He presented a scroll that included these words: "Under repeated fire from the skies, Malta stood, alone but unafraid in the center of the sea, one tiny bright flame in the darkness—a beacon for the clearer days which have come. Malta's story of human fortitude and courage will be read by posterity with wonder and gratitude through all the ages."

On August 23, 1942, eight days after the *Ohio* reached Grand Harbour, Captain Dudley Mason was lionized by the London Sunday papers. GREATEST DRAMA OF THE YEAR! screamed one headline. THEY SAILED INTO HELL; HE DEFIED THE NAZIS' BOMBS AND WON THROUGH. The next day Mason pardoned the seaman who had thrown his dinner dishes over the side: "Owing to the subsequent good behavior of A. Byrne Messman the entry's [*sic*] made on page 30 & 31 are hereby cancelled." It was Captain Mason's final entry into the *Ohio*'s log.

He was awarded the George Cross Medal, along with Charles Henry Walker, who swam the backstroke into the flames around *Waimarama* to rescue survivors. They were the only men from Operation Pedestal to receive Britain's highest civilian honor. Mason resumed his career as a master for Eagle Oil and Shipping a few months later.

After the oil in the *Ohio* was off-loaded in Malta, she sank to the bottom of the shallow harbor; it was the oil that had kept her afloat. She was dragged to a dock in a far corner, where she was used for storage and barracks by the Yugoslavian Navy for the rest of the war. In 1946 the rusty hulk was towed ten miles out to sea, her back finally broken. She was scuttled by charges placed in her holds and sank in two pieces on an undersea shelf. She cries out to be raised and restored.

Fred Larsen nearly died the week after he rode the Bofors into Malta. He was hospitalized in Gibraltar for six days, suffering from severe stomach ills as well as his fractured spine. He steamed back to New York on the *Queen Mary* and took a taxi to his sister, Christina's, house, where he saw his son, Jan, for the first time. Minda was at the movies, so he went to the theater and found her. He sat in the seat behind her in the dark, put his hands over her eyes, and whispered the lyrics to "You Are My Sunshine," as if they had never been apart.

The most heavily defended and heavily attacked naval convoy in history.

<small>FOURTEEN MERCHANT SHIPS</small>

Ohio   Torpedoed by an Italian submarine; bombed repeatedly; two shot-down Stukas crashed on her decks; suffered one direct hit and many near misses; lost engines and rudder; towed by destroyers, minesweepers, and tugboats into Malta; scuttled offshore in 1946.

Santa Elisa   Torpedoed by two E-boats; afire, abandoned, sunk by direct hits from a dive-bombing Junkers Ju 88.

Almeria Lykes   Torpedoed by an E-boat, down by the bows; American crew took to lifeboats, refused to reboard; ship was assumed to have sunk.

Waimarama   Two thousand–plus tons of aviation fuel ignited by four bombs from a Ju 88, quickly sunk; all but about twenty men burned to death in the inferno.

Deucalion   Holed by a near miss, later torpedoed and set afire by a phantom bomber in a dead-stick dive; abandoned, survivors boarded a destroyer, which left the ship in flames.

Empire Hope   Three direct hits and many near misses from an attack of Ju 88s, afire, abandoned, scuttled by a torpedo from the destroyer *Penn*.

Clan Ferguson   Torpedoed by a bomber; up in ferocious flames and down in seven minutes.

Glenorchy   Torpedoed by an E-boat in the middle of the night; flooding, abandoned except by the captain; sunk in the morning by an explosion aboard, believed to be the captain scuttling her and going down with his ship.

Wairangi	Torpedoed by an E-boat; flooding, abandoned, presumed to have sunk.
Dorset	Ahead of the convoy, within sight of Malta, turned back and rejoined convoy; attacked by fourteen Stukas; afire, abandoned, attacked by Ju 88s; direct hit, more fire, sunk by a torpedo from U-73.
Port Chalmers	Turned back toward Gibraltar; chased by a destroyer and ordered to rejoin the convoy; arrived in Malta undamaged.
Melbourne Star	Arrived in Malta charred after being caught in the flames of Waimarama, missing thirty-three men who jumped overboard into the fire.
Rochester Castle	Damaged by an E-boat torpedo; bombed; fire in the hold carrying ammunition, extinguished; arrived in Malta.
Brisbane Star	Holed in the bows by a torpedo dropped from a Heinkel He 111; arrived in Malta after limping along the coast of Africa.

FOUR AIRCRAFT CARRIERS

Indomitable	Attacked by a hundred bombers; three direct hits and many near misses; fifty men killed; returned to Gibraltar, listing and in flames.
Eagle	Sunk in eight minutes by three torpedoes from U-73; 231 men killed.
Furious	Flew off thirty-eight Spitfires to Malta; returned to Gibraltar.
Victorious	Returned to Gibraltar with Force Z.

TWO BATTLESHIPS

Nelson	Flagship of Admiral Syfret; returned to Gibraltar with Force Z.
Rodney	Returned to Gibraltar with Force Z.

SEVEN CRUISERS

Nigeria	Torpedoed by Italian submarine Axum; fifty-two men killed; returned to Gibraltar listing and afire.
Cairo	Stern blown off by two torpedoes from the same salvo by Axum; twenty-six men killed; abandoned; scuttled by torpedoes from destroyers.
Kenya	Damaged by an E-boat torpedo; returned to Gibraltar with Force X.

Manchester	Disabled by two torpedoes from two E-boats; fifteen men steamed to death; abandoned; scuttled with depth charges; her captain court-martialed.
Phoebe	Returned to Gibraltar with Force Z.
Sirius	Returned to Gibraltar with Force Z.
Charybdis	Returned to Gibraltar with Force X after being sent forward from Force Z.

THIRTY-TWO
DESTROYERS

Ashanti	Flagship of Admiral Burrough after cruiser *Nigeria* was damaged; returned to Gibraltar with Force X.
Ledbury	Towed *Ohio* into Malta.
Penn	Towed *Ohio* into Malta.
Bramham	Towed *Ohio* into Malta.
Foresight	Disabled by dive-bombers; scuttled by depth charges from destroyer *Tartar.*
Tartar	Towed *Foresight* until scuttling her; returned to Gibraltar.
Wolverine	Rammed and sank submarine; returned to Gibraltar.
Ithuriel	Rammed and sank submarine; returned to Gibraltar.
Amazon *Antelope* *Bicester* *Derwent* *Eskimo* *Fury* *Icarus* *Intrepid* *Keppel* *Laforey* *Lightning* *Lookout* *Malcolm* *Pathfinder* *Quentin* *Somali* *Vansittart* *Venomous*	Returned to Gibraltar with either Force Z or Force X, or damaged.

Vidette
Westcott
Wilton
Wishart   Returned to Gibraltar with either Force Z or Force X, or damaged.
Wrestler
Zetland

Plus a fifth aircraft carrier for exercises, as well as oilers, corvettes, minesweepers, motor launches, tugboats, and nine submarines on patrol.

PART I

FATE IN THE CONVERGENCE

The seed of *At All Costs* was sown in 1963, when a small boy in a dark theater in London watched in awe as Stukas dived straight down from the sky at ships of the Operation Pedestal convoy, in battle footage used in the movie *The Malta Story*. Thirty years later, living in New York, he learned that two American merchant mariners and a U.S. tanker had played the pivotal role. It took him another decade to put it all together to bring their story to these pages, and more. The boy was Peter Riva, and in 2003, together with Random House editor Bob Loomis, he and I began working on *At All Costs*.

In the spring of 2004 I traveled to Malta and spent seven days with Jan Larsen, the three-year-old boy in this book. We explored the island and dug for its history, in particular during the siege of 1940–43. We met Simon Cusens, whose efforts to track down veterans for the Operation Pedestal reunions in 1992 and 2002 have brought closure to those men, along with some good times over grog. Cusens opened his library to me, as well as some pages of his painstakingly acquired address book, cooperation that got the research off to a rolling start.

All the material accumulated during more than two years of researching and writing, including some forty hours of recorded interviews with the convoy's veterans, will be contributed to the Operation Pedestal museum that Cusens plans to build on Malta.

The three volumes of *Malta at War*, coffee-table books edited by John Mizzi (who was a boy during the siege) and Mark Anthony Vella, provided insight, illumination, and details in Chapter 1 and throughout the book. They include hundreds of black-and-white photos, articles, and items written in and about Malta during the war years, many of them from *The Times* of Malta daily newspaper. Their publication is a priceless contribution to world history; nowhere else can such a comprehensive picture of Malta during that period be found.

Quotes in the first chapter and subsequent comments by Admiral Cunningham come from his 674–page autobiography, *A Sailor's Odyssey*, which was one of the two hundred books that squeezed all others out of my office for those two years, including seventy-eight books from the Multnomah County Library in Portland, Oregon, and another seventy-one that were purchased—often used, because they were long out of print. The analysis and opinions of Admiral Weichold, commander in chief of the German Navy in the Mediterranean, appear in an essay he wrote at the direction of the Allies while awaiting trial for war crimes at Nuremberg. Winston Churchill's quotes are from various writings and speeches, most notably the fourth volume of his World War II memoirs, *The Hinge of Fate*. Governor-General William Dobbie's quote is from an obscure softbound book he wrote after the war, *A Very Present Help: A Tribute to the Faithfulness of God*, which reveals his religious fanaticism that led to his replacement by Churchill. More but not all Dobbie quotes come from this book.

In Chapter 2, *The Great Influenza* by John Barry contained the information on the flu pandemic of 1918. At Minda Larsen's home in New Jersey, I began a series of interviews and a friendship with her, amazed by the way she frequently sprang up from a chair in the living room to answer the phone in the kitchen and by how she enjoyed being outside in the cold winter air. Minda emptied the file cabinet containing records of her flight from Nazi-occupied Norway, as well as those of the career of her husband, Fred, including the folder he had labeled "Bad." He never talked about bad things, so the folder was thin, although it might easily have been substantial. He was a quiet, positive man.

Some information in Chapter 3 came from the book *Operation Drumbeat*, a remarkable event about which relatively little has been written, save this definitive work by Michael Gannon. Other details came from *Hitler's U-Boat War*, a Random House book researched for nearly a decade by its author, Clay Blair.

Frank Dooley, currently serving his second term as president of the American Merchant Marine Veterans and a shipmate of Fred Larsen in 1959, helped to explain the story of the collision between the *Santa Elisa* and *San Jose* and cleared up many other technical mysteries. Frank introduced me to Toni Horodysky, whose Web site www.usmm.org is a comprehensive reference about the American Merchant Marine at war. Toni's research ability and initiative cracked open the door to more Internet discoveries. Toni also read the manuscript to catch technical errors, for which I'm especially grateful.

Visits to the New York Public Library turned up microfilm clips from *The New York Times* pertaining to both Operation Drumbeat and the *Santa Elisa/San Jose* collision, while Grace Line documents and some merchant ship records were found at the National Maritime Museum Library in San Francisco, by Bill Kooiman, another ex-mariner who sailed with Grace Line and author of *The Grace Ships, 1869–1969*. And Miriam Devine at the tiny Amenia, New York, library found some books that even the NYPL didn't have. Miriam was a very young girl in Malta during the siege; more than the bombs, she remembers the hunger.

Theodore Roosevelt Thomson appears in Chapter 3. His daughter, Peg Thomson-Mann, born on the day the *Santa Elisa* was sunk, mailed me a gold mine, a nineteen-page report full of ship's details, written by her father after the fire. Later quotes come from a 1943 article in *The New Yorker* written by a young Brendan Gill, a wordsmith even then; Gill apparently chose Thomson because the master was only thirty-three. More personal information about Thomson and Fred Larsen was provided by Captain Warren Leback, a Grace Line master for many years and U.S. Maritime Administrator in the Bush, Sr., administration.

Much of the dialogue that takes place on the *Santa Elisa*, and details such as the keg of Jamaican rum kept in Captain Thomson's head, came from an unpublished manuscript, "Swans in the Maelstrom," written by the ship's purser, John Follansbee, who was Larsen's close friend and who died in 2002. After much searching, I located his son John, who provided the only existing copy of this memoir, as well as a rare copy of a spiral-bound, self-published work by Ensign Gerhart Suppiger, titled *The Malta Convoy*. The descriptions of Suppiger's thoughts and actions come from this work.

I spoke on the phone to Peter Forcanser, the junior engineer on the *Santa Elise*, who calls Larsen a "square-head," and has sharper things to say about Ensign Suppiger. "I know them like it was yesterday," he said. "I think of that ship a hell of a lot. I know how lucky I was."

Larsen's sextant hangs on the office wall of his engineer grandson, Scott Larsen, who contributed the sextant story as well as more insight into the character of his grandfather.

That summer, I spent a steamy five days in Augusta and Waynesboro, Georgia, getting to know the Dales family. Marjorie Dales, Lonnie's widow, covered her kitchen table with five towering scrapbooks and spent the next two days answering my questions with unwavering patience and grace. It's easy to see why Lonnie left the sea for her.

PART II
THE SECOND GREAT SIEGE

On Malta, Jan Larsen and I spent time with Louis Henwood, a veteran of the Royal Navy and merchant navy, and former mayor of the city of Senglea. Mr. Henwood is also a diver and believes he knows where the *Ohio* lies. His Web site, www.louishenwood.com, has more information about Malta than any other, and some of it appears in Chapters 6 and 7.

Jan and I saw as much as we could in one week. We stood on the bastions surrounding Fort St. Elmo in Valletta, where thousands of Maltese had cheered and cried when the *Ohio* came in and where the cannons of the Knights of St. John had fired the Turks' chopped-off heads across the harbor. We sidled into the dank caves around the docks, where families had lived during the war. We walked around the towers and pillboxes at the edge of cliffs over the sea and through a cemetery with the tombstones of too many children, as well as those of Axis airmen shot down over Malta. We gazed in silence at the prehistoric Tarxien Temples. We spent an afternoon at St. John's Cathedral, raided by Napoleon, and were chilled by an all-too-real display deep in the caves under the cathedral, where Maltese had been tortured during the Inquisition.

We took a bus to the ancient walled city of Mdina, where off-duty RAF pilots and Maltese farmers had watched dogfights in the sky. We visited the National War Museum and spent an afternoon at Takali airfield, now the site of the Malta Aviation Museum, where we examined a restoration of one of the original Gladstone Gladiator biplanes. We spent a fascinating few hours with Ray Polidano, director of the museum foundation, who worked in a hangar in back; he walked us around and told stories of the men and planes at Takali.

Most of the information on the Malta Gladiators, both the men and the machines, came from this visit and the book *Faith, Hope and Charity* by Kenneth Poolman, an old paperback found, like so many, after searching the Web sites of rare-book sellers. More material in Part II came from Michael Galea's *Malta: Diary of a War* and *Raiders Passed*, by Charles B. Grech, one of the Maltese boys who collected shrapnel like arrowheads during the siege.

Chapters 8, 9, and 10 were by far the most challenging to write, because they span two years, and there are three or four more unwritten books in there, in particular regarding the bombing of the *Illustrious*, Admiral Cunningham's biggest (and maybe only) blunder, which historians have yet to address.

In using so many sources and voices, it was difficult to reconcile the differences and contradictions, which demanded choices about credibility and probability. These chapters include quotes from autobiographies, memoirs, or diaries by Admirals Cunningham and Weichold and General Dobbie; Field Marshal Albert Kesselring, commander in chief of the Luftwaffe; Field Marshal Erwin Rommel, the legendary leader of the Afrika Korps; Admiral Erich Raeder, commander in chief of the German Navy; Admiral Karl Dönitz, the U-boat commander; Count Galeazzo Ciano, Mussolini's son-in-law and minister of foreign affairs; Air Marshal Sir Hugh Lloyd, the RAF's commanding officer on Malta; Admiral G.W.G. "Shrimp" Simpson, commander of Malta's 10th Submarine Flotilla; General Hastings "Pug" Ismay, Churchill's chief of staff; General Alan Brooke (later Field Marshal Lord Alanbrooke), chief of the Imperial General Staff and Churchill's closest military adviser; Sir Charles Wilson, Churchill's personal physician, who wrote his memoir as Lord Moran; Elizabeth Layton Nel, Churchill's young and resolute Canadian secretary; and of course Churchill himself.

There were also biographical books in the pile, for example of Admiral Dudley Pound, the First Sea Lord of the Admiralty, and of the 10th Submarine Flotilla. And *The Italian Navy in World War II* by Marc'Antonio Bragadin, the official Italian history, along with *The Naval War in the Mediterranean, 1940–1943* by Jack Greene and Alessandro Massignani—a British and an Italian historian, allies in accuracy. Another invaluable reference was Captain Arthur R. Moore's *A Careless Word . . . A Needless Sinking,* a heavy encyclopedia of all the American merchant ships lost in World War II.

Among five memoirs by fighter pilots, two were particularly evocative, and they found their way into Part II. Insight and beauty float off the pages of *Tattered Battlements* by Tim Johnston, DSC, and *War in a Stringbag* is unique because its author, Charles Lamb, DSO, DSC, bombed Taranto and lived to tell about it and witnessed the brutal bombing of the *Illustrious* from the air as Stukas swarmed around his shabby biplane and paid him no mind.

The statement in Chapter 9 from the Luftwaffe pilot who flew into the Royal Malta Artillery box barrage and dropped his bombs prematurely was taken from a letter he wrote after the war to *The Times* of Malta. With all the aircraft action in Part II, technical books on the planes, such as *Aircraft of WWII* and *Jane's Fighters of World War II* were used. But my favorite was *Wings of the Luftwaffe* by Captain Eric Brown, the RAF's chief test pilot, who flew captured German planes and wrote about them as if he were doing road tests for a British car magazine.

There were many discrepancies in the reports of the number of Axis aircraft involved in the various attacks. But the books *Malta: The Hurricane Years, 1940–41* and *Malta: The Spitfire Year, 1942* by Christopher Shores and Brian Cull with Nicola Malizia solved most of them. These reporters worked more than ten years to acquire the accurate documents.

PART III
ALLIES

From Malta I flew to London and spent two weeks researching in England, beginning at the Imperial War Museum and the National Archives, where I pored over documents: books, films, audiotapes, cables, and especially Letters of Proceeding, the action reports written by Royal Navy officers and masters of merchant ships. The plot thickened. With each report, questions arose that added two or three more reports to the list. There was far too much information at the National Archives to note or even photocopy during four days there, so I recruited a researcher, Tim Hughes, who caught the detective bug and continued to dig for documents at my request. Tim found pieces of the puzzle into the final chapter.

Many of the documents we found and examined were declassified by the British government only in 2002. If the reader wonders how the full story of such a significant World War II battle could have been untold for so long, this is part of the answer; also the fact that Tim Hughes looked in places historians had apparently missed, in response to my wondering what was under every rock and my being struck by the heretofore undrawn connections between events.

Beginning in Chapter 12 with Operation Harpoon, it was those intriguing and often mysterious Letters of Proceeding that defined the convoy stories. They weren't always accurate, because they were written after the battle and colored by the fog of war; but when there were four or five of them to compare incidents and times and places, reality usually emerged. There were times when I had charts on my desk full of Xs and arrows, a deductive process to find the common fact and reach a small conclusion to complete one sentence. It was slow going.

The LOPs from Operation Harpoon are an excellent example. Most of the story lies between the rambling lines in the reports of Captain Hardy in the cruiser *Cairo*, who commanded the convoy; the direct lines of Captain Roberts, master of the tanker SS *Kentucky*; and the misguided lines of Admiral Harwood, the new C in C of the Mediterranean—with the bottom line coming from the Italian history. Harpoon has been called the "forgotten convoy," but a better name might be "disowned convoy." Somebody should write a book about this dramatically balzupped naval action.

Speaking of balzup, a word that first appears and is explained in Chapter 22 with Operation Bellows, that's my spelling for "balls-up." It's a word that might have been used to death. This is a war story, after all. Balzups are the nature of the beast.

And speaking of untold stories, there's a lot about Colonel Bonner Frank Fellers that's untouched in this book; maybe someday someone will find and tell the whole story. Some of my information on Fellers in Chapter 12 and later came from TNA documents that were secret until 2002, and there were more bits in the books *The Battle of Alamein*, *Trading with the Enemy*, *The War in the Mediterranean*, and *The End of the Beginning* by Tim Clayton and Phil Craig.

Rick Atkinson's Pulitzer Prize–winning *An Army at Dawn*, about Operation Torch, set the stage for the others. In some ways, *At All Costs* might be seen as a prequel, although decidedly narrower—Pedestal as prequel for Torch. *An Army at Dawn* provided background for Chapter 13, which was probably the most entertaining chapter to write. What a day that Father's Day in the White House must have been!

I read a number of accounts of Churchill's trip to Washington and Hyde Park in June 1942, and with the messages Tim Hughes found in TNA pertaining to the SS *Ohio*, in particular the cable cited in Chapter 13, it all fell into place. There's no record of the points of discussion that Churchill verbally listed with Harry Hopkins and that Hopkins passed on to President Roosevelt, but there's little doubt that the SS *Ohio* was among them. Regarding the final sentence of Chapter 13, the order signed by Admiral King, the powerful man behind the scenes in so many World War II naval actions stretching in both directions around the globe, involved more than just the *Ohio.*

This version of the rest of that trip to Washington comes primarily from the writings of Churchill, General Brooke, General Ismay, and Sir Charles Wilson, who were all intensely there.

Still sitting here on my desk are two remarkably detailed six-inch scale models of the SS *Santa Elisa* and SS *Ohio,* which I examined so many times that teeny merchant mariners began to appear on their decks. Further descriptions in Chapter 14 of the equipment, weapons, and guns on the *Santa Elisa* came from her Royal Navy liaison officer's LOP, as well as the record of Ensign Suppiger, who headed the U.S. Naval Armed Guard.

Neither Larsen nor Dales wrote about his life, but they passed on a few oral stories to their families. About five years before his death, Larsen had reluctantly sat down for an interview with a fellow from his local New Jersey chapter of the American Merchant Marine Veterans; many of his quotes came from this transcript.

And in the final year of his life, when he was eighty, he penned a reply to a letter from another veteran, a British Eighth Army soldier named Leonard Fisher, who had been stationed on Malta during the siege and who had read about Larsen and wrote to thank him. "We all felt that this was the end of the road," said Mr. Fisher. "But when the tanker came into Grand Harbour, you could feel the love that was poured toward you and the crews and those who gave their lives. Today in Malta they still talk of the Santa Marija miracle convoy, and the story of your part in bringing the Ohio home is legend."

Larsen never finished his handwritten reply, which ended at twelve pages. Some of what he wrote appears in this book.

There were fewer words from Lonnie Dales to work with. Marjorie Dales found one good letter, and there was a brief taped telephone interview with Simon Cusens when Dales was quite ill; more of Dales's quotes came from the two reports he wrote for the merchant marine after the convoy—the first was a required report of the *Santa Elisa* sinking, the second was requested after the commandant of the Cadet Corps heard from Captain Thomson about Dales's heroism. Dales hadn't mentioned it himself.

Elizabeth Layton Nel's 1958 memoir, *Mr. Churchill's Secretary,* offered an inside look at the prime minister. She worked closely with Frank Sawyers, Churchill's valet, and enjoyed his company. Between her description of Sawyers, as well as General Brooke's, a discreet but clear picture pops up. When General Marshall invited Sawyers into that convertible in South Carolina, it must have been with a sense of mischief, to shock the class-conscious Brooke. After the war, there was an issue with Sawyers's homosexuality; Churchill spoke for him, and the issue went away. "The nation will get over this nonsense one day," he said.

A piece of the story of the Norwegian tanker king Torkild Rieber, the father of the *Ohio* and a larger-than-life character, is told in Chapter 15. There was just one dramatic degree of separation between Rieber and Fred Larsen. The trail of the Rieber story began with documents from the Chevron Texaco archives, sent by historian John Harper, which led to the University of Texas Center for American History archives, which had a Rieber interview, although, not surprisingly, he didn't address his trading oil to the Axis while Britain was at war with it and while Nazi soldiers were occupying his homeland. Much of that information, from the British perspective, came from TNA documents that were secret until 2002. The American side of the story came from the *New York Times* microfilm pieces and the *New York Herald Tribune.* As for Rieber's last blast, his run in the *Ohio* from New Jersey to Texas, I simply put the little facts together. After Rieber resigned in disgrace from the Texas Company, he went to work for a Guggenheim company building secret ships for the U.S. Navy. "I want to beat the hell out of those Nazi bastards," he said.

There's one intriguing thing that's not in the chapter, mostly because it roams away from Fred Larsen. Days after Rieber cut his first deal with the Gestapo's Hermann Göring to sell oil to the Germans, his Norwegian wife committed suicide by jumping out the window of their penthouse apartment on Central Park South in Manhattan. It would have been stretching too far to peer into that dark tunnel for a moral about love and happiness, or money and values, and find Fred and Minda in the light at the other end.

Some of the technical information on the *Ohio* came from the archives of the old Sun Shipbuilding in Chester, Pennsylvania, and the book *The* Ohio *& Malta* by Michael Pearson. Useful line drawings of the inboard profile and deck plans appeared in *Steamboat Bill* magazine in the fall 1994 issue.

PART IV
OPERATION PEDESTAL

Leaving London, I drove 1,600 miles over the next five days to interview eleven Operation Pedestal veterans in all four corners of England; Volvo Cars of North America supported this mission by arranging the loan of a turbocharged five-speed S40 sedan. I drove at night on the high-speed motorway and interviewed a vet in the morning; drove more miles on narrow twisty roads between towns and interviewed another vet in the afternoon. My conversations with these men remain the most rewarding and memorable part of writing *At All Costs.* I'm privileged to have met them. They were the eleven best veterans for this story—the right minds with the right experiences from the right ships.

Going all the way north first, to Blyth on the North Sea, near Glasgow, I spoke to Allan Shaw, who is the only living veteran from the original crew of the *Ohio,* except for one other, who has been in a mental institution since shortly after Operation Pedestal. Shaw told me that this fellow has never spoken about the attacks on the convoy and has said he never will; he didn't reply to my letter. The nineteen-year-old Shaw is introduced in Chapter 16 and becomes an important presence, providing details about what happened on the *Ohio* and making observations about her master, Dudley Mason.

Captain Mason's journal is buried deep on the Internet, on a site devoted to the tankers of the *Ohio*'s owners, Eagle Oil and Shipping Company, Ltd.; and Tim Hughes found records of the movement of Mason's prior ship, which revealed his near miss with the U-boats of Operation Drumbeat off the Atlantic coast. There was also a wildly inaccurate 1960 story in *The Saturday Evening Post* that offered some color.

The official log of the *Ohio* is kept in a humidity-controlled room with precious maps on the top floor of the National Archives. The entries about the aluminum dinner plates that appear in Chapter 17 and the Afterword, intriguing for their pettiness and their indication of Captain Mason's focus, reflect the kinds of things that the log was used for. There aren't many entries between the Clyde and Malta; Mason was too busy dodging torpedoes and fighting fires to do much writing.

Admiral Burrough's comments to the captains and liaison officers at the Clyde came from his own LOP and various journals. Surely Captain Mason and Captain Thomson of the *Santa Elisa* met at that meeting, and in the first draft of this manuscript I made up a conversation between them; they had so much in common, including being rookie masters of state-of-the-art ships who were stalked by U-boats on the Caribbean run. Their imagined conversation was fun, and funny, and it might even have been close to reality, but it didn't work in this nonfiction book.

It took scores of hours of reading and searching for books to get the events in Chapter 18 reduced to 820 words; small parts of *Winston S. Churchill: Road to Victory, 1941–1945* by Martin Gilbert helped. Churchill's multilayered reasons for firing General Auchinleck had to be reduced to a sound bite and his adventure-filled trip to Cairo squeezed down to a few symbolic moments. But there were so many other wonderful pieces, including a sweet and romantic letter from Clementine Churchill to her husband, after she watched him fly off into the night in the Liberator bomber. The quote describing Churchill with his cigar sticking out of his oxygen mask came from *The Sky Belongs to Them*, by Roland Winfield, an RAF officer on the Liberator, whose pilot was a young American hot dog whom Churchill instantly liked.

The quotes from the chief engineer of the *Santa Elisa*, Ed Randall, beginning in Chapter 19, came from an article he wrote for *The American Magazine* of January 1943; the piece avoided certain military specifics, but it was still controversial because of what it revealed about convoys, which were still a new thing. He's quoted in the present tense, as it appears in his story.

Captain Mason's words to his men were taken from the pioneering Pedestal work, *Malta Convoy*, by Peter Shankland and Anthony Hunter, published in 1961. *Pedestal*, by Peter C. Smith, followed in 1970. Both books were very useful. I envied their authors' opportunity to interview so many of the Pedestal sailors (in particular Captain Mason and Admiral Burrough), as they might envy my discovery of documents that were unavailable to them thirty-five and forty-five years ago.

Frank Pike was one of the two veterans who liked to use e-mail, and his quotes came from e-mail correspondence with him from Auckland, New Zealand, where he now lives.

Admiral Syfret didn't leave behind memoirs, nor has his biography been written, but he was one of the subjects of the obscure 1945 book *Seven Sailors* by Royal Navy Commander Kenneth Edwards, and there were eighteen appetite-whetting pages about him.

Roger Hill's memoir, *Destroyer Captain*, provided many of his quotes in Chapter 20 and the rest of the book; and his Letter of Proceeding was long, because his actions during Operation Pedestal were so expansive. I spent a moving afternoon with his mate on the destroyer *Ledbury*, the brilliant Dr. Nixon, who took me out to his local pub near Salisbury for chicken and chips. He was over ninety at the time and passed away before I ever got to speak to him again. He said he had sometimes been criticized for treating burned or wounded Axis airmen the same as he did Allied seamen, but that there had never been any question in his mind about doing so.

I drove from Salisbury to the southeast tip of England, near Dover, to visit with Don Allen, a retired osteopath and widower, who's quoted in Chapter 20 and more significantly later on.

During dinner at the home of Charles Henry Walker, GC, his daughter Anne, who cooked for us, kept teasing her father about his "birds," during and after the war and until that day. I had a couple of pints with him but couldn't manage the malt whiskey. He was exceptionally sturdy at ninety (and still going strong at ninety-two), and it was easy to imagine him being the toughest of seamen. He revered Roger Hill, his commanding officer on the *Ledbury*. Walker reappears in Chapter 38, when all humor is lost.

PART V
INTO THE MEDITERRANEAN

Beginning in Chapter 22, the reader can use the eyes and ears of correspondents on Royal Navy warships. First comes Norman Smart of the London *Daily Express*; in Chapter 23 we hear from Arthur Thorpe of the *Daily Telegraph*; and in Chapter 24 the BBC commentary by Anthony Kimmins begins.

The astonishing story of the Air France flying boat begins in Chapter 22, with a quote from the journal of Desmond "Dag" Dickens, a descendant of Charles; his purplish prose is sprinkled around a bit. The end of the French airliner story comes in Chapter 26.

Explaining the balzupped Operation Bellows was especially challenging, because all the available accounts were vague, contradictory, or improbable. After weeding out the impossible, this version prevailed. Geoffrey Wellum should know, because as a twenty-one-year-old lieutenant he led a group of eight Spitfires off the *Furious*; his wryly hilarious anecdote comes from his wonderful memoir, *First Light*, which he waited sixty years to write.

The brief story of the ramming of the Italian submarine *Dagabur* by the destroyer *Wolverine* (originally an entire chapter) came from the LOP of *Wolverine*'s twenty-nine-year-old captain, Lieutenant Commander Peter Gretton, a Royal Navy golden boy who went on to become an admiral and Fifth Sea Lord. It was years before Gretton learned that it wasn't a German U-boat he rammed that night, because the Italians never acknowledged the sinking of their submarine and records were chased by Italian historians only long after the war.

The veteran George Amyes contributed much of the exclusive information that's in Chapter 23, on the sinking of the venerable *Eagle*. When I visited Amyes in the industrial city of Hull on the North Sea, he handed me the log and journal of the famous U-boat captain Helmut Rosenbaum. Amyes believed this was the only copy in Britain, having been given to him by Rosenbaum's widow. Amyes later mailed me his "Memories of Eagle," along with a manuscript he had written about his time at sea, "Trampship," which revealed arcane things about life at sea that made their way into the book elsewhere.

His friend and former *Eagle* shipmate Les Goodenough, whose story about the "toboggan team" also appears in Chapter 23, told me about the rats glaring down from the beams, adding a gruesome description of his lip after it was bitten by one of these rats as he slept in his hammock. Goodenough also directed me to the Inverness Library in Scotland, which sent biographical material on Captain Mackintosh of the *Eagle*, adding to that which appears on Web sites of Scottish clans.

Chapter 25 opens with comments from Keith Park, the RAF commanding air officer on Malta during Operation Pedestal. The broken promise of the Liberators was a very big deal and might have blown the whole thing. Park's bold complaint in his LOP was a message to Air Marshal Tedder, the chief of the RAF, who was in Cairo with Churchill during the early days of Pedestal. The "shootup" of the airfields on Sicily was actually more of a balzup; Park puts a positive spin on it.

Admiral Da Zara wrote his own book, *Pelle d'ammiraglio* ("Admiral's Skin"), which hasn't been translated into English, but an Italian-speaking journalist friend skimmed relevant parts of it for me. Another Italian book he looked through was Gianni Rocca's *Fucilate gli ammiragli* ("Shoot the Admirals").

The stories about the *motobombe* and the remote-controlled flying buffalo, like others, came from about half a dozen sources—a piece of information here, a piece there. *Malta at War* usually got me started on these puzzles.

Mark Whitmore, director of collections at the Imperial War Museum, made it easy to see what was needed there. Like Peter Riva forty-three years before, I sat in a dark room in London and viewed footage shot during Operation Pedestal, of screaming Stukas diving absolutely vertically at ships. The description in the opening of Chapter 26 of the depth charge being launched from a destroyer comes from one of these films.

The IWM sound archives turned up dozens of segments of relevant interviews on cassette with war veterans; Richard McDonough's IWM program to conduct and record as many interviews as possible before we lose these men is an important unsung project, deserving of recognition and support in Britain.

The LOP of Lieutenant Commander Maitland-Makgill-Crichton, commanding officer of the destroyer *Ithuriel*, which rammed the Italian sub *Cobalto*, might have been the most entertaining; he called the rescued Italians "scared stiff" as they were kept out on *Ithuriel*'s decks during attacks by Italian dive-bombers, and his description of balzups on his ship were wild, at least by Royal Navy standards of prose. As these Letters of Proceeding were all addressed to Admiral Syfret, his LOP might have been part of the reason he was scolded by Syfret, while Lieutenant Commander Gretton, who rammed a sub with his destroyer *Wolverine*, was praised; both young destroyer captains had immediately made the decision to ram, but for a number of reasons, Gretton's was correct and Maitland-Makgill-Crichton's was not.

The profound book *Observations*, written by *Indomitable* airman Hector Mackenzie, included his firsthand descriptions of the result of the direct hits on *Indomitable*. Captain Tom Troubridge's LOP offered a bit more. Troubridge had served at the Admiralty in 1940, as an expert on the German Navy; he had been the naval attaché in Berlin from 1936 to 1939, and knew Admiral Raeder, its commander in chief, quite well. He said that Raeder had never believed in Hitler's war, nor that U-boats could ever be a decisive factor.

At the end of Chapter 26, the Air France flying boat lands in the sea. Most of the rare references to this incident, including from veterans, were brief, only suggestive, and confused. However, *Malta: The Spitfire Year, 1942* tells the story, including a photo of the plane in the water.

In Chapters 27 and 28, the excerpts from Captain Ferrini's log came from *The Naval War Against Hitler* by Donald Macintyre. The quote from Alfred Longbottom appears on the BBC Web site, on a link called "warmemories." Captain Mason's comments come from his report to Eagle Oil and Shipping, as well as his journal, the *Ohio*'s log, and one clip that Peter Riva tracked down of a piece by Movietone News, which was shown in theaters in 1942; it was especially good because his voice was there. He did seem to be unflappable, as others had described him. As he smoked a cigarette with one bandaged hand, he discussed his George Cross medal matter-of-factly, almost abstractedly, without any indication of chagrin for having received the medal despite having abandoned his ship.

Ray Morton's quotes come from the transcript of an interview that's been floating around for some time. I phoned him in Australia, but the interview told his story with more detail.

PART VI
HELL IN THE NARROWS

On the first page of Chapter 29, it seems fair to wonder here if the attack by *Axum* might have been less successful, or even prevented entirely, if Admiral Syfret had sent *Charybdis, Eskimo,* and *Somali* with Admiral Burrough's Force X when the fleet had first split up, especially since Force Z made it back to Gibraltar without needing them. But because Syfret never wrote his memoirs, there's no indication he ever second-guessed himself.

The instructions from the young gunner on the *Almeria Lykes* was one of the best lines in *Malta Convoy.* The fact that it was probably made up makes it no less fun, or likely.

I used some license myself in describing Larsen's shooting down the Stuka. But the motive was confirmed, the kill was confirmed, and that's how it was at the trigger of an Oerlikon.

The stories in Chapter 30 all come from the Letters of Proceeding. Mr. Black's story was not only surreal, it was also long and vivid and weird—there could be a movie in it. Although Mr. Black doesn't say how they got back, they appeared to have escaped from their camp and been towed to Algiers, hiding in the back of a railroad ore car.

Chapter 31 was constructed from the writings of Churchill and Sir Charles Wilson, or Lord Moran as he would become. The juxtaposition of moments and events between Moscow and the Mediterranean is accurate, give or take a few minutes and allowing for the difference in time zones.

Allan Shaw and I talked a lot on the phone, in order to get straight what happened on the *Ohio* after they put out the fire and got the ship going again, in Chapter 32. He also sent me a twenty-eight-page handwritten letter.

My statement in Chapter 32 that Commodore Venables ran from the fight is supported by quotes from the LOPs. His actions have been overlooked or glossed over in previous historical accounts.

I met the veteran Reg Coaker, who was the ordinance artificer on the destroyer *Bramham,* in a hotel near Bournemouth where he was attending a reunion of the survivors of the sinking of the twin battleships *Prince of Wales* and *Repulse* (three days after Pearl Harbor), of which he was one. He told me the story about passing the *Port Chalmers* in the night, as it was headed back toward Gibraltar. Coaker's mind is precise; he's the other veteran who's comfortable with e-mail, and he has written a lot about his war experiences, some of which material is in the Imperial War Museum.

Chapter 33 is the crux of this story. It might be going too far to suggest that World War II was decided the moment Mussolini made the middle-of-the-night decision to turn his fleet of warships back to Sicily, but maybe not. Follow the dominoes.

The Wellington airman Dennis Cooke mailed me his written account of that night, and afterward we spoke on the phone a couple of times, to get the rest of his fascinating firsthand story.

Admiral Burrough's final succinct word came from the source notes in *Pedestal* by Peter Smith.

The beginning of Chapter 34 feels like the scene in *Apocalypse Now* after Captain Willard goes down the river to find only insane chaos and spectacular explosions in the night sky. My description of an E-boat is a generic one, because there were many different types. Some of the information about the E-boats being hit came from Francesco Mattesini's book *La battaglia aeronavale di mezzo agosto*, which is what the Italians call Operation Pedestal; passages were translated for me by Matthew Riva and Milena Di Tomaso.

The quote from petty officer Cunningham, and the postscript to the scuttling of the *Manchester*, came from the 2004 documentary *Running the Gauntlet*, produced and directed by Crispin Sadler and narrated by the actor Freddie Treves, who appears in Chapter 37 as a seventeen-year-old cadet on the merchant ship *Waimarama*.

The tale of the *Almeria Lykes* in Chapter 35 is told in and between the lines of the LOPs, and a bit more. Patrick Osborn, in Modern Military Records at the National Archives and Records Administration in College Park, Maryland, tracked down a number of casualty records, including those of the *Almeria Lykes* and *Santa Elisa*. Bill Chubb, chief of the Mariner Records Branch at the U.S. Coast Guard National Maritime Center, found more, including a slim file on the *Almeria Lykes*, which included one note on a little piece of paper about the fate of the junior engineer Henry Brown. I left it at that.

PART VII
SURVIVORS

The account in Chapter 36 of the E-boat attack on the *Santa Elisa* is taken from sources previously mentioned, except for Dales's quote about the bodies and blood, which comes from *The End of the Beginning*, an excellent book whose coauthor Phil

Craig interviewed Dales. The rest of Dales's quotes come from his report to the merchant marine. Many of the quotes are passages from John Follansbee's manuscript.

I interviewed George Nye at his home in Dartford, near London, after he had just come in from a round of golf with his wife. He said he could remember Dales standing up in the lifeboat and taking control as clearly as if it had happened that afternoon on the eighteenth fairway. He said it had changed his life, because he had been so affected by the fact that Dales, this born leader with such presence and authority, was just a teenager like him. It made him realize possibilities within himself.

In Chapter 37, my description of the *Waimarama* on fire came from viewing clips at the Imperial War Museum. John Jackson's words came from his LOP. The moving interview with Freddie Treves was conducted at his home in Wimbledon. After the war he began a long and rich career as an actor. The poem at the end of his story is from the beginning of a play he wrote about Operation Pedestal, which was presented more than fifty years ago on the BBC's *Saturday Night Radio Theatre*.

When the *Waimarama* went up in flames, Admiral Burrough mistakenly believed it was the *Clan Ferguson*. The LOPs contain many such errors. "What ship?" was a signal often passed in the night. But mostly the question wasn't asked, because it rarely mattered.

The passage that follows is from Roger Hill's *Destroyer Captain*. And finally, in Chapter 37, the interview with Charles Henry Walker is resumed.

In Chapter 38, I edited the report by the *Ohio*'s engineer, James Wyld, for the sake of brevity, omitting some parts but changing no words. And I enjoyed putting together the story about the *Ledbury* pirates drunkenly raiding the bushes of the Tunisian coast, as told mostly by Roger Hill.

Ron Linton, who tells the story in Chapter 39 about his ship actually getting close enough to Malta for him to see it, died without ever learning that it was his own captain who had turned the *Dorset* back to rejoin the convoy, where it was promptly dive-bombed and sunk. His candid quote about the instructions received by the gunners explains a lot about the convoy's frequent fire on friendly aircraft.

The brief description of the dogfight by the RAF ace "Buzz" Beurling came from his own book, *Malta Spitfire: The Diary of a Fighter Pilot*.

The first quote in Chapter 40 comes from John Follansbee; he was there in the wardroom of the *Penn*, along with Mason, Thomson, Larsen, Dales, and other officers. Ensign Suppiger's story came from a BBC television show made in 1992, at the fiftieth reunion of Operation Pedestal on Malta.

Because it wasn't made clear by Captain Mason that the *Ohio* was officially abandoned, it was important to show that her liaison officer, chief officer, and chief engineer all declared that they had been ordered to abandon ship.

It remains a small mystery why Admiral Burrough returned to Gibraltar instead of staying to protect the *Ohio,* which he knew was under fire. He might have had orders from the Admiralty; in Gibraltar, he took a saltwater shower on the decks of the *Ashanti*—the men were apparently more embarrassed by the naked admiral than he was—and rushed off to command another operation.

PART VIII
TWO MEN, ONE WARRIOR

By using the many memoirs, journals, and accounts like interviews and writing large parts of the story like a newspaper reporter covering a natural disaster, the context and time of the words "he said" were lost, because they would have been impossible to keep in place and didn't matter in the big picture anyhow. Nowhere was this more true than in the final nine chapters.

The characters took control of the story to its conclusion, so few of the sources in Part VIII are new. The voices reappear. There are more Churchill, Lord Moran, Larsen, Dales, other veterans, and Letters of Proceeding.

I'd like to thank each individual mentioned here as a source. I was moved by the help I received from so many people who took an interest in this project. The research began and ended twenty-three months later at a borrowed table in a corner of the Oasis Internet café and smoothie bar in Los Barriles, Baja, on the Sea of Cortés. My friend Carol Pogash read two chapters at a time when I was buried by the bulk of the story and made two simple suggestions that helped the voice be heard through the din of the action. My friends John and Suzanne Mockett invited me into their home in Northampton to recover on Easter Sunday between legs of my drive around England. Moira Terry steered me around communication traps in London and turned over her cell phone to use on my drive. Jan Larsen fed me in Malta and was there for anything I needed. Cliff Dales and Donna Dales Lovett showed me Georgia hospitality. Peter Riva's research skills sometimes surpassed my own—certainly his knowledge did—and copy editor Lynn Anderson caught scores of flaws in the manuscript. Finally, Bob Loomis's vision of this story was clearer than my own. Without his wisdom, guidance, and patience, *At All Costs* would have been lost at sea.

SELECTED BOOKS

Atkinson, Rick. *An Army at Dawn.* New York: Henry Holt, 2002.

Attard, Joseph. *The Battle of Malta.* London: Kimber, 1980.

Barry, John M. *The Great Influenza.* New York: Viking, 2004.

Beurling, George, and Leslie Roberts. *Malta Spitfire: The Story of a Fighter Pilot.* New York: Farrar & Rinehart, 1943.

Bierman, John, and Colin Smith. *Alamein: War Without Hate.* London: Viking, 2002.

Blair, Clay. *Hitler's U-Boat War.* New York: Random House, c. 1996–1998.

Bradford, Ernle. *Siege: Malta, 1940–1943.* London: H. Hamilton, 1985.

Bragadin, Marc'Antonio. *The Italian Navy in World War II.* Annapolis, Md.: Naval Institute, 1957.

Brodhurst, Robin. *Churchill's Anchor.* London: Cooper, 2000.

Brown, Eric, Captain. *Wings of the Luftwaffe.* Marlborough, Wiltshire, U.K.: Crowood, 2002.

Bryant, Arthur, Sir. *The Turn of the Tide, 1939–1943.* London: Collins, 1957.

Bungay, Stephen. *Alamein.* London: Aurum, 2002.

Callo, Joseph R. *Nelson Speaks.* Annapolis, Md.: Naval Institute, 2001.

Cameron, Ian. *Red Duster, White Ensign.* Garden City, N.Y.: Doubleday, 1960.

Campbell, John. *Naval Weapons of World War II.* Annapolis, Md.: Naval Institute, 1985.

Churchill, Winston S. *The Second World War.* London: Cassell, 1975–1976.

Ciano, Edda Mussolini, Contessa. *My Truth.* London: Weidenfeld and Nicolson, 1977.

Ciano, Galeazzo, Count. *Diary, 1937–1943.* New York: Enigma, 2002.

Clayton, Tim, and Phil Craig. *The End of the Beginning.* New York: Free Press, 2003.

Coleman, Terry. *The Nelson Touch.* Oxford and New York: Oxford University Press, 2002.

Cunningham, Andrew Browne, Viscount. *A Sailor's Odyssey.* London: Hutchinson, 1951.

Dahl, Roald. *Going Solo.* London: Cape, 1986.

Dobbie, William, Sir. *A Very Present Help: A Tribute to the Faithfulness of God.* London: Marshall, Morgan and Scott, 1955.

Dönitz, Karl. *Memoirs: Ten Years and Twenty Days.* New York: Da Capo, 1997.

Edwards, Kenneth, Commander. *Seven Sailors.* London: Collins, 1945.

Farago, Ladislas. *The Game of the Foxes.* New York: McKay, 1971.

Felknor, Bruce, ed. *The U.S. Merchant Marine at War, 1775–1945.* Annapolis, Md.: Naval Institute, 1998.

Galea, Michael. *Malta: Diary of a War, June 1940–August 1945.* Malta: Publishers Enterprises, 1994.

Gannon, Michael. *Operation Drumbeat.* New York: Harper & Row, c. 1990.

Gilbert, Martin. *Winston S. Churchill: Road to Victory, 1941–1945.* Boston: Houghton Mifflin, 1986.

Goldberg, Mark H. *Going Bananas: 100 Years of American Fruit Ships in the Caribbean.* Kings Point, N.Y.: American Merchant Marine Museum, 1993.

Grech, Charles B. *Raiders Passed.* Malta: Midsea, 2002.

Green, William. *Famous Fighters of the Second World War.* Garden City, N.Y.: Doubleday, c. 1975.

Greene, Jack, and Alessandro Massignani. *The Naval War in the Mediterranean, 1940–1943.* London: Chatham, 1999.

Griehl, Manfred. *Junkers Ju 88: Star of the Luftwaffe.* London: Arms and Armour, 1990.

Hague, Arnold. *The Allied Convoy System, 1939–1945.* St. Catherines, Ont.: Vanwell, 2000.

Higham, Charles. *Trading with the Enemy.* New York: Delacorte, 1983.

Hill, Roger. *Destroyer Captain.* London: Kimber, 1975.

Holland, James. *Fortress Malta.* New York: Miramax/Hyperion, 2003.

Holmes, Tony. *Fighters of World War II* (Jane's Pocket Guide). London: Collins, 1999.

Ireland, Bernard. *The War in the Mediterranean, 1940–1943.* London: Arms and Armour; New York: Sterling, 1993.

Ismay, Hastings Lionel, Baron. *Memoirs.* New York: Viking, 1960.

Johnston, Tim. *Tattered Battlements.* London: Kimber, 1985.

Keegan, John, ed. *Churchill's Generals.* New York: Grove Weidenfeld, 1991.

Kersaudy, François. *Norway 1940.* London: Collins, 1990.

Kesselring, Albert. *The Memoirs of Field-Marshal Kesselring.* Novato, Calif.: Presidio, 1989.

Kimball, Warren F. *Forged in War: Roosevelt, Churchill and the Second World War.* New York: Morrow, 1997.

———. *The Most Unsordid Act: Lend-Lease, 1939–1941.* Baltimore: Johns Hopkins University Press, 1969.

King, Ernest J., Admiral. *U.S. Navy at War, 1941–1945*. Washington, D.C.: U.S. Navy Department, 1946.

Kooiman, William. *The Grace Ships, 1869–1969*. Point Reyes, Calif.: Komar, 1990.

Lamb, Charles. *War in a Stringbag*. London: Cooper, 1987.

Lloyd, Hugh Pughe, Sir. *Briefed to Attack*. London: Hodder and Stoughton, 1949.

Macintyre, Donald G. R. *The Naval War Against Hitler*. London: Batsford, 1971.

Mackenzie, Hector. *Observations*. Edinburgh: Pentland, 1997.

Macksey, Kenneth. *Kesselring: The Making of the Luftwaffe*. London: Batsford, 1978.

Mahan, Alfred Thayer. *The Life of Nelson*. Annapolis, Md.: Naval Institute, 2001.

Mattesini, Francesco. *La battaglia aeronavale di mezzo agosto*. Rome: Edizioni dell'Ateneo, 1986.

Mizzi, John A., and Mark Anthony Vella, eds. *Malta at War*, vols. 1, 2, and 3. Malta: Bieb Bieb.

Monsarrat, Nicholas. *The Kappillan of Malta*. London: Pan, 1975.

Moore, Arthur R., Captain. *A Careless Word . . . A Needless Sinking*. Kings Point, N.Y.: American Merchant Marine Museum, 1983.

Moran, Charles McMoran Wilson, Baron. *Churchill, Taken from the Diaries of Lord Moran*. Boston: Houghton Mifflin, 1966.

Nel, Elizabeth Layton. *Mr. Churchill's Secretary*. New York: Coward-McCann, 1958.

Pearson, Michael. *The Ohio & Malta*. Barnsley, South Yorkshire: Cooper, 2004.

Poolman, Kenneth. *Faith, Hope and Charity*. London: Kimber, 1954.

Raeder, Erich, Admiral. *Grand Admiral*. New York: Da Capo, 2001.

Renehan, Edward. *The Kennedys at War, 1937–1945*. New York: Doubleday, 2002.

Rocca, Gianni. *Fucilate gli ammiragli* (Shoot the Admirals). Milano: Arnoldo Mondadori, 1987.

Rommel, Erwin. *The Rommel Papers*. Edited by B. H. Liddell-Hart. New York: Harcourt, Brace, 1953.

Roskill, Stephen W. *Churchill and the Admirals*. London: Collins, 1977.

———. *The War at Sea, 1939–45*. London: Her Majesty's Stationery Office, 1976.

Rudel, Hans Ulrich. *Stuka Pilot*. Dublin: Euphorion, 1952.

Shankland, Peter, and Anthony Hunter. *Malta Convoy*. London: Collins, 1961.

Sherwood, Robert E. *Roosevelt and Hopkins*. New York: Enigma, 2001.

Shores, Christopher, and Brian Cull, with Nicola Malizia. *Malta: The Hurricane Years, 1940–41*. London: Grub Street, 1987.

———. *Malta: The Spitfire Year, 1942*. London: Grub Street, 1991.

Simpson, George Walter Gillow. *Periscope View*. London: Macmillan, 1972.

Smith, Peter C. *Eagle's War*. Bristol: Crecy, 1995.

———. *Into the Assault*. London: Murray, 1985.

———. *Pedestal*. London: Kimber, 1970.

Spooner, Tony. *Warburton's War*. Bristol: Crecy, 1994.

Stokesbury, James L. *A Short History of World War II*. New York: Morrow, 1980.

Suppiger, Gerhart. *The Malta Convoy.* Chicago: self-published, c. 1992.

Thomas, David A. *Malta Convoys, 1940–1942.* Barnsley, South Yorkshire: Cooper, 1999.

Warner, Philip. *Auchinleck, the Lonely Soldier.* London: Buchanan & Enright, 1981.

Weichold, Eberhard, Admiral. *The War at Sea in the Mediterranean.* Washington, D.C.: U.S. Navy Department, 1945.

Wellum, Geoffrey. *First Light.* Hoboken, N.J.: Wiley, 2002.

Williamson, Gordon. *German E-Boats, 1939–45.* Oxford: Osprey, 2002.

Wilson, Stewart. *Aircraft of WWII.* Fyshwick, A.C.T.: Aerospace, 1998.

Windrow, Martin. *German Air Force Fighters of World War II.* Garden City, N.Y.: Doubleday, 1971.

Wingate, John. *The Fighting Tenth.* London: Cooper, 1991.

Winton, John. *Cunningham.* London: Murray, 1988.

Young, Desmond. *Rommel.* London: Collins, 1972.

MAGAZINES

Bartimeus. "Malta Invicta." *National Geographic* (March 1943), pp. 375, 376, 378, 379, 386, 387, 388, 389, 390, 392, 393, 394, 395, 396, 398, 399, 400.

Bogart, Charles. "Operation Pedestal." *Steamboat Bill* (Fall 1994).

Caruana, J. "Ohio Must Get Through." *Warship International* 4 (1992), pp. 333–48.

Gault, Owen. "The Tanker That Saved Malta: SS *Ohio.*" *Sea Classics* (August and September 1997), pp. 32–42 and 56–62.

Gill, Brendan. "A Reporter at Large." *The New Yorker* (July 3, 1943), pp. 43, 44, 46, 47.

Morganstierne, Wilhelm. "Norway, an Active Ally." *National Geographic* (1942), pp. 333–57.

Randall, Edwin J. "Convoy to Malta." *The American Magazine* (January 1943), pp. 18, 19, 80, 81, 84.

Robertson, Terence. "The Ordeal of the *Ohio.*" *The Saturday Evening Post* (January 9, 1960), pp. 14, 15, 75, 76, 77.

"World Battlefronts." *Time* (October 26, 1942), pp. 25, 26, 27, 28.

NEWSPAPERS

Smart, Norman. *Daily Express* [London] (August 13, 14, 15, 17, 18, and 20, 1942).

Thorpe, Arthur. *The Daily Telegraph* [London] (August 14 and 17, 1942).

Daily Mail [London] (August 17 and 18, 1942).

The Times [London] (August 13, 14, and 15, 1942).

The New York Times (various issues, 1940–42).

DOCUMENTARIES

"Running the Gauntlet." Produced and directed by Crispin Sadler (2004).
"True Stories: Convoy." Produced by Noreen Molloy for BBC4 television (c. 1995).

JOURNALS, DIARIES, TRANSCRIPTS, UNPUBLISHED MEMOIRS, REPORTS, CORRESPONDENCE, COMMENTARY

George Amyes
Dennis Cooke
Francis Dales
Desmond Dickens
Anthony Kimmins
Frederick Larsen
John Follansbee, "Swans in the Maelstrom"
Douglas Hunter Gray
Captain Dudley Mason
Ray Morton
Frank Pike
Kaptein Helmut Rosenbaum
Allan Shaw
Theodore Roosevelt Thomson (Captain Tommy Thomson)
James Wyld

INTERVIEWS

Don Allen (veteran, HMS *Ledbury*)
George Amyes (veteran, HMS *Eagle*)
Rusty Bailie (cousin of Francis Dales; family historian)
Frank Balcombe (veteran, HMS *Eagle*)
Alan Barnett (veteran, SS *Waimarama*)
Reg Coaker (veteran, HMS *Bramham*)
Dennis Cooke (veteran, RAF Malta)
Simon Cusens (organizer, Operation Pedestal reunions)
Clifford H. Dales (son of Francis Dales)
Kitty Dales (Mrs. Bertram Dales, sister-in-law of Francis Dales)
Marjorie Dales (Mrs. Francis Dales)
Joe Darmanin (child veteran, siege of Malta)
Miriam Devine (child veteran, siege of Malta)
Tony DiMicoli (child veteran, siege of Malta)
Francis J. Dooley (former shipmate of Captain Fred Larsen)

John Follansbee (son of John "Jack" Follansbee)

Peter Forcanser (veteran, SS *Santa Elisa*)

Andrew Forrest (veteran, HMS *Penn*)

Les Goodenough (veteran, HMS *Eagle*)

Rollin Hansen (former shipmate of Francis Dales)

Mary Stone Hargrove (childhood friend of Francis Dales)

Sandra Larsen Hosay (daughter of Fred Larsen)

Charles Johnson (childhood friend of Francis Dales)

Eleanor Johnson (childhood friend of Francis Dales)

James Johnson (veteran, SS *Santa Elisa*)

Bill Kooiman (author; veteran of the Grace Line)

Jan F. Larsen (son of Fred Larsen)

Minda Larsen (Mrs. Fred Larsen)

Scott Larsen (grandson of Fred Larsen)

Captain Warren Leback (former Grace Line shipmate of Captain Tommy Thomson)

Ron Linton (veteran, SS *Dorset*)

Donna Dales Lovett (daughter of Francis Dales)

Peg Thomson-Mann (daughter of Captain Thomson)

Captain Arthur Moore (author; veteran, U.S. Merchant Marine)

Ray Morton (veteran, SS *Ohio*)

Harold Myers (veteran, SS *Almeria Lykes*)

Dr. John Nixon (veteran, HMS *Ledbury*)

George Nye (veteran, SS *Santa Elisa*)

Danny O'Mara (veteran, SS *Brisbane Star*)

Frank Pike (veteran, SS *Santa Elisa*)

Ray Polidano (Malta Aviation Museum Foundation)

Peter Rothwell (veteran Spitfire pilot, RAF Malta)

Allan Shaw (veteran, SS *Ohio*)

Freddie Treves (veteran, SS *Waimarama*)

J. T. Turner, Jr. (former employer of Francis Dales)

Charles Henry Walker (veteran, HMS *Ledbury*)

ROYAL NAVY LETTERS OF PROCEEDING,
FROM THE NATIONAL ARCHIVES, LONDON

Operation Pedestal

Rear Admiral Harold Burrough, Commander, Force X

Admiral R. Leatham, Vice Admiral, Malta

Rear Admiral A. L. St. G. Lyster, Commander, Fleet Air Arm

Air Vice Marshal Keith Park, Commanding Air Officer, RAF Mediterranean

Acting Vice Admiral Neville Syfret, Commander of the Fleet

HMS *Ashanti:* Commander R. G. Onslow

HMS *Bramham:* Lieutenant Eddie Baines

HMS *Cairo:* Commander C. C. Hardy

HMS *Eagle:* Captain Lachlan D. Mackintosh

HMS *Eskimo:* Commander E. G. Le Geyt

HMS *Furious* (Operation Bellows): Captain T. O. Bulteel

HMS *Indomitable:* Captain Tom Troubridge

HMS *Ithuriel:* Lieutenant Commander D. H. Maitland-Makgill-Crichton

HMS *Kenya:* Captain A. S. Russell

HMS *Ledbury:* Lieutenant Commander Roger Hill

HMS *Manchester:* Sub-Lieutenant F. H. Munro

HMS *Nigeria:* Captain S. H. Paton

HMS *Pathfinder:* Commander E. A. Gibbs

HMS *Penn:* Lieutenant Commander J. H. Swain

HMS *Somali:* Commander E. N. Currey

HMS *Wolverine:* Lieutenant Commander Peter Gretton

SS *Almeria Lykes:* Lieutenant Commander H.D.S. Marshall, liaison officer

SS *Brisbane Star:* Lieutenant E. D. Symes, liaison officer

SS *Clan Ferguson:* Mr. A. H. Black, second officer

SS *Deucalion:* Captain Ramsay Brown

SS *Dorset:* Captain Jack Tuckett

SS *Dorset:* Lieutenant P. T. Bernard, liaison officer

SS *Empire Hope:* Captain Gwilym Williams

SS *Glenorchy:* Mr. B. H. Skilling, second officer

SS *Melbourne Star:* (signature illegible), liaison officer

SS *Ohio:* Lieutenant D. E. Barton, liaison officer

SS *Port Chalmers:* A. G. Venables, commander (RN retired), Commodore of the
    Merchant Fleet

SS *Rochester Castle:* Captain Richard Wren

SS *Rochester Castle:* Lieutenant E. J. Reisfield, liaison officer

SS *Santa Elisa:* Lieutenant Commander A. Barnes, liaison officer

SS *Waimarama:* Mr. John Jackson, third wireless operator

SS *Wairangi:* Captain H. R. Gordon

Boarding of Italian Submarine

HMS *Ithuriel:* Lieutenant J. R. Evans

Operation Statue (the towing of Ohio *by tugboats)*

HMS *Robust:* Commander H. J. Jerome

J. P. Pilditch, commander (RN retired), Assistant King's Harbour Master

Operation Harpoon/Vigorous

Admiral Henry Harwood, Commander in Chief, Mediterranean
HMS *Cairo:* Acting Captain C. C. Hardy
HMS *Partridge:* Lieutenant Commander W. A. Hawkins
SS *Kentucky:* Captain C. J. Roberts
SS *Kentucky:* Lieutenant Huntley, liaison officer
SS *Troilus:* J. P. Pilditch, commander (retired), Commodore of the Convoy

Operation Hats

HMS *Illustrious:* Captain Denis Boyd

INDEX • • •

SAM MOSES is the author of the acclaimed race-driving memoir *Fast Guys, Rich Guys and Idiots.* He began writing as a U.S. Navy seaman on a heavy cruiser in action off Vietnam, and was for eighteen years a feature writer for *Sports Illustrated.* He lives with his two sons, Tai and Makani Kai, in White Salmon, Washington.